ROUTLEDGE LIBRARY EDITIONS: MANAGEMENT

Volume 35

ASSOCIATIONS AND CONSULTANTS

ASSOCIATIONS AND CONSULTANTS

External Aid to Management

STANLEY HYMAN

Routledge
Taylor & Francis Group

LONDON AND NEW YORK

First published in 1970 by George Allen & Unwin Ltd

This edition first published in 2018
by Routledge
2 Park Square, Milton Park, Abingdon, Oxon OX14 4RN

and by Routledge
711 Third Avenue, New York, NY 10017

Routledge is an imprint of the Taylor & Francis Group, an informa business

British Library Cataloguing in Publication Data
A catalogue record for this book is available from the British Library

ISBN: 978-1-138-55938-7 (Set)
ISBN: 978-1-351-05538-3 (Set) (ebk)
ISBN: 978-1-138-57051-1 (Volume 35) (hbk)
ISBN: 978-1-138-57054-2 (Volume 35) (pbk)
ISBN: 978-0-203-70346-5 (Volume 35) (ebk)

Publisher's Note
The publisher has gone to great lengths to ensure the quality of this reprint but
points out that some imperfections in the original copies may be apparent.

Disclaimer
The publisher has made every effort to trace copyright holders and would welcome
correspondence from those they have been unable to trace.

Associations and Consultants

EXTERNAL AID TO MANAGEMENT

STANLEY HYMAN

London

GEORGE ALLEN AND UNWIN LTD

FIRST PUBLISHED IN 1970

SBN 04 658033 6

PRINTED IN GREAT BRITAIN
in 11 on 13 pt *Times Roman*
BY BLACKFRIARS PRESS LTD
LEICESTER

Acknowledgements

The studies reported here were made possible by grants from the Social Science Research Council and by its predecessor, the Human Sciences Committee of the Department of Scientific and Industrial Research. I am grateful to them for their generous support and particularly to Professor Albert Cherns, formerly scientific secretary of the D.S.I.R. Committee.

The pilot project interviewing was carried out by my first research assistant, John Haywood, and Richard Pulfrey was the research assistant on the main three-year project. I should like to thank them both for their very hard and conscientious work. Mr Pulfrey's task has been extremely arduous and it is a remarkable testimony to his powers that he was able to cope successfully with so many organisations—and with me.

Mrs M. Thomas was the secretary on the pilot project and Mrs B. Mulhall on the major project. The projects could not have been carried out unless they had supported its main burdens so willingly. I am most grateful for their valued contribution.

We interviewed 216 organizations in the pilot project and we studied twenty-one organizations over three years in the major project. We also discussed aspects of the projects with members of about twenty other organizations. I suppose about one thousand people have contributed to our knowledge. My thanks to all of them and my apologies for the inadequacies of the final product.

STANLEY HYMAN

December 31, 1968

Kingston Polytechnic, Surrey.

Contents

Trade associations and consultants in their many varieties are the most important of our economic organizations. The people that manage those organizations are among the most influential members of modern society. There is no systematic knowledge available about the performance of these vital organizations.

Associations and consultants help managers to overcome obstacles to survival. The obstacles may be internal or external. The obstacles may be obvious or obscure and they may be concerned with the present and the future. These helpers of management bring together the knowledge and experience of successful organization and transfer them from leader firms to follower firms. The dissemination of valuable knowledge is the essential process of economic progress. Unless these links between the pioneer and the copiers exist there can be no substructure to support the peaks of isolated achievement. The knowledge does not in itself guarantee progress but the absence of knowledge makes progress impossible. Once the knowledge is integrated and distributed, resources such as money and people can be mobilised for a useful purpose. In advanced economies money is always available for the soundest projects.

The research reported in this book constitutes one of the very few attempts to obtain systematic knowledge about the process of helping management. It began as a general survey of aid in one small area and it could have developed into a much larger national survey. Instead, however, I decided to undertake a detailed study of a very few organizations, despite the obvious risk that any findings would be dismissed as peculiar to the participants. Yet such small detailed studies are unavoidable if any foundation is to be provided for the more elaborate studies that will in time justify statistical generalizations. The organizations in this study may not be typical but there is just as much chance that they are. The reader looking for guidance about his own organization should hesitate to dismiss the peculiarities of these organizations and might well derive more benefit by concentrating on the similarities that do exist.

The suppliers of aid to management have been subjected to severe criticisms by many who have used their services and even more so by those who have not used them. They arouse considerable emotion in many managers and the attitudes towards them range from great respect to extreme contempt. Much of the unbalanced assessment of these organizations stems from a misunderstanding of the role of the user of aid. The manager who makes use of his trade association or engages the services of a management consultant is a party to the process that emerges from these requests for help. If he appreciated his own role more clearly he would derive more benefit from them.

Many suppliers of aid deserve criticism. Yet there is no simple means of assessing their performance. The prosaic use of profit is a superficial guide in the best of cases and is entirely irrelevant for some types of suppliers of aid. But some appraisal has to be made by all those who participate in the process of aid to management—the officials of the association and consultancy firms, the members of councils and boards, the consultants, the client or user, and the public authority concerned with the wider implications of aid supply and use.

The reader of this study will derive most value from it if he formulates some guiding questions that will more readily enable him to appraise the information offered. I suggest that he includes the following in his check list:

(1) Why do associations and consultants exist?

(2) How many should there be?

(3) Should each serve (a) one particular occupation, (b) one industry, or (c) one special function such as production or personnel that is common to many firms and industries?

(4) Should they obtain their income from their retaining or membership fee, or should they be paid for each service rendered?

(5) How can their performance be assessed?

(6) How should they be related to government? Should government be regarded as their enemy or ally or simply as another client or member?

(7) Should each aid organization provide its own comprehensive service or should several join together for such activities as publishing, organizing conferences, and investing reserves?

(8) What is the essence of aid to management? Is it knowledge? Or is the personality of the individual who provides aid more important? Or is aid concerned primarily with encouraging managers to understand and solve their problems for themselves?

The answers to these questions are embedded in the case studies of suppliers and users of aid that follow. I have reserved my interpretation of the evidence until the reader has had an opportunity of examining it for himself. I hope he will then draw his own tentative conclusions and compare them with mine. From this joint examination he ought to be able to construct a guide to the use of aid or to the management of an aid organization, whichever is his main concern.

Such collaboration in an enquiry may sound unusual. But I believe the reader to be unusual: he will be intelligent, experienced, and sceptical. He will also be used to collaboration, because our economy is based on a very vast amount of joint activity, springing from a frequently disproportionate contribution from each participant. Many successful businessmen devote a great deal of time to trade associations, many successful members of professions give their time to institutes, and many successful workers give much time to trade unions: the professional institute and the trade union are similar to the businessman's association. Much collaboration is provided indirectly and possibly unintentionally: every firm using a management consultant is helping the consultant's unknown future clients. Every firm obtaining export information from the Board of Trade is helping it to provide a better, more experienced service to future users.

There is a considerable range of external aid available to management. 'External aid' cannot be defined precisely but includes the services provided by consultants, trade and research associations, some professional institutes, a number of public bodies such as the Industrial Liaison Service of the Ministry of Technology, and unbiased information and advice given by suppliers and customers.

This is a report of an investigation into the availability and use of such external aid to management.

The project began in 1964 with a one-year pilot survey of 216 firms, mainly in the Kingston area. That was followed by a three-year investigation planned to study sixteen firms and four organizations supplying aid. The aim was to investigate the supply and use of aid by a range of different organizations, to assess problems, and to consider whether changes were needed.

It is in no degree assumed that the use of external aid is a 'good thing'. Some of our organizations did not use outside aid and suffered no observable ill effect.

The information in the main study was built up from a series of visits over three years. Several informants were interviewed at each organization, and particular activities and projects undertaken by an organization were studied wherever possible.

The information has been analysed and assessed, and some conclusions have been reached that lead to proposals for changing the existing structure of aid and for increasing its effective use.

In addition, I have tried to examine the problems involved in carrying out this study and in employing a number of research methods. This critical concern with methods seems particularly important in view of the paucity of knowledge about research into management. The frank discussion of difficulties may help others working in this field, after the model of *Sociologists at Work*.[1]

The roots of this enquiry are to be found in an investigation of management consultancy that I began in 1958.[2] My interest in consultancy arose after devoting much of my last year of full-time work in industry to persuading my board of directors that they ought to make use of the services of a reputable firm of consultants, with valuable experience in dealing with the problems of a similar company. The directors produced numerous objections, and when each was demolished, they resorted to an unexplained negative. Some years after I left, the firm was absorbed in a 'take-over' and closed down.

Later, I became interested in the exporting problems of small firms. Despite the existence of many sources of information and advice, these small firms were largely unaware of, or failed to use, the help that was available, even when it was free.

These two experiences indicated that there was at least a problem of communication and motivation in the field of aid. At the same time, there were many outside relationships that brought indirect benefits to management, some of them through contact with competitors. Trade

---

[1] *Sociologists At Work*, P. E. Hammond (ed.), Basic Books, 1964.
[2] See my *Introduction to Management Consultancy*, Heinemann, 1961.

and research associations are the most obvious examples.

On further reflection, wider issues emerged. Business managers assume that they control and guard autonomous organizations against all comers and that their task is to be as self-sufficient and independent as possible. But much management work is concerned with problems involving other organizations, such as trade unions and customers.[1] The fundamental problem is the relationship between organizations, and the use of external aid is merely one kind of inter-organizational relationship. I wanted to tackle this general phenomenon through a study of the major problems of managers and of their use of external relationships, particularly external aids.

I applied to the Department of Scientific and Industrial Research for a grant so that a research worker could be employed. But the broad project I favoured was considered too elaborate. D.S.I.R. was interested, however, in that part of the scheme concerned with the use of external aids. After discussion, it was agreed that I should seek answers to a number of specific questions within the field of aids, based on a survey of firms in the Kingston area.

This pilot project was completed in one year. It demonstrated that surveys of this kind are inevitably superficial and unable to present a comprehensive explanation of the problem under investigation. We found out that external aids were numerous and widely used. But managers did not give much thought to aid, and they were often unable to maximise the benefits obtainable from aid. I decided that a much deeper and longer study of a small number of organizations was necessary. I applied for a second grant to the successors of D.S.I.R.—the Social Science Research Council—and they agreed to support a three-year investigation of twenty organizations.

I hope that the publication of this report may provide some independent evidence for policy-makers concerned with external aids in government, associations, and firms.

I should like to stress that my aims were modest, as are my achievements. I have endeavoured to collect relevant information by appropriate means, mainly through direct observation of a flow of behaviour from which particular activities have been isolated, and therefore distorted to some extent.

The first part of this report surveys the supply of aid and describes

[1] See my *Society and Management,* Chapter 2, Business Publications, 1964.

15

the four suppliers that collaborated with us. The existence of the suppliers indicates that aid is used and that some at least is needed. It seemed logical therefore to present that information first. The second part summarizes the information that we obtained from the farmers, builders, manufacturers, and distributors in our sample. The accounts in these two parts are factual and have been agreed as accurate with the organizations. Comment has been reserved for the third part that also attempts to present our findings systematically and to draw some conclusions. Reports on the pilot study and on our research methods are given in appendices. Some readers may find it helpful to read the appendices first.

PART A

The Supply of Aid

Chapter 1

Existing Facilities

Many organizations supply aid to management. That is one of the few hard facts of the external aid situation. This work therefore begins with an analysis of the suppliers of aid before approaching the more subtle problems of the use of such aid by management. After a general review of existing aid facilities, the activities of the four suppliers that collaborated on this project will be described.

In a paper read to the 1958 conference of the British Institute of Management, an authoritative review was given of the aid supplies situation as it then was. It was not based on a survey carried out by investigators but summarized the knowledge of one individual.[1] In December 1968 the National Economic Development Office published a pamphlet of 162 pages entitled *Business Efficiency: An ABC of Advisory Services*. That listed 247 organizations offering aid, ranging from the Advisory Services for the Building Industry to the Zinc Development Association. It excluded the names of management consultants but included a list of forty organizations which provide names of individual consultants or consulting firms in a wide variety of industries and subjects.

There is no reason to believe that the pamphlet includes every sort of aid organization. A comparison between the 1958 and the 1968 surveys indicates a considerable growth in organizations and in the range of topics that are covered. It is difficult to assess the scale of operations of these organizations and the number of users. Some help can be obtained from an unpublished survey carried out by NEDO as a result of the 1966 National Productivity Conference. A special working party concerned with productivity advisory services was set up by NEDO after the conference and it was given the tasks of: (a) carrying

[1] Summarized in my *Introduction to Management Consultancy*, pages 75-8.

out a quantitative and qualitative examination of existing productivity advisory services; (b) examining the forward programmes of the main advisory bodies and their financial implications; and (c) considering the need for expansion or development of productivity advisory services and for better collaboration between organizations providing them. That study excluded advisory services available in agriculture.

The working group concluded that there was some overlap between some services and that some gaps still remain. They noted that many advisory services were sponsored in whole or in part by government departments but that the reason for departmental responsibility for these services was not always clear. They believed that there were considerable differences in the amounts spent on these services which did not appear to reflect their relative importance or effectiveness.

They estimated that about £5 million of public money was provided directly or indirectly for those advisory services to industry, commerce and the building industry.

A second major activity of this working party was to carry out a survey among firms who had used or were likely to use these advisory services. A postal questionnaire was sent to approximately 1,100 firms, comprising 700 in manufacturing and construction and 400 in other sectors of the economy. The sample was roughly proportionate to the total number of companies in the sectors covered and was selected to represent a proportion of small, medium, and large companies. Very small companies were however somewhat under-represented. About two-thirds of those approached replied.

The aim of the survey was to find out from the companies whether they were aware of the services available and how they had come to learn about them, the use they made of the services, the extent to which their expectations had been realized, and their intentions about future use of advisory services. Companies were also invited to give their views about duplication, overlaps or gaps and to make comments or suggestions for future improvements. Some of the findings will be considered in the final part of this study, but a postal questionnaire cannot obtain reliable information on such a complex subject.

The working party interviewed a number of the organizations supplying advisory services and a further questionnaire was prepared and sent out. 172 organizations replied to the questionnaire, saying that they offered productivity advisory services. The picture that emerges is summarised in the following table:

TABLE A *Survey of organizations providing productivity advisory services (i)*

Subjects which services cover:

	Total sample	Pro-fessional organiza-tions	Trade associa-tions	Research insti-tutes	Other organiza-tions (ii)
	Number	Number	Number	Number	Number
Total organizations (100%)	172	37	53	51	31
Services offered by them	%	%	%	%	%
Method study and ergonomics	33	27	36	39	26
Labour utilization	34	27	36	35	35
Plant utilization	45	30	51	61	26
Production control	36	24	34	57	29
Stock control	24	22	32	24	13
Personnel	23	22	32	8	35
Marketing	17	8	32	6	23
Management accounting	22	27	32	10	19
Technical problems requiring research	59	35	51	98	35
Interfirm comparisons (iii)	35	14	62	31	23
Safety	5	—	8	—	13
Testing	6	—	—	16	10
Product utilization	2	—	—	2	6
Lighting	1	3	—	—	3
Training	7	11	6	4	10
Administration	3	5	4	2	3
Design	9	5	6	12	16
Financial advice	2	3	—	—	6
Computerization	3	—	4	6	—
Exporting/importing	2	3	2	—	3
General advice/consultancy	10	8	6	16	13
No answer given	12	30	9	—	16

(i) Survey only included organizations to whom the questionnaire was first sent.
(ii) Includes organizations giving general or specific services to industry as a whole.
(iii) Categories above the line were specifically mentioned in the questionnaire; those below the line were volunteered.

THE MAIN TYPES OF AID ORGANIZATIONS

It is difficult to classify so many and such a variety of aid suppliers. Many of them have a number of different functions, some of them have income from industry and from government, some are entirely private, some entirely public. Any classification must therefore be somewhat arbitrary and imperfect. It seems that nearly all aid suppliers can be divided among four main categories. The precise location of any one

21

organization with multiple functions ought to be decided on the basis of a detailed analysis of the work it does in a year, but unfortunately such analyses have not been published.

The first category, management consultant, covers individuals and firms who supply advice to management for a fee, usually after objective investigations of problems. There are now seventeen member firms of the Management Consultants' Association who carry out most of the consultancy in this country. However, there are a large number of other firms who do not qualify for membership of the Association or have not applied to join, and there are a number of individuals practising as consultants who cover a very wide range of managerial and technical matters. The title of 'management consultant' is thus broad and imprecise; and it is frequently used for technical or specialist consultants who concentrate on problems that do not concern general managers. The management consultant is primarily concerned with matters that are of direct concern to the general manager and board of directors.

The second category, the trade association, is made up of a number of firms that manufacture similar products, supply similar services, make use of particular raw materials, or exist to supply specified groups of customers. Some trade associations include within their activities the negotiation of wages and conditions of work with trade unions. But other associations exist, known as employers' associations, whose primary task is within the field of industrial relations. The trade association that took part in this study is not concerned with industrial relations. Some trade associations are concerned with research, and some with publicity and public relations.

The third category is the research association. There are now forty-three research associations and their primary characteristic is the joint membership of (a) private firms in a particular industry, and (b) government departments and nationalized industries and services, organized to carry out research on problems of general interest, mainly in their own laboratories. These associations receive part of their income from government and are subjected to considerable scrutiny by the Ministry of Technology before grants are made. Most research associations operate independently but in some industries, such as wool textiles and furniture, they are inter-linked with a development council and a trade association. Some research associations take on consultancy duties and public relations activities but the majority restrict themselves to scientific and technological research and the dissemination of findings. The Production Engineering Research Association is exceptionally well organized, being based on a wide-ranging industrial membership.

The fourth category is the public body supplying aid. The National Agricultural Advisory Service was the public body that co-operated in this study, and it epitomizes public aid bodies because it is entirely dependent on public funds, and is legally part of a ministry. There are numerous other public bodies supplying aid in one form or another both to industry and to individual citizens. Some of them work closely with industry and receive much of their income from industry. The 1968 NEDO guide mentioned above includes twenty organizations listed under ministries that offer advisory services to industry and the number is constantly growing. *The Sunday Times* on December 1, 1968, reported on the work of the Manpower and Productivity Service of the Department of Employment and Productivity, which is concerned with the better utilization and deployment of manpower. The Service is under the control of Mr George Cattel, a former director of Rootes Motors, and at the time of the report had thirty projects in hand for a number of large firms. There were seven members of staff and the aim was to expand this to twenty as soon as possible. Its concern with labour productivity involved the Service in many other aspects of the activities of firms, and the report suggested that they were to all intents and purposes management consultants. But their services were available without charge.

In view of their diverse and essentially technical activities, little more can usefully be said about public aid bodies. But a more detailed survey of the other three categories of aid bodies is needed for a proper appreciation of the aid situation and its relationship with management.

MANAGEMENT CONSULTANTS

The extent and use of management consultancy has increased enormously in recent years. The first firm of consultants in this country was set up by Charles Bedaux in 1924. Most managers now know about consultants and many have strong views about using their services. Consultants have a very mixed reputation and managers who have not used them tend to be most sceptical about their value, suspecting their competence and honesty. But I have not been able to find one authoritative example of their delinquency. A number of managers have engaged the services of consultants without discovering whether they are qualified to carry out the particular assignment, and without fixing a fee. Management dissatisfaction, where encountered, may well spring from such causes.

In 1967 there were seventeen member firms of the Management Consultants' Association in Britain. These firms have together dealt with about 20,000 clients, of whom 4,000 were overseas customers. In 1967, they had 3,347 clients, 106 of whom (4 per cent) employed fewer than twenty-five people. 14 per cent of the fees earned in that year were concerned with assignments on company development and policy formation, 41 per cent on production, 10 per cent on marketing, 28 per cent on finance and administrative matters, and 7 per cent on personnel matters. Their total income in that year was £12,527,000—a decline (the first ever) of about 10 per cent on 1966.

The prestige and status of management consultants has increased enormously in recent years. Their respectability was confirmed by the appointment to the National Economic Development Council of Mr W. Coutts Donald, chairman of Urwick, Orr & Partners Limited and 1964 chairman of the Management Consultants' Association. A more recent indication of official favour is the government scheme to subsidise consultancy for small firms, initially on an experimental basis in Bristol and Glasgow. It began in June 1968. The Board of Trade has absolute discretion about the type of project it will support and can pay up to 50 per cent of the cost of an assignment. £500,000 has been allocated for this scheme. It is heavily weighted in favour of established and reputable consultants and the scheme should not lead to the setting up of new firms of consultants.

One of the few attempts at assessing the value of management consultancy was made by Professor J. Johnston.[1] He based his analyses on a random sample taken from the records of the four largest British firms of management consultants who appear to employ about 80 per cent of all consultants and undertake 80 per cent of all management consultancy.

The sampling was based on the job summary completed by the consultant at the end of an assignment with a client firm. The resident

---

[1] *The Productivity of Management Consultants,* Journal of the Royal Statistical Society, Vol. 126, Pt. II, 1963.

consultant normally writes a number of reports during the assignment but a final report summarises the work that has been done and, if possible, estimates the results that have been achieved. This final report 'has to be, and is, agreed with the client and his staff and, indeed, any quantitative assessments of results that may be made is normally based upon the figures produced by the client's accounting system. In assessing the results achieved, a comparison is usually made between the situation ruling at the end of the job and that obtaining at an earlier reference period before the start of the investigation, which will have been agreed between the consultant and client. After the completion of the final report the consultant is required to complete a short job summary solely for the internal files of the consultancy firm, and this summary draws on the information developed in the final and other reports. Job summaries are filed alphabetically by clients' names and our sampling method has been to take a systematic sample from the job summaries, after excluding all work outside the British Isles and also excluding any job which ended before January 1950 . . . An attempt was made to apply the same framework of questions to all sets of records so that a common analysis could be applied to the pooled data from all four firms. Fortunately, there was sufficient homogeneity of records for this to be partially, but not wholly, achievable.'

One of the four firms apparently had unsuitable records as most of the analysis is based on three firms only. Taking a sample fraction ranging from one in five to one in ten, a total sample of 604 jobs was analysed. 47 per cent of them fell into a category where a quantitative assessment was feasible and an actual assessment was positive—that is, it had been made and could be used.

In 211 jobs of this quantitatively assessable nature, there was an average productivity increase of 53 per cent. That figure is based on work study principles of measuring increased productivity. One half of all these jobs had an achieved productivity increase of between 30 and 70 per cent. Professor Johnston then attempted to assess the monetary value of these increases and the cost of achieving them. The monetary assessment was based on direct savings, additional overhead recovery, and net profit on additional turnover. After some elaborate calculations, Professor Johnston concludes that the average assessable job takes 12 consultant months to complete, yields net savings of about £14,000, gives a net return on fees of about 200 per cent per annum, and achieves a productivity increase of over 50 per cent with an applied labour force of about 110.

'The current impact of management consultancy on the economy may be *very roughly* assessed as follows. Starting with an estimated current total figure of 2,000 consultants, we apply a proportion of three in the field to every one at base or temporarily unassigned, giving 1,500 active consultants in the field at any one time.' He calculates that 1,125 of those consultants are working on the assessable jobs, which he calls Class C jobs. 'The latter average about 110 applied labour force each, which gives about 125,000 workers involved in a given year in Class C jobs, with an average productivity improvment of over 50 per cent. Spreading this productivity increase over the nine million workers employed in manufacturing industry gives a productivity increase of about 0.7 per cent per annum. If it were averaged over the fourteen million employed in manufacturing, construction, public utilities and distributive trades it would come to roughly 0.5 per cent per annum, that is about one quarter of the annual productivity increase achieved in recent years.'

Professor Johnston concludes his paper by pointing out that he is not taking into account the many jobs undertaken by consultants that do not appear to be quantifiable and he is also ignoring the internal work done by companies on improving productivity. His final thought is 'the real, long-term benefit of consultants, however, lies probably not so much in the measurable short-run changes in productivity and costs as in inculcation of an enquiring habit of mind and a continuing search for ever better ways of dealing with the industrial and commercial problems of tomorrow'.

It is very difficult to decide the value of this article and in particular to assess the reliability of its statistics; we are given very little information about the basic statistical records on which the calculations are made. It is unlikely that each of the four independent, competing consultancy firms maintains exactly the same records and calculates benefits to the client by the same methods. It is equally unlikely that every client would take the trouble to consider whether he agrees with the estimated savings of the consultant, particularly when the assignment has been completed. Many clients derive considerable benefit from using consultants that cannot be expressed in statistical or financial terms, and if they felt that such benefit had been obtained they might not wish to challenge the calculations of benefit. Quiescence by clients need not prove agreement on calculations.

More difficult problems arise over national estimates. The most important is the projection of this calculation of the benefits of assignments involving 125,000 workers on to a national estimate of productivity benefit of 0.5 per cent. Do those 125,000 workers constitute a meaningful sample of fourteen million employees from many different industries and occupations? There are some elementary statistical grounds for doubting the justification of this estimate. It is not Professor Johnston's fault that this calculation has been too widely accepted as a precise measurement of the benefits to the national economy of the work of management consultants. If such a calculation is needed, a much more elaborate enquiry would be necessary and it may well be impossible to carry it out under any forseeable circumstances.

Laura Tatham in her book *The Efficiency Experts*,[1] published in 1964, has provided a more popular, impressionistic view of the management consultant. It is based on twenty interviews with consultants and twenty interviews with clients. Her interviewing methods were somewhat unsystematic and it is very difficult to draw any conclusions from her work. She does highlight some problems relating to the size of both parties to an assignment.

The situation in the United States of America is different. Management consultants are in much greater demand. According to one study published in 1963, there were 2,500 management consultancy firms employing 24,000 professional staff, and several thousand full- or part-time independent consultants. In addition, the eight major certified accounting firms employed approximately 1,650 professional staff in their management services divisions. American industry was spending about 650 million dollars a year on outside consultants. Nearly half went to general management consultants, and the specialists took the rest.

The American Association of Consulting Management Engineers stated in 1968 that there were approximately 2,600 management consulting firms in North America. Most of these firms were small and offered specialized services. Several hundred medium size firms offer a wide variety of managerial services, and approximately 125 large con-

---

[1] Tatham, L. *The Efficiency Experts*, Business Publications, 1964.

sulting firms offer a broad range of management services to clients. In addition, there are several thousand individual practitioners of management consultancy.

Despite this achievement, the Association continued to be concerned at the lack of organization and regulation of the profession. 'There is at present no means available to prevent the ready entry of individuals or firms with little or no training, experience or ability to the practice of management counsel.' As a result of the Association's endeavours, nine existing associations in America and Canada agreed to collaborate in a five-year programme to raise the status and practice of consultants. They have established the National Academy of Management Consultants which will aim at recruiting individual management consultants. 'Its principal purposes are to advance management consulting as an art and science; to develop and enforce professional standards for admission to the National Academy of Management Consultants Incorporated; to establish practical standards of ethical conduct; to promote and organize a programme of research, publications, seminars, conferences, education, and training in the field of management consulting; to take all the other necessary steps to help individual management consultants achieve professional status; and to promote constructive working relationships with related professional groups.'

Management consultants are not the only group offering consultancy services. As is apparent from the previous paragraph, the leading American organizations operating in this field are known as 'consulting management engineers', mainly due to the pioneering influence of the engineer Frederick Winslow Taylor. In the United Kingdom, and presumably in most other countries, there has been an equally important expansion of services akin to management consultancy in many industries and services. The Association of Consulting Engineers, for example, with a distinguished reputation of professional expertise and ethics, and whose members are used by clients throughout the world, has been in existence since 1912.

In 1967 the National Economic Development Office published a handbook of advisory services entitled *Productivity*. It listed 197 organizations offering a variety of services to members or to relevant firms. Eighty of them offered consultancy of some kind or another, stretching from regular visits to firms by a member of the organization, to a full consultancy service available from management consultancy firms. These consultancies include the Advisory Centre for the Building Industry, the Council of Industrial Design, the Independent Stores' Association, the Institute of Cost and Works Accountants, and the National Association of Retail Furnishers.

No one knows how many people are employed on this work. Rough calculations suggest that at least 5,000 people are involved in full-time consultancy of one kind or another in British organizations. There has been separate development of 'internal consultancy'; a group of employees within large organizations offer services to individuals, departments, or operating units within their company's structure. There does not appear to be any value in stretching 'consultancy' to cover these internal activities, for the primary characteristic of the consultant is his independent status: he is not dependent on one client and certainly not an employer-client.

TRADE ASSOCIATIONS

The only comprehensive study of industrial trade associations in the United Kingdom was carried out by Political and Economic Planning between 1953 and 1955.[1] They defined a trade association as 'a voluntary non-profitmaking body formed by independent firms of manufacturers to protect and advance certain interests common to all'. They listed 1,300 national associations in 1955. They excluded associations of wholesale and retail distributors, merchants, importers, trade unions, professional institutions whose members are individuals and not firms, geographically based associations (principally Chambers of Commerce), research associations, employers' associations concerned primarily with labour matters, and export groups. Local or regional associations representative of an industry concentrated in a particular part of the country were included. Some forty national associations and twenty smaller associations provided detailed case studies of their history, activities, organization, and administration. The impact and effectiveness of associations were studied through interviews with government departments, public corporations, local authorities, about fifty large firms, and over 600 small firms. The aim of the enquiry was to present a balanced and comprehensive account of all aspects of industrial trade associations and it was hoped that the study would show trade associations in proper perspective as industrial institutions.

[1] *Industrial Trade Associations*, P.E.P. Allen & Unwin, 1957.

According to an early sample enquiry by P.E.P. there appeared to be about 2,500 trade associations of all kinds in existence in 1944. The standard reference book of trade associations, defined in the widest possible sense, now includes about 3,000 entries.

One trade association started in 1799, and many were set up between 1875 and 1900. Most associations were created to restrict competition and to set up common prices, to deal with labour problems and to agree on wages to be offered to workers and unions, and to defend firms against foreign competition and the influx of foreign goods. Concern with labour matters often came first and firms then realised the advantages of joint action in other matters. In some cases, international problems came first, as with the Manufacturing Confectioners' Association, set up in 1901 to deal with problems of world sugar supplies.

Trade associations proliferated during the First and Second World Wars. As governments became increasingly involved in wartime economies, ministries needed to discuss problems of rationing and output with representatives of numerous industries and trades. National bodies representing industries were established in 1917 and have grown into the present Confederation of British Industry. As early as 1919 the report of the Committee on Trusts said: 'We have found that there is at the present time in every important branch of industry in the United Kingdom, an increasing tendency to the formation of trade associations and combinations, having for their purpose the restriction of competition and the control of prices.'

Between the two wars, economic depression encouraged the growth of trade associations concerned to control imports and protect home industries.

There is no need to repeat the very competent description and analysis of the P.E.P. report here. Trade associations deal with problems common to their members, and among these are representation to government in a very wide range of activities, particularly about proposed legislation and new administrative policies. Many common services to the benefit of most members are also carried out by associations: intelligence services, export opportunities, the collection of statistics about the industry, for example. Fixing prices was a common activity until the Restrictive Trade Practices Act 1956. It is only permitted now for export markets.

Some people thought that the 1956 Act would destroy many associations. But there have been many new problems to occupy them. With the growing participation of government in industry, and recurring economic crises, consultation between government and industry has been increasing and will continue to increase, irrespective of the political party in power.

Trade associations have numerous management problems. The smallest associations frequently appoint firms of accountants or solicitors to administer their simple activities. Full-time executives are necessary when the work becomes too much for part-time paid or voluntary managers. The move towards bureaucracy creates problems about the proper division of responsibilities between members and officials. That usually involves problems of finance, and many associations have to struggle to obtain adequate income from members.

Only a small number of members is seriously concerned with an association's affairs and those enthusiasts devote a great deal of time to its needs. The chairmen of associations may well give up one or two days a week during their period of office. There are usually many committees in an association, each dealing with a different aspect of the industry's problems; there are national and regional meetings, conferences, annual dinners, and annual meetings that have to be attended by officers. The associations may also be involved in negotiations with official bodies, both domestic and foreign.

The P.E.P. study approached 882 firms each employing fewer than 200 operatives, and fifty larger firms, to find out what use member firms made of the services provided by trade associations and the extent to which firms took part in the work of their associations. The data was obtained from personal interviews with the managing director or another senior executive of the firms. 626 firms supplied information.

The first aim was to find out how many firms were members of associations. 473 or 76 per cent were members; the range of membership ratios extended from 50 per cent in the plastic goods and fancy articles industry to 97 per cent in the cocoa, chocolate and sugar confectionery industry. Of the 473 firms, 255 belonged to one association only, 153 to two associations, forty-six were members of three, twelve belonged to four, four belonged to five, and three belonged to six or more associations. In some industries, similar associations exist side by side with no major functional differences; each retains the loyalty and preference of some firms. Some firms belong to several associations because their range of products makes them members of a number of industries. Some firms believe they should join associations in the industries that supply their main raw materials. Many firms believe that they should join national as well as industrial associations. Many firms do not review their memberships and, once established, they continue indefinitely.

348 firms (73 per cent) had no representative on any governing body or committee of the association to which they belonged. Seventy-six (16 per cent) were represented on a committee, and twenty-eight (6 per cent) had a representative on the governing body. Only twenty-one firms (4 per cent) were represented on both the governing body and at least one committee of their association.

Eighty-three firms (17 per cent) said they made no use of a list of the services associations offered. 121 firms were concerned with representation to government departments, and 102 were interested in representation on British Standards Institution committees. 156 welcomed and used services for the circulation of business enquiries, 164 accepted market information, 136 wanted technical information, and 117 benefited from information on costs and prices. 142 valued the interpretation of government regulations, and 142 made use of export information provided by the trade association. A number of publications were issued by associations and used by their members.

THE AMALGAMATION OF TRADE ASSOCIATIONS

Associations are being set up and disbanded continually, reflecting social and economic changes. In the Preface to the fourth (1968) edition of *Trade Associations and Professional Bodies of the United Kingdom* Mrs P. Millard says: 'New technologies give rise to new associations and included are the most recent bodies formed as we went to press— the Computer Services Bureaux Association is one, others cover data processing, infra-red equipment and similar. New management techniques similarly give rise to their own special interest societies: methods-time measurement, research and development, ergonomics, organization and methods, long-range planning are some examples, a far cry from the oldest body listed—the Royal Society of Musicians founded in 1738.'

She included 500 more organizations in the current edition than in the previous one. About half of them had been established for some time but have not appeared previously. The remainder of the additions were new bodies. Between the third and the fourth editions, there were about 160 closures, mainly in the craft industries. Other associations have disappeared because of the creation of a more comprehensive body. Some have disappeared because legislation has created monopolies, and associations thus become unnecessary.

There have been a number of mergers and changes in function, particularly in textiles and the metallurgical industries. The research association and the trade association in the welding industry have recently merged (as in the timber industry) and similar mergers may occur elsewhere in the future.

Mrs Millard's definition of a trade association is very wide: 'As before, we define a trade association, professional body or learned society as representing the interest and welfare, in the broadest sense, of any trade, industry or profession, collectively or individually on a national or near-national scale.' Thus she has been concerned with many organizations beyond the scope of this investigation but the boundaries are in many cases indistinct. For example, she has noted that the smaller learned societies continue to proliferate, ' . . . thus showing the need for the individual to have a voice and a platform where views can be aired. Techniques as they are developed, particularly in the engineering fields, give rise to special interest societies— one of the reasons why this present edition has increased to such an extent.'

Merging associations and disbanding redundant ones is a difficult and lengthy process. There are numerous vested interests that operate against any initiative for change. In some cases, however, there is no simple solution to the overcrowding that exists within many industries through the haphazard development of associations over many years.

One interesting case of merger occurred in mechanical engineering. The Confederation of British Industry were asked by the British Mechanical Engineering Federation to help in undertaking a review of the trade associations in the industry. The C.B.I.'s report was produced after many discussions and enquiries over several years.[1]

The mechanical engineering industry is important through its rela-

[1] *A Review of Mechanical Engineering Trade Associations*, C.B.I., 1966.

B

33

tions with many other industries that use its products. Its efficiency affects many sectors of the economy. In 1965 its sales amounted to £3,085 million and contributed 4.6 per cent of the gross domestic product. In 1964 nearly 50 per cent of the country's total fixed investment was on plant and machinery. Mechanical engineering sales amount to roughly 10 per cent of the sales of all manufacturing industry and employment in the industry comprises 14 per cent of all manufacturing employment. The industry provides 20 per cent of all UK exports and has a consistently favourable trade balance, amounting in 1965 to £560 million.

The report estimates that there are about 6,500 mechanical engineering companies in Britain and about 72 trade associations representing their interests. One of these associations, the British Mechanical Engineering Federation, is the only body which regularly seeks to speak for a substantial proportion of the industry at the national level on a broad range of subjects. At the beginning of 1966 its membership comprised 286 companies and nineteen trade associations. The report says that the Federation is attempting to fulfil four distinct functions: it provides normal specialist trade association services for its member companies; it provides the services expected of a federation to its trade association members; it provides secretarial services to four of the associations; and it tries to act as a body representing the whole industry on occasions. The staff consisted of four senior and two junior executives.

One member association, the Engineering Industries' Association, embraces many industries outside mechanical engineering and includes a large number of small and very small firms among its 3,000 members. It has a regional structure and provides services that appear to be distinctly different from those of the average specialist trade association.

Most trade associations work closely with associations serving other industries. Mechanical engineering, for example, is frequently involved in the activities of the Society of Motor Manufacturers and Traders, the Shipbuilding Conference, and the British Electrical and Allied Manufacturers' Association.

No exact figures about finance or staff exist for trade associations, and the report had to make some estimates. It believed that the total income of the seventy-two trade associations was about £550,000, and that they employed altogether about 250 people. These figures do not represent the total real cost of associations as they exclude the value of the time given by company staff to trade association matters.

The working party that prepared the report recommended that there should be a new central organization for the industry consisting only of trade associations. Efforts should be made to achieve a reduction in the number of associations but the investigators were impressed by the strength of feeling among many people that specialist associations were needed and were valuable. Thus they felt that the central organization should be a federation of associations. It should be run by a central council and each association would be entitled to a number of seats in proportion to the total number of employees among its member firms. The income of the central organization should be based on the total wages bill for employees engaged in work of the type covered by the association and the central organization.

The report recommended that the day-to-day work of the central organization should be under the care of a small committee selected by the president of the central body to represent the industry in current activities. The central organization would be able to speak for the whole industry and would become the reference point of all matters affecting the industry. The central organization would identify areas of common interest in the work of specialist associations, encourage mergers where practicable, and provide better specialist services and information than many associations can now afford themselves.

The report was published in November, 1966. The new British Mechanical Engineering Confederation came into existence in October 1968.

The P.E.P. study was only concerned with associations in manufacturing industries. There are many other trade associations in service industries and in distribution. In 1967 the National Economic Development Office published a report on *Trade Associations in the Distributive Trade*, summarizing a survey of the services provided by associations in the distributive trades. They sent a questionnaire to 110 known associations and received replies from 'over eighty' (it appears from other information in the report that ninety-five associations have been analysed). The questionnaire asked about their methods of communication with members, training, recruitment and labour turnover, wages and employment, consultancy, inter-firm comparison, group trading, merchandising and marketing, liaison with manufacturers, general services, and special activities. It is difficult to summarize the results in any shorter form than the pamphlet. It provides a review both by subject of enquiry and by twenty-three trades or types of association.

The report has some interesting information about advisory and consultancy services. 'The answers to the questionnaire showed that the consultancy services provided by associations vary considerably, ranging from the comprehensive service provided by some associations, such as the National Federation of Ironmongers, to the informal general enquiry service given by other associations.'

Eighteen associations provided consultancy services dealing with shop layout and design, eleven associations offered work study, thirteen market research, sixteen accountancy, and fifteen stock control.

Twenty-five associations employed experts for these services, nineteen made use of firms of consultants, thirty relied on 'the association's own access to the knowledge and experience of its membership at large', and eighteen associations based their consultancy service on 'collective guidance by panels of experts employed in member firms'.

Thirty-four associations provided free consultancy services to their members, nineteen associations subsidised consultancy services, and fourteen associations charged an economic rate for consultancy.

Seventeen associations that did not provide their own consultancy service knew of members who had employed consultants and found them satisfactory. Twenty-two associations kept a list of consultants for use by their members.

In a related field, thirty-four associations collected data from member firms on a number of subjects for use in inter-firm comparison or similar studies.

Nine associations operated some form of group central buying. Fifteen associations had helped their members to form voluntary buying groups. Another seventeen associations who had not been concerned with buying groups believed that they could encourage their formation.

The report gives some detailed account of the unusual activities of the National Federation of Ironmongers. The Federation had 6,000 members in forty-eight regional branches. Training is provided through the National Institute of Hardware, operating from the same address as the National Federation of Ironmongers. Training is available for junior trainees, junior management, and higher management in the form of seminars, summer schools, one-day courses, evening classes and correspondence courses.

The Federation offers a comprehensive consultancy service for its members for which it employs a permanent staff of eleven. The service deals with about one hundred cases a year and many more enquiries, and is subsidized by the Federation because smaller member firms could not afford realistic fees. The Federation staff give consultancy advice on market research, accountancy, stock control, stock turn, warehousing, transport, showrooms, office layout, statistics, and work study.

In 1966 three hundred members took part in an inter-firm comparison scheme, costing £3,000 per annum. Some participants go on to use the consultancy service.

The Federation operates group central buying and local buying groups. The Federation owns its own wholesale company which will eventually have branches and depots in various parts of the country. It has an annual turnover of over £1 million.

Other services provided by the Federation include: (1) advice on legal matters; (2) a debt collecting service; (3) a clearing house operation whereby members can settle accounts with 2,400 suppliers each month; (4) advice on accounting matters; (5) provision of a wide variety of publicity and display material; (6) advice on and installation of shop fittings; (7) insurance facilities; (8) an enquiry department for trade matters, staff pension schemes, and private hospital treatment; (9) its own finance company to give advice on hire purchase and to provide cash; and (10) a direct mail service for suppliers to the hardware trade.

RESEARCH ASSOCIATIONS
Research associations arose from the inadequate application of scientific knowledge to manufacturing, particularly to armaments in the 1914-18 war. Government aid seemed necessary but public funds could not be used to promote the profits of the private firm. Some type of partnership between government and industry seemed desirable, one that any appropriate firm could join.

British dependence on German chemicals in 1914 led to many discussions between industry and government. It was decided to promote a number of research associations, financed jointly by both industry and government. A special Committee of the Privy Council committee and an advisory council were set up in 1915, and the Department of Scientific and Industrial Research was established in 1916. One of its duties was to promote appropriate research associations. The first association was established in 1918.

The early history of the associations and their problems at the end of the second world war have been described by Professor Sir Ronald Edwards.[1] He was much concerned with an appropriate method of financing associations, and whilst there is still considerable variety, member firms are usually levied on the basis of turnover and the government adds 50 per cent of the total collected from industry above a stated minimum. The official contribution does not usually increase as the association grows. Most associations now undertake paid research sponsored by one or a few member firms; the results are not available as public information. The general research programme is concerned with problems common to most member firms, and all members receive copies of those research reports.

The value of research associations has often been doubted. Some people believe that as there is so much more research in industry and in colleges than in 1918, associations are no longer necessary. But several investigations have shown that most research is carried on in modern, science-based industries like electronics; whilst in the older, more traditional industries, such as food manufacturing and brewing (where the need is presumably greater) little research occurs.

Directors of research associations may nowadays be more concerned with finance than science: research opportunities exceed income. As subscriptions are based on size, it would not be surprising if the larger firms had greater influence in determining the association's research programme than the smaller firms. But that situation makes many small firms doubt the advantages of membership: they feel that priority will be given to the interests of the large firm if only because its managers can more easily attend association meetings.

Perhaps because of these possible conflicts, there may be a tendency to concentrate on work that will lead to quick results and easy application. The separation of pure research from applied research is definite

---

[1] *Co-operative Industrial Research,* Pitman, 1950. A more up-to-date description is given in *Industrial Research Associations in the United Kingdom,* A. B. Hammond and others, O.E.C.D., 1966.

in most fields, and associations tend to have a practical, mundane bias.[1]

There have been numerous investigations into industrial research and research associations. The three volumes by C. F. Carter and B. R. Williams, beginning with *Industry and Technical Progress* in 1957, are the most comprehensive. The Federation of British Industry investigated research in 1944, 1946, 1951, 1955, 1958 and 1959. A report of the last enquiry — *Industrial Research in Manufacturing Industry: 1959-60* — was based on questionnaires to over 4,500 firms of all sizes. The total income of grant-aided research associations in 1959 amounted to £7.3 million, of which £1.7 million was derived from D.S.I.R. grants. Manufacturing industry, either directly or through trade associations, probably contributed about £5 million. In addition, industry probably paid about £¾ million for research work in universities, about £600,000 for work done by D.S.I.R. laboratories, about £800,000 to research associations which are not in receipt of D.S.I.R. grants, and over £1 million to private consultants and research institutes. This gave an overall total of about £8 million external expenditure.[2]

At the time of the enquiry, five industries paid a compulsory levy that aided the incomes of research associations.

The report is based on replies to a lengthy questionnaire by 300 firms accounting for over 85 per cent of the total expenditure on research and development in all the 771 firms that replied to either the long or the short questionnaire that were used in this study. Of the 300 firms, 103 had submitted specific problems to research associations. Most of those enquiries came from large firms. Firms were asked to estimate the value of the work done by research associations on the specific problems which were referred to them, and they found it extremely difficult to make such estimates.

Over 90 per cent of large firms in the sample were members of one or more associations, and of these nearly half were members of four or more different associations. Six large firms, four of them in chemicals, were members of more than twenty research associations each. Among

---

[1] However, part of the basic work on chromatography which earned Martin and Synge the Nobel Prize for Chemistry in 1952 was carried out at the Wool Research Association. Hammond, p. 85.

[2] The total income of the forty-four research associations in 1963 was £10 millions, of which official grants amounted to £2,420,000. In 1967, forty-three associations employed 1,800 graduates, had a total income of £13 millions, and served industries responsible for 55 per cent of industrial output. They had 19,000 members. Official grants totalled £4 millions.

medium firms, only 7 per cent of those belonging to an association belonged to four or more, and of small firms only one belonged to four or more.

Firms completing the full questionnaire were invited to comment on the services they received from research associations and similar bodies. Of 143 that did reply, seventy-five made favourable comments and forty-four made critical comments. Thirty-nine said that they valued the associations for information services and informal background discussion.

Co-operative research associations have been set up in many countries, in some cases antedating the British system, and the Organization for Economic Co-operation and Development has made a study of them in several countries. Many appear to face the same problems of finance, recruitment of members, and relations with government. There is some variety in the attempted solutions. In France, for example, there are government regulations about the organization and membership of associations but no public money. In Germany, the system is more centralized, although without close examination it is impossible to assess whether central control is any greater than in Britain, as exercised now by the Ministry of Technology. In Belgium, the associations cover only a small part of industry; very few associations possess their own laboratories but make use of facilities offered by universities and similar institutions.[1]

Research associations are not the only sources of research. Several organizations exist in many industries. The position of the wool textile industry is illuminating and a valuable 'case study' now exists in the report prepared for the Wool Textile Research Council by Urwick Technology Management Ltd. (a subsidiary of Urwick, Orr and Partners Limited, management consultants) published in 1967.[2] The investigation aimed to 'advise the Wool Textile Research Council on its future organization of the co-operative research activities of the Wool Textile industry, with the general object of assisting the Council to establish proper priorities for research, to accelerate the pace of scientific and technological advance and to ensure the results of research are applied speedily so that effective use is made of research

[1] *Industrial Research Associations in France, Belgium and Germany*, O.E.C.D., 1965.
[2] *The Organization of Co-operative Research in the Wool Textile Industry*, Wool Textile Research Council, 1967.

and development in increasing the productivity and profitability of the industry'.

The industry has been in existence for centuries. There has recently been some contraction of sales—they totalled £550 million in 1966. The investigators studied the structure of the industry and reported: 'the picture which emerges is thus a complex one, characterized by a delicate dynamic balancing of mutual and of conflicting interests, which is reflected in a rich pattern of organization, co-operation and competition'.

The industry came twenty-ninth out of thirty industries in the 1959 F.B.I. survey for the number of qualified scientists and engineers employed per hundred employees. The wool textile industry's proportion was 0.03, whereas the highest, in specialist pharmaceutical firms, was 2.62 per hundred employees.

The Wool Textile Research Council was constituted mainly by trade associations with the objective of 'fostering and encouraging research on the materials, methods, and processes of the Wool Textile Industry, including the study of textile design'. It was set up in 1952 and it administers the scientific research levy imposed under the statutory powers granted by the Industrial Organization and Development Act 1947. The levy raised £286,000 in 1967. The Council grants about 12 per cent of its income to universities and technical colleges, and most of the rest to the Wool Industries Research Association. The research association was established in 1918 'to promote research and other scientific work in connection with the production of wool and its utilization in industry'.

Any firm paying the statutory research levy is eligible for membership of the research association without further charge. Of about 2,000 firms paying the levy, 1,200 are registered with the W.I.R.A. Most of the 800 non-members are presumed to be merchant firms. The total income of the research association in 1966 was £370,634, the statutory levy yielded £198,000 and Ministry of Technology grants were £82,500.

The report says: 'Our impression, and it must be appreciated we were only required to enquire into the functions and methods of the W.I.R.A. and not into the scientific merit of the research programme, is that with the passage of time W.I.R.A.'s objective has become blurred, and that consequently the work has become too diffuse. . . . The causes, we believe, go very much deeper than simple questions of

41

management and arise from a failure on the part of the industry to set clear objectives and to appreciate the fundamental issues which the industry must first resolve before settling on the most desirable methods of organizing co-operative research'.

Despite the long history of the research association, the investigation found as a result of numerous interviews and surveys, that the satisfaction felt with the W.I.R.A. was closely correlated with the extent to which a company sets out to make use of it. There were few research and development departments in the industry although all companies were clearly concerned with quality control. 'Most companies' objectives are simply stated as improvement of machinery and processes. Very few are interested in, or seem to have grasped the value of, fundamental research as an essential step in understanding these processes or in initiating new ones. Perhaps this is due to the notion that fundamental research is only concerned with the structure of the wool fibre, whereas it is equally necessary to study the physical and chemical properties of the machinery and processes.'

Nevertheless, most companies—including many who were critical of the association—were in favour of co-operative research being continued.

In a very careful analysis of the differing interests involved in co-operative research, the report emphasizes that the needs of the large firm, the small medium firm, and the small firm do not coincide and that a policy for co-operative research must be based on an integration so far as is possible of these differing requirements. The large firm is more likely to undertake pure research whereas, at the other extreme, the small firm, through a lack of technical staff, will not even understand the reports of research and through a lack of managerial time will not be able to implement a report. The small firm requires direct assistance from an association to enable it to assess, understand, and apply a particular piece of research that is directly related to the firm's needs.

The report attempts to work out a basis for the integration of these differing needs. It proposes a number of organs in the industry with different, essential functions that should not overlap. The structure of the relationship between these differing organs must be logical and effective. The first organ should be concerned with enabling the industry to set commercial objectives that should be undertaken without

42

concern for scientific or technological potentialities. It should consider market trends and the economic evaluation of situations which might follow if certain objectives could be reached.

The second organ should be concerned with the translation of the commercial objectives into a scientific research programme.

The third group should then re-examine the scientific research programme and decide priorities and expenditure by the commercial interest of the industry.

Once projects have been approved, the director of research would have the assistance of expert technical panels to oversee the research work and these panels should be set up for a specific purpose. Members should be willing to carry out work for the projects in their own premises.

A fifth organ should be concerned with the consideration of scientific and technological trends in the future. By digesting science on behalf of the industry it would deduce the effects coming from the advance of science on textile technology, living habits, sources of raw material, new machines and processes, etc. This group would consist of scientists and engineers.

The investigators then contrast that ideal system with the existing situation. They believe that the various sub-committees of the research council and the research association are inadequate; that they have failed to assess the economic benefits of the research programme, failed to provide estimates of research project costs, failed to examine the feasibility of a project precisely, and failed to discuss with enough thoroughness the technical aspects of reported research projects.

On the basis of that analysis, the report makes the following major recommendations:

(1) The links between the Wool Industry Research Association and the universities should be considerably strengthened and there should be an interchange of staff;

(2) The Wool Textile Research Council should form a joint textile business committee with the cotton and hosiery industries to propose suitable business objectives towards which joint research programmes should be directed;

(3) Eventually the three industries should appoint a director of joint textile research together with a joint project secretariat. In the mean-

time, the three industries should appoint a co-ordinator for a period not exceeding two years;

(4) A proportion of the statutory levies should be administered by this new joint business committee;

(5) The Ministry of Technology should be asked to match the industry contribution;

(6) The Wool Textile Research Council should continue to exist but its duties should now include the formulation of the commercial objectives towards which research programmes should be directed;

(7) The industry should take steps to bring the research association more directly under the control of the research council and its executive organ. The research association should centre around fundamental research, applied research and development, technical services, and information;

(8) There should be two assistant directors of the research association, one to be in charge of fundamental and applied research, and the other in charge of consultancy and information services.

In an important statement of government policy towards research associations on November 26, 1968,[1] Mr G. T. Fowler, M.P., Joint Parliamentary Secretary to the Ministry of Technology pointed out that the general purpose grant had been gradually reduced since 1964 and grants for particular projects increased. Sponsored work had also been increased. 'The former emphasis on the virtues of long-term research has been abandoned, and research associations are now encouraged to take part in various quasi-research matters, such as inter-firm comparisons. We should like to see R.A.s charging for advisory and consultancy services . . .

'It must be borne in mind that the Ministry does not in any circumstances offer grant to an R.A. if it is considered that industry is well able to afford to fund projects on its own account, or if there is a more appropriate place than an R.A. to carry out the work. Co-operative research is not to be supported simply for its own sake. We feel that the time has come when more research should be done directly by firms themselves; the encouragement of this is a primary objective of my Ministry.'

Whilst that statement indicated an important shift of emphasis, there

[1] Reported in part in *The Times*, November 27, 1968.

seems little doubt that research associations will continue, if only because of the interest of their industrial members.

But how many associations should there be? There have been as many as fifty, there are now forty-three, and expert opinion suggests that there will be about thirty-five ten years hence.

It is not difficult to see where amalgamations are possible and desirable. Associations concerned with the textile industries present one area, and those serving iron and steel manufacturing and user industries another. Most mergers seem to take an extraordinarily long time, due presumably to vested interests and the penalties of consultation. But there is another question not usually asked: are additional associations required? Nearly all associations have been linked to a manufacturing industry, and that was certainly sensible fifty years ago. Since then, however, the economy has changed, and the majority of workers are now employed in non-manufacturing activities. Government grants can be made to any research body. The numerous organizational inventions of the Ministry of Technology since 1964 demonstrate the ease with which new types of technological and research bodies can be established, such as the National Computer Centre and the special engineering research institute at East Kilbride. We may now need research associations in banking, insurance, education, and government itself.

Decisions about the number and type of associations ought to be based on the widest appraisal of available research resources. For example, the Launderers' Research Association works closely with the unofficial Dyers and Cleaners Research Organization. One research association has been converted into a private limited company providing testing services to its former members. There are a number of private research companies, joint research organizations, research units in colleges and universities, research activities within companies in nationalized industries, and in other official organizations such as the training boards. It would be useful to build a very careful map of research resources in all their many forms.

Whatever the number of associations, the problem of ensuring their efficiency and effectiveness is extraordinarily difficult. It seems almost impossible to ensure that the right work is being done in the best way in research associations. However, a very conscientious branch of the Ministry of Technology is responsible for the recommendation of grants

45

to associations, and in order to carry out that function it is in close contact with the work of associations. At five-yearly intervals it reviews exhaustively the organization, finances, and work of each association and undoubtedly the Ministry can stimulate the activities of associations. It is almost certainly an imperfect control device but nobody knows what would be adequate.

One considerable determinant of the general level of efficiency is the degree of collaboration and co-ordination between associations. The entirely unofficial Committee of Directors of Research Associations appears to do much in comparative privacy to avoid conflict and undesirable duplication, and to promote the common interests of research associations.

The phenomenon of the research association presents a number of fascinating sociological problems. In a competitive economic system— or at least in a system where businessmen claim to favour competition —it is strange to find an organization deliberately set up at the behest of government to bring competitors into active collaboration with one another, particularly in the crucial area of research. Having undertaken this unusual interference with the market fifty years ago, little seems to have been done particularly for small firms; a strong case justifying official support could be made for them. The associations more and more are concerned with the application of existing knowledge. Yet even with that bias, the associations cannot usually supply detailed and continuing on-the-job assistance to the firm that wishes to make direct use of research.

These anomalies are reinforced with a complex financial system that aims at ensuring a partnership between the government and industry but entails considerable financial insecurity for the associations. As a consequence, the directors of many associations are much concerned with raising adequate income from members, although they know that if deficiencies arose in an association that was otherwise considered socially useful, the government would step in and ensure its survival.

If national need makes research associations necessary, it is surprising that there is no central body concerned with the creation and enforcement of a comprehensive research programme. The Ministry of Technology stimulates each association and ensures that the efficiency level is not too low. But as the research associations are surrounded by a number of other organizations concerned with research, each association has to consider which of them are allies and which enemies. There is a continual process of amalgamation and disbandment, but it is not entirely a rational process.

None of these oddities would of themselves condemn the research association and the British system of governmental involvement. If the associations work satisfactorily and efficiently despite their lack of logical structure and method, they would be fully acceptable to the modern industrial economy. Unfortunately, there are no clear criteria against which the performance of these associations, nor even their need to exist, can be judged. It is this failure to provide any system of evaluation, above all in the field of research, that makes the entire outlook mystifying.

From the point of view of the individual firm, the looseness of the system to a considerable extent may suggest that the odd firm out is the one that bothers to join and pay a subscription. The less scrupulous firm may glean the benefits of an association's work indirectly. Most associations seem willing to supply information to almost anybody, and although there may be valuable information distributed only to members, it is generally agreed that the really secret work is done within the research departments of individual firms and not in the research associations.

Thus there must be important social as well as practical motives for membership. Some managers enjoy meeting people with similar responsibilities, particularly when they have similar intellectual, academic and scientific abilities and interests. The information obtained will often be valuable but it could be obtained elsewhere. Perhaps the integration of a company's own private research programme with that of a research association is a rational justification for membership. But that cannot often happen. Apart from those factors, the research association system appears to exist because government departments have so decided, in the somewhat indefinite national interest.

There is no doubt that research (in the widest sense of systematic and tested knowledge) and its application, is essential to the modern firm and the advanced economy. Some of the influences that led to government initiative at the beginning of the century persist. But there is still no way of ensuring that every firm will seek and apply new knowledge, even if its competitive status is worsened through such neglect. So long as the firm earns an income that meets the goals of management, there need be no automatic pursuit of excellence.

Assistance with research has been officially encouraged on the implied assumption that there are firms anxious to innovate who need help to overcome obstacles. There are almost certainly such firms still in existence. There is a second category of firms who are fully alert to the role of research and recognize that some of it is better done jointly than singly. But there is a third category that is unconcerned with research and has never considered what part it should play in the firm's activities.

A national research policy must take account of all three categories (and their many intermediate variations). It may thus be necessary to provide a network of approaches and organizations that will embrace the peculiar needs of each.

To do that, the proper function and location of public concern with research must be clarified. Either government undertakes research that is judged necessary but neglected, or government could simply encourage improved standards of research within firms or groups of firms. The present system appears to support the view that more research is better research, and that it will meet the needs of management if the findings exist. Such views may be misguided in contemporary society. A radical review of this situation would be beneficial and should begin with an investigation of the modern research needs of firms in all sections of the economy.

There can be little doubt that research associations would be more helpful to industry if some of their avoidable difficulties were eliminated. But, as the present situation of the laundry industry indicates, there is little point in government encouraging research if economic policies prevent the optimum use of its findings. Research, particularly aided research, is too important to be wasted, and national research policy must link up with national economic policy.

Chapter 2

The Management Consultant

The management consultant is in something of a dilemma. He is increasingly used, achieving a higher status each year, yet beset by critics and suspected of nefarious practices. He seeks to overcome these disadvantages by promoting professionalism, but the private regulation of professional conduct may take many years to show its effect in a universal acceptability of the consultant.

This somewhat unsympathetic atmosphere is likely to complicate the work of the reputable consultant and may reduce the quality of his help to management. It seemed essential to study the work of the consultant from his perspective as well as from the client's in order to appreciate his difficulties. It may then be possible to propose changes that would benefit both consultant and client.

Industrial Administration Limited readily agreed to co-operate with us when asked for their help. We made heavy demands on their time and we have been able to learn a great deal from them and some of their clients. Industrial Administration were able to arrange for us to visit their staff engaged on three assignments in different parts of the country and on various types of work.

Industrial Administration Limited was set up in 1949 by Mr E. L. G. Robbins, then joint managing director of Production Engineering Limited. P-E is now one of the four largest management consultancy firms in Britain. Mr Robbins joined P-E in 1932 and left them because he wanted more independence. He believed that would be possible in an organization small enough for the chief executive to influence directly all major activities. Mr Robbins launched a scheme for training apprentices for the Engineering Industries Association and that scheme has grown into a nationwide training organization employing eighty people. It is now entirely separated from Industrial Administration and does not form part of its consultancy activities.

Industrial Administration employed twenty consultants in 1967.

We were supplied with the following information about 18 consultancy staff in February 1968:

Industrial Administration Ltd. Consultancy Staff 1968

Age	Service	Qualifications	Annual Income
43	8 years	B.A., M.I.C.E.	£5,000
35	7 years	B.Sc.(Eng)	£2,900
58	14 years	B.Sc.	£2,400
32	4 months	Ass. Member I.P.E.	£2,200
45	8 years	A.M.I.Mech.E., A.M.I.Prod.E.	£3,100
26	2 months	C.A.	£2,000
42	4 months	M.A., A.M.I.C.E., M.S.E.E.	£4,000
40	6 years	B.Sc.	£3,600
28	1 year	Ll.B.(Hons), Dip.M.S.	£2,300
38	2 years	B.A., A.M.B.I.M.	£2,500
31	3 years	D.L.C.(Hons)	£2,500
37	6 years	B.A.	£4,000
29	2 years	Dip.(Mech.E.)	£2,500
50	12 years	B.Sc.(Mech.E.)	£3,500
35	7 months	B.Sc.	£2,900
35	7 years	B.Sc.(Econ.)	£2,400
31	2 years	A.C.W.A.	£2,400
39	8 months	Grad.R.Ae.Soc.	£2,500

The type of work carried out is summarized in the following table:

Industrial Administration Ltd. — Assignments 1966 and 1967

Clients' Industry	Activity	Number of Clients		Fees	
		1966	1967	1966	1967
Food, drink and tobacco	Production, Personnel	2	2	£50,000	£70,000
Engineering and electrical goods	Organization, Production	22	21	£29,000	£25,000
Metal goods	Organization, Production, Marketing	5	4	£12,000	£11,000
Bricks, pottery, glass	Production, Personnel	1	2	£35,000	£30,000
Timber, furniture	Management Accountants and Clerical Procedure		1	—	£1,000
Paper, printing and publishing	Organization, Personnel	1	2	£500	£1,000
Professional and Scientific Services	Management Accountants and Clerical Procedure, Personnel	2	3	£1,700	£2,000
		33	35	£138,200	£140,000

The company's fees are 250 guineas per week and each consultant is expected to be earning fees for about 70 per cent of the year. With twenty consultants that would produce an income of about £175,000, and 10 per cent profit before tax is normally earned.

Mr Robbins aimed to maintain the highest professional standards, and as part of that philosophy no deliberate 'selling' is undertaken by the company and clients are not persuaded to use the firm's services. He realized that this anti-selling attitude was the main reason for the smallness of the firm; he preferred to remain small and to rely on reputation and recommendation as the basis for earning the company's income. The engineering training scheme has only brought in three small assignments in the last twelve years and the training staff have been told that they were not to seek assignments for the consultancy side of the firm. He anticipated that the firm might grow to having thirty consultants.

Every firm of consultants ought to take very great care in selecting its staff. Industrial Administration follow the same procedure that they offer to clients who ask them to recruit senior executives; it consists of a series of interviews and consultation by telephone with referees. Mr Robbins said he looked firstly for integrity in an applicant, secondly acceptability, and thirdly knowledge, but knowledge was less significant because it could always be supplemented. However, he preferred applicants to possess a university degree or a professional qualification. Consultants usually spent about five years with the firm and many then left to take up senior posts in industry at a much higher salary. He did not believe that the firm would ever suffer from a shortage of suitable applicants.

I interviewed the youngest consultant on the staff after he had worked for the firm for about eighteen months. This relative beginner was likely to provide some insight into the firm and I wanted to find out about his selection, training, initial assignments, and his assessment of the organization's efficiency. Industrial Administration selected the information and the individuals made available to us but I am satisfied that no deliberate or accidental bias occurred in selecting individuals and clients for our study.

Mr A. was twenty-six years of age in 1968 and had a law degree from Manchester University. He did a year's course at the Manchester Business School and a term at Leicester University Business School on a job evaluation project. He had decided some years before that he wanted general industrial experience, and after leaving college he spent two years in a variety of jobs in several different firms, including a period on the shop floor. He is a small man with considerable self-confidence that appears to be largely justified, highly intelligent and I would guess very able. He is self-critical, keen on his work, and conscientious. He seems to lead a balanced life with a variety of interests. He is a bachelor. He expects to spend up to seven years with the firm and then to become a general manager.

He spent his first six months with Industrial Administration at their head office. He had experienced a very gruelling series of selection interviews, lasting about ten hours altogether, before he was offered the job. As a result of those interviews, the senior staff must have known his major weaknesses and proceeded to reduce them in a number of informal training discussions. He was also encouraged to attend a number of carefully selected short courses of various kinds provided by several other organizations; such outside courses are considered an important part of the firm's training policy. He also spent a week or two as an observer on some exacting assignments. That does not appear to be very systematic and there was no one person integrating the programme of training. It would appear that Mr. A. acquired considerable quantities of knowledge of a factual kind and a great deal of hearsay and anecdotalism. It is debatable whether in the case of this recruit such lengthy, varied and somewhat extravagant training was essential. For most other candidates and recruits it would seem a good recipe that could be improved with a little more careful preparation.

The first long-term assignment that he joined was concerned with job evaluation, working with two other consultants. He thought it was carried out reasonably well and he felt that his relationship with everybody concerned was satisfactory. The resident and supervising consultant found time to talk to him and pointed out his limitations. His second assignment was one of those that we observed and it is described later. Mr A. found this assignment stimulating. (It says something for the complex emotional nature of the management consultancy situation that Mr A. and one of the other consultants believed that the research assistant that visited him had been sent by I.A. to check up on them!) His third assignment was in charge of an industrial marketing research problem. He has no special knowledge of this field but he was working with an associate of Industrial Administration who is a specialist.

Mr A. had a high opinion of the organization and the efficiency of Industrial Administration but was aware of some faults. He believed that they were weak in certain areas of management and that they were not planning far enough ahead. He felt that too much was decided by senior people and that the juniors are not being encouraged sufficiently to express their ideas.[1]

Mr Robbins retired in 1967 and Mr P. Fatharly became managing director in his place. Mr A. believes that the same high professional standards were being well maintained and was only worried about the difficulties of maintaining them as the firm becomes larger. He expected it to double in size over the next ten years.

I asked Mr Robbins how he ensured that the efficiency of the organization was properly maintained and that the staff continued to observe high standards after they had been appointed to the company. The answer is partly provided by the organization of the company. Each assignment is in the hands of a resident consultant, and there is a supervising consultant for each five assignments. The supervisor spends one day per week on average at each assignment. There are also three directors who are partly employed in ensuring the quality of work of the supervisors. Mr Robbins believed that standards were maintained by providing extensive on-the-job training that could last up to two years, and by the energies of the supervising consultant and the director in charge of consultancy who ensured that the supervisors worked properly. Mr Robbins said that they aim to make their consultants capable of tackling all management problems and that there was therefore a great deal of exchange of knowledge and opinion in relation to assignments. That was continued at the top level, where irregular meetings were held between the supervisors and the directors at which current assignments were reviewed and procedures being followed were commented upon and criticised.

Every client benefits from all the resources of a consultancy firm such as Industrial Administration and not simply the skills of the resident consultant. The supervising consultant takes overall responsibility for the assignment and maps out the programme of work that the resident will carry out. Assignments are carefully planned, and

---

[1] It must be remembered that he was not aware of the secret development planning that was taking place and described in the postscript to this chapter.

defined quantities of work must be completed within specified periods of time. If the assignment takes longer than scheduled merely because the consultants misjudge the period needed, the firm cannot ask the client for additional fees. The weekly visits of the supervising consultant will thus be very relevant to the task that the resident is carrying through and they are not merely concerned with inspection.

We observed the following three assignments in the course of several visits whilst they were being carried out, with the consent of the client concerned:

Firm I are machine tool manufacturers, and the assignment concerned one of their factories in Southern England employing 240 people. Our information is based on three visits over a period of thirteen months; the project began before we first visited the factory and continued after it. The assignment involved a complete overhaul of the firm's production system and included responsibility for the selection and induction of a new factory manager, and the setting up of and output planning for a new product line.

The assignment was in the hands of one supervising consultant and one resident consultant, assisted by a consultant under training. The occasional services of a consultant specializing in accountancy were also involved, and for a three-week period a consultant specializing in personnel management was available to investigate the labour supply in the area.

The project involved the modification of production schedules and the elimination of a number of models, the strengthening and reorganization of factory management (including advice about the selection and appointment of three new members of middle management), the changes in design for a major product line, the improvement of production schedules, the conduct of market surveys of competitive products, converting the financial situation from loss to profit, and all related changes to company organization.

A very close relationship had been built up between the consultants and the factory manager and the company's directors. The resident consultant became almost an associate factory manager, and most decisions appeared to be taken jointly by the two men. The firm have in effect acquired a superior executive director for a limited period, able to apply his experience gained from a number of firms in different industries. He was able to assess problems objectively and to provide precise guidance to the firm. Although the assignment was primarily concerned with major reorganizations, a large number of day-to-day problems were considered by the resident consultant and he gave advice that was acted upon frequently by management. This assignment will lead to major changes of policy and convert the firm from manufacturing 'made-to-measure' machine tools into manufacturing standardized machine tools.

Firm II is a well-known firm of manufacturing confectioners. They have several factories around the country, and this assignment was in the north-west of England. Our information is based on a two-day visit, and interviews were held with the director in charge of the factory and with the team of five consultants engaged on the assignment.

The origins of the assignment go back to the appointment of the present Factory Director. Shortly after his appointment there was a three-day strike, the longest in the factory's history. The director decided that there was a need to review labour procedures, and after discussion with his personnel manager he decided to employ consultants in view of the complex industrial relations situation in the area. The company had never used consultants, and he decided to be as scientific as possible in selecting the consultants.

He began by consulting the register of consultants maintained by the British Institute of Management. Although he found the register somewhat less helpful than anticipated, he decided to approach five consultants. Two of the biggest appeared to the director to go in for 'high pressure' salesmanship and offered him expensive luncheons in order to persuade him of their virtues. The opposite effect was achieved: he was looking for consultants prepared to work hard, not entertainers. The third firm had a better approach but they failed to consider the individuality of the prospective client, and were rejected. The fourth firm was another large firm of consultants, but the factory director did not like the staff in the region, although they did endeavour to offer a service that took account of the individual circumstances of the client. They carried out a two-day survey and presented proposals. These did not appear to be sufficiently deep to win the respect of the manager and they may have carried out the survey too quickly. Industrial Administration were the fifth firm and they carried out a five-day survey of the situation.

In addition to interviewing consultants, the factory director and the personnel manager visited a number of other former clients of the two most favoured firms of consultants. They investigated thoroughly the experience of these clients with the consultancy firms.

This selection process lasted about six months, and in the end Industrial Administration were offered the assignment and accepted it. Later, another firm of consultants were called in by the head office of the company to undertake a general review of company organization, and the two firms of consultants were able to work amicably together without overlapping.

The client decided that consultants were essential because the task to be carried out was beyond the experience of the company's own staff, although they were of a very high calibre. The factory had been established for fifteen years and had grown rapidly to a labour force of 4,500. Industrial Administration were to assist with the application of a productivity agreement that had recently been concluded with the engineering unions; it covered rates of pay and a number of work practices. The agreement would also involve changes in recruitment policy and the reorganization of the engineering department. At the time of our visit, the client believed that his confidence in Industrial Administration was justified, although he felt that the consultants should only be judged after a further year's work. It was clear that their high standards of competence and integrity coincided with the philosophy of the client.

A major part of the assignment was concerned with job evaluation and with training. That involved a number of complex cases where similar trades were to become interchangeable and possess a common standard of pay. The unions, being parties to the productivity agreements, co-operated in this study, but considerable patience was needed to win support as the investigation progressed. The analysis of training needs was a long process and the collaboration of many people inside and outside the factory had to be obtained.

The following report on part of one day's activities during his visit was made by the research assistant. He was visiting the consultants with the consent of the client and he had interviewed the factory director on the previous day.

The working day started at 9.20 a.m. when one of the consultants began drawing up the agenda for the following Monday's regular planning meeting with senior executives of the factory. The meeting was to be concerned with the job evaluation programme due to start on that day. A working party and a review committee were to be set up.

'From 9.45 to 11 a.m. I toured the factory with Mr Z (a consultant). He showed a ready awareness of the total layout of the various production lines. He commented that the client company does not rush to replace satisfactory equipment if the replacements will not necessarily yield greater productivity. He pointed out the odd instance where the lines appeared to be over-manned, or where a more successful flow line for production could be established.

At 11 a.m. Mr Z and Mr Y (another consultant) had a meeting with Mr X, the factory manager.

This meeting was essentially an 'ironing-out' session. The thinking was presented essentially by I.A., but Mr X produced cases, made comments and represented the views of the client staff at appropriate intervals.

Two of the matters under discussion were (a) the location of a chargehand and whether he should have a telephone and office against the 'normal' factory procedure, and (b) the difficulties of implementing a double day shift.

The productivity agreements at present being implemented cover a total of 330 engineering workers who provide the essential services to back production. The aim of Industrial Administration is to provide enough fitters to cover all shifts.

Production continues throughout Friday night until six o'clock on Saturday mornings. Graphs and appropriate plans were presented during the discussion. Mr X expressed some surprise that the new night shift rate would be £5 12s 6d. Also discussed were (a) the implementation of the double day shift and (b) providing supervision for overtime. There is a trend towards telling the production manager what is proposed, i.e. consultation after the decision has been taken but before the event takes place. Mr X fully realizes the difficulties of foremen being allowed to sanction overtime and knows that the weaker ones are likely to sanction overtime to curry favour. There is some difficulty because the electricians are seeking to go their own way rather than join up in the most effective manner with the departmental heads.

At 11.45 a.m. Mr Y had a meeting with the chief engineer. Names for various posts in the factory are to be changed following the recommendations of the other firm of consultants working at head office. Industrial Administration readily agreed to alter their proposed names to come into line with those suggested. For example, the projects foremen are to be promoted to projects engineers.

Mr Y explained that the consultants always ring up first when visiting a senior member of management. At this interview he was letting the chief engineer play a directive role. This meeting was in effect further liaison following the discussions with Mr Y. The consultants spend a large part of their time preserving the most effective communication lines and channels as the total plans are implemented.

At 12.05 we returned to the office to discuss various aspects of the consultants' work. They pointed out that for the last three months they have suggested that a pocket paging system should be installed so that engineers not in their offices could be easily contacted. Although this recommendation was made three months ago the client still had not agreed to its implementation.

A fortnight's management course is to be held at head office. One of the aims of this course is to widen the experience of managers who have only specialist knowledge. Industrial Administration staff are sufficiently friendly with members of middle management to help them select their topics and write their papers in preparation for this course.

Lunch (free for consultants) was served from 12.45 to 1.40 p.m.

At 1.45 p.m. a working party met to consider the allotment of offices for managers following the reallocations about to take place. At this meeting the consultants were assigning jobs to all of the members of the teams present. The client's team was made up of a foreman, deputy chief engineer, and a junior member of the engineering department. It was obvious that all three members were prepared to defer to the consultants, and the amount of work given out was quite considerable. The consultants, I would presume, will be on hand sufficiently often to give advice and stimulation where necessary to ensure the working party produces its results to a required standard in the appropriate time. The youngest member of the group had to liaise with head office about planning boards, order forms, envelopes and workshop order forms. The other members of the client team were concerned to build up the necessary information for scheduled maintenance. Throughout the meeting the consultants adopted tones of careful, quiet explanation. Among items to be considered by the working party are stores, part stores, stock items, offices, and the location of the seven planning assistants. A most interesting point arose about the movement of lockers, drawers, or trolleys for the engineering craftsmen whilst moving from the different sites of their locations.

The team appeared to take a reasonable management line as regards smoking and acceptance of the value of de-centralized clocking. The working party took away sufficient information to consider the problems of movement of tools, and where to clock. Also the establishment of a co-ordination office. Throughout this meeting there was frank speech by the client team. There was also discussion about the people in the fitting shop.

The frankness and lack of inhibition to communication were the outstanding impressions gained from this working party.

At 2.55 p.m. we went to see the industrial relations manager. He was concerned with the agenda for a meeting next week about the distribution of the night shift and double day working. He was currently involved in an internal dispute with one of his engineering staff. The nub of the problem concerned double day working, and clearly all that is necessary is some further thought. The industrial relations manager is undoubtedly correct in stating his view about the need to preserve a management front after the main negotiating body and joint craft consultative committee have been approached. Other facts having come to light, however, it is essential to uphold the Industrial Administration view that further negotiations are necessary.

The industrial relations manager took a line which was correct and orthodox but it seemed that the apportionment of blame for what after all was a human situation probably involved both the consultants and the client's staff. Mr Z showed much tact and commonsense throughout these discussions, and was able at the end of them to promise to smooth out the difficulties in the future.

My main general impressions of the assignment are:

1. Industrial Administration's consultants, except perhaps the most junior one, have appreciated that the client may have overall strategies and policies for growth and development which are equal to any firm in the industry. Mr Y and Mr Z both pointed out that they appreciate the need for a careful speed of change within the client's organization. Whilst a hire and fire approach is inappropriate to the firm's traditions, they appear to combine the better aspects of market-

orientated firms with above average concern for the individual employee. For example, the promotion of all foremen is still dependent upon Board approval.

2. The need and importance of the personal touch was stressed. Mr Z has clearly shown great skill and expertise in bringing his personal influence to bear in an appropriate manner. For example, the client director has appreciated being involved in the annual managing directors' conference organized by Industrial Administration.

3. This respect for the factory director and the client's traditions cannot be too strongly emphasized. The other consultant firms failed to secure a most useful piece of business and the possibility of many more assignments because they ignored this factor.

4. Given their age, both the more mature resident consultants, Mr Y and Mr Z, appeared to have great skill, capability and flexibility. They possess the ability to mix with all levels of staff, to be on first name terms with senior management without abusing the privilege, and also to be able to nod to operatives or very junior ranks without becoming involved. The client's dining system helps considerably in this matter. They have provided a self-service cafeteria and a 'waitress service' dining-room. There are no other distinctions but this system in itself enables those who prefer to exploit their status through withdrawing at meal times to do so.

5. The consultants have been concerned to initiate, plan, co-ordinate, consult, and build up confidence and acceptance of the need for innovation. They have been and are an essential adjunct to the factory organization. They have let the management of the factory perform their routine tasks, and involved them to a sufficient degree for the client management to feel responsible for the successful outcome of the reorganizations. The job the consultants have done is necessarily peculiar to skilled outsiders with specific and specialist areas of expertise. By recruiting new staff, reallocating duties of staff, and generally aiding management development where appropriate, when the assignment is complete the factory will be in a better state of ongoing productivity than when they initially arrived. They showed throughout this visit that they are aware of the need to help the organization to carry on without them by being an essential catalyst to the whole reorganization process.'

Firm III are cosmetic manufacturers with a Midlands factory. They had brought in Industrial Administration to carry out a job evaluation assignment for all managerial posts. It was estimated that the project would last for six months. Mr P, the resident consultant, had an engineering background and had become a specialist in personnel matters. He was about fifty years of age. Mr Q, the supervising consultant, spent one day a week at the factory in accordance with the normal practice.

Our information is based on a half-day visit and it was not possible to interview representatives of the client in private. However, it appeared that the assignment was progressing to the satisfaction of both parties, and the only unusual aspect was the decision to employ consultants instead of engaging a full-time specialist. The assignment was likely to cost the clients about £6,000 and therefore it would have been more economic to engage their own staff. The consultants were expected to be more acceptable to the staff of the client firm because they would be somewhat more objective in the complex process of evaluating managers. The company is prosperous and expanding, and they were not trying to economize. They believed that the consultants should be able to do a better job and avoid the difficulties faced by management when introducing job evaluation without outside help.

We were curious to know whether suppliers of external aid such as management consultants themselves made use of other forms of external aid. Industrial Administration are members of the Management Consultants' Association and Mr Robbins was for some time a member of the Council of that Association. The Association, being a trade association, supplied a number of benefits to its members and perhaps its main task has been the defence of the consultant's reputation. It is a very small organization employing only two officials and meets the existing requirements of its members. It was instrumental in establishing the Institute of Management Consultants in 1962 and they have offices at the same address. Most of the members of the Institute are employed by member firms of the Management Consultants' Association.

Most of the training of the firm's consultants is done on the job and to that extent, like most consultants, they do not practice what they usually preach. They imply that consultancy is primarily an intuitive aptitude and much of it cannot be systematically learned. There is no evidence to support that view and in practice the on-the-job training testifies to the inadequacy of this particular hypothesis—some training is clearly recognized as being necessary. However, the nature and content of training by Industrial Administration is varied to suit the calibre of each individual.

The consultants we visited appeared to derive considerable educational value from a wide range of publications. Published material provides the opportunity for continual training as the consultant spends long periods away from home and has some empty leisure hours in isolated places.

The company is a member of the European Consortium of Management Consultants which is a private international alliance of experienced firms offering management consulting services throughout the world.

The consortium was established on the initiative of Industrial Administration in 1960 with a view to meeting the expected requirements of clients in relation to the European Economic Community. It was thought undesirable to set up a special European department or offices in a number of European countries in view of the considerable expense involved. Instead, it was decided to seek relationships with similar consultancy firms in each of the main European countries, and a network has been built up of eight such firms, plus an arrangement with three American firms specializing in particular management problems.

The scheme for the consortium was clearly described in the following document prepared by Mr Fatharly in 1964. He was elected chairman of the consortium at the beginning and has held that office continually since it began operations in 1962:

EUROPEAN CONSORTIUM OF MANAGEMENT CONSULTANTS

STATEMENT OF TERMS OF AGREEMENT EVOLVED DURING THE
FIRST TWO YEARS OF OPERATION

1. The original object in forming the Consortium was to enable any one member to offer to his clients expert consulting services in any of the countries represented by other members. This would greatly widen the scope of each member's operations and offer a much higher operating potential to existing and future clients without the disadvan-

tages of each member carrying the high overhead costs that are associated in setting up individual offices in various European cities.

2. It is essential that as far as possible member companies should be of similar type—that is, they should not be widely different in size and composition. They should also be fairly matched in respect of experience and services offered, and, most important, have a common outlook on the ethical aspects of consulting.

3. It is most important that all members should be compatible professionally and personally.

4. Further members will be admitted to the Consortium only after full agreement by existing members.

5. Not more than one member will be admitted from any one country, as it is not intended to promote competition between members in their own countries.

6. The Chairman of the Consortium shall be elected annually, and he will be responsible for nominating a Secretary from his own company to function during the Chairman's period of office. In general, the company from whom the Chairman is elected shall act as the 'post box' for inter-communication between members and for the dissemination of Consortium news and information.

7. English will be the language used at all Consortium meetings, and wherever practical, it shall also be used in written communication.

8. Full Consortium meetings will be held three times a year, spaced by approximately four months, and each member will, in turn, act as host in his own country for these meetings. In the early stages of the Consortium's existence, some part of each Consortium meeting shall be set aside for the host company to present case studies or some aspects of his consulting operations.

9. It is intended that Consortium meetings shall be held during Sundays and Mondays so as to minimize interference with the normal working week.

10. It is intended during the early stages that the association between members shall be a loose one, and that members shall observe the general code of behaviour that is set down from time to time at Consortium meetings. At this time, May 1964, the principal operating practices are as follows:

(a) There shall be no formal bond between members.

(b) Any one member is free to operate in another member's country, but as a matter of courtesy the foreign member shall notify the local member that he will, in fact, be so operating.

(c) Any member when operating in another country may call upon the member from that country to provide staff or any other assistance that may be necessary. The fees charged for this work shall be agreed separately on each occasion.

(d) Whenever a member is negotiating with a client for an assignment that takes him into another member's country, he is free to lead the job personally, with or without assistance from the local member, or to pass the assignment over to the local member. In this case he may also want some of his own staff to participate.

(e) Whenever any member requires assistance in another member's country, it is agreed that he will first contact the local member, who in turn will give a factual answer as to whether his is the best company to provide assistance in each particular case. If his company is not, then he will recommend to the foreign member another local company who will be able to provide expert service.

(f) The method of charging fees, both between members and between members and their clients, will be agreed locally on each occasion.

(g) Whenever there is joint working in any of these ways, the local member will be responsible for keeping the foreign member advised on progress at regular intervals and all problems as they arise.

(h) On all occasions at this stage arrangements will be simply on a bilateral basis. This will provide adequate opportunity for members to come to know each other and to assess various strengths in consulting operations.

(i) Opportunity will always be given for members to meet potential clients from other countries.

(j) All members will provide information for other members when requested to do so. Charges, where appropriate, will be agreed on each occasion before the work is undertaken. Clearly where the work is of a very minor nature, it is not expected that individual charges will be made.

The members of the consortium are now actively discussing the development of its activities to extend membership into other countries and to set up a full-time secretariat.

POSTSCRIPT

The preceding description of Industrial Administration was submitted to them for discussion towards the end of the project, and they were invited to point out any errors in fact or comment. Some useful corrections were made as a result of that discussion. However, I was then given some additional information that made it clear that I had not fully appreciated the company's forward thinking and planning. That is not surprising as the development of the firm involved confidential negotiations before any publicity was desirable.

Before Mr Robbins retired in 1967 the problem of the disposal of his majority shareholding began to be examined. Mr Fatharly, who had already been designated his successor, designed a five-year development plan that began with proposals for overcoming the problems inherent in a closed company. He held discussions with a number of city investors and eventually a scheme emerged for three well-established trusts to join with some of Industrial Administration's senior executives to purchase Mr Robbins' shares and establish a new holding company that would act as the parent for a number of other companies. One of the main subsidiaries was to be Industrial Administration, and another was to be concerned with financing a number of new business ventures. The intention was to provide finance for the development of Industrial Administration and also to offer a financial service to clients in need of additional capital. Another possible use of the finance company would be to provide specialized industrial knowledge in assessing business proposals, particularly in unquoted companies, that the investment trusts might receive in the course of their normal activities.

A major part of Mr Fatharly's plans was to ensure that Industrial Administration grew but did not exceed a size that made possible close collaboration between all its members. He plans to reach a size of fifty consultants within the next two years and to stay at that figure. However, partly to ensure that there are opportunities for competent consultants to develop their own abilities in their own companies, a network of small subsidiaries is envisaged that would cover specialized consultancy services in such fields as marketing. The new group structure could also lead to the provision of temporary or permanent senior executive opportunities for consulting staff in a number of manufacturing and service companies financed by the holding company. The group has already invested in various companies in engineering, entertainments, and publishing.

One other major development was the decision to buy the firm of John Tyzack and Partners Limited who specialize in management selection, management training, and remuneration studies as well as offering management consultancy services. That merger was also linked to the problem of operating a closed company that has become very successful in its own field. It is also a relatively small organization, and in accordance with Industrial Administration's policy about size, it will continue to exist in its own name and to operate independently. The selection and the training work now undertaken by Industrial Administration may gradually be transferred to John Tyzack.

Thus the problem of growth is to be solved by a network of small units under the umbrella of a holding company that will in no way interfere with the specialist activities of each subsidiary. It is particularly important for the consulting companies that the holding company should act as a buffer between the institutional shareholders and the consulting operations to avoid their interests conflicting with those of the clients.

This very interesting attempt to deal with the problem of growth without magnifying the consultancy organization into a giant company is unusual, possibly unique. It will be valuable to observe its future experiences as it may well provide a suitable guide for many other consultancy firms to follow.

CONCLUSIONS

Professor Johnston's study of management consultancy has already shown the difficulties of assessing its value. Probably some fairly precise method of evaluating the work of consultants could be constructed but it would need thorough research involving many more subtle techniques than statistical multiplication and financial estimates.

Nevertheless, some attempt at overall assessment of Industrial Administration is a necessary part of this enquiry. There is no important evidence of inefficiency or incompetence, although like every other human organization there is almost certainly scope for marginal improvements and economies. The main basis for judging management performance must be associated with the goals that management has set and its degree of success in achieving them. The goals must of course be carefully constructed and not simply be the minimum that would occur even without managerial effort. Once adequate goals have been defined, it would then be necessary to work out criteria for assessing the quality and rate of achievement.

Industrial Administration had no clearly defined goals for future growth during the main part of our enquiries. The founder of the company wished it to remain small in order to maintain the highest professional standards and there seems no reason to doubt that those standards are reasonably maintained. But it is difficult to know whether smallness is a necessary condition of professionalism, and the four large firms of management consultants in this country would not accept that largeness necessarily involves lack of integrity or ability. Perhaps the question of size is irrelevant; the main problem is the process of consultancy and its supervision, irrespective of the number of consultants employed by one organization. One characteristic of professionalism is independence for the professional worker, and reputable consultants achieve considerable independence because of their relative scarcity and geographical distance from their employers in most assignments.

Thus the ultimate test of Industrial Administration's competence would involve a judgment about the appropriateness of the size of the management consultancy firm. But nobody knows the necessary relationship between efficient consultancy and size. It is obvious that consultants require an increasing superstructure of specialists' services, and the ease of access to those specialists is more important than their formal incorporation within the consultancy firm.

The major challenge for most firms of consultants is their ability to retain their highly skilled staff, most of whom are capable of earning higher salaries in senior executive positions in industry or commerce. Most will stay in consultancy so long as they enjoy it and so long as they can expect an adequate career as a consultant. The test of Industrial Administration's preference to remain small lies in its consequences for unwanted labour turnover. Growth is frequently unavoidable if highly valued staff are to be retained, because most of them do require opportunities for expanding experience and that cannot usually be obtained within a static population of employees. The network of small firms that Industrial Administration is promoting may ensure the benefits of both small and large firms. But there are inevitable dangers in expansion, however great the independence of operating units.

One other major criterion of competence (apart from the obvious one of obtaining clients without difficulty) is the firm's concern with standards of knowledge and performance by its consultants. There would seem an unavoidable need for considerable attention to research in technical and scientific fields and more importantly in the fields of the social sciences and psychology. Industrial Administration seems no more concerned with this behavioural aspect of its functions than most consultancy firms, and until the evolution of consultancy away from its primitive engineering attitudes occurs there will be a neglect of opportunities to benefit clients through the use of consultants skilled in the social sciences.

Is it possible for a firm like Industrial Administration to reach the standards of sociological and psychological knowledge that are increasingly necessary and possible? Fortunately, their high professional standards have taken them most of the way required by present knowledge, and their responsible attitudes should encourage the necessary recruitment of social scientists in the future. But there must be considerable problems for any firm, particularly a small one, in adapting to the changing demands of clients and of knowledge.

The probable high cost of research in all relevant areas, including the social sciences, may well be a major obstacle to the firm's long-term prosperity. The answer is not to become as large as possible, because that might destroy many of the firm's sensitivities. But a search for an alternative will be vital. It may be found in the provision of research and information centrally, possibly by the Management Consultants' Association, or by a federal arrangement between several small firms of consultants.

Chapter 3

The Trade Association

The British Chemical Plant Manufacturers' Association was established in 1920 and was originally called the Association of British Chemical Plant Manufacturers. It was formed at the suggestion of the Association of British Chemical Manufacturers which represented its principal customers, and B.C.P.M.A. was affiliated to that Association until 1963. It was initially concerned with standardization, chemical engineering education, publicity, and acting as a clearing centre for plant enquiries. From that beginning many other activities have developed. It is the trade association of British engineering companies engaged in the design, manufacture and installation of plant, machinery and ancillary equipment for the chemical and process industries. Apart from these immediate concerns B.C.P.M.A. was set up because a representative body was needed with which the rapidly expanding chemical industry could discuss its equipment problems.

The Association, in December 1967, had 170 ordinary members and eighty-one associate members. Members are concerned with all aspects of chemical engineering including manufacturers of, and contractors for, complete process plant and manufacturers of plant for unit operations and unit processes, and producers of specialist fabrications in a wide range of materials. The associate members are manufacturers of ancillary equipment such as instruments, pumps, and valves, and suppliers of specialist services such as thermal insulation and chemical plant lining, and manufacturers and suppliers of materials used in construction of plant and of plant components. Membership subscriptions range from £40 to £350 on an annual turnover exceeding £4 million. Associate members pay a flat rate of £25 a year. During 1967, seventeen firms joined and nineteen resigned. Six of the resignations were due to firms ceasing to manufacture chemical plant, and three were absorbed into associated companies already in membership.

In 1968, the Association had an income of £000000 including £00000 from the Food Machinery Association for its share in the cost of administrative services. It had a surplus of £00000 of income over expenditure that brought its accumulated reserves to just over £00000 and current assets exceeded current liabilities by £00000.

The Association occupies premises near Trafalgar Square and shares offices with the Food Machinery Association. Its permanent staff consists of the director, the secretary, a technical officer, a commercial officer, and clerical staff—a total of eleven. The staff are shared with the Food Machinery Association. B.C.P.M.A. is incorporated as a guarantee company without share capital. It is managed by a Council consisting of a chairman, all past chairmen, the honorary treasurer, and up to fifteen elected members, and from that is appointed an executive committee. There are sub-committees dealing with exports, finance, publicity, and research.

The objects of the Association as stated in its memorandum of association are:

(1) to foster the manufacture of British chemical plant;
(2) to promote co-operation and interchange of information between British chemical plant manufacturers;
(3) to co-operate with the Association of British Chemical Manufacturers (now the Chemical Industries' Association) with a view to providing so far as practicable British chemicals shall be made with British plant;
(4) to place before government, the chemical and allied industries, and others the views of members on matters affecting the chemical plant industry.

The Association supplies its members with a number of commercial services, which include negotiations with the Board of Trade about duty on imported chemical machinery. The Association helps members engaged in export trade by maintaining extensive records on overseas countries; liaising with the Board of Trade and the Export Credits Guarantee Department; handling enquiries on such matters as tariffs, licensing, import and exchange controls, and agencies. An extensive collection of reports and directories is available for consultation. Desk surveys on the chemical and allied industries in a number of overseas markets have been undertaken, while in 1966 the Association organized a joint mission with the Food Machinery Association to South Africa.

The Association publishes a biennial directory entitled *British Chemical Plant*. This should be specially noted as such publications are not generally undertaken by trade associations. It is, the Association says, 'a compact, comprehensive, and authoritative guide to members' products and a first-class advertising medium'. The circulation is 6,500 and it is distributed free to chemical and allied manufacturers at home and abroad. Whilst charges are made to members for display advertisements, the directory includes without charge a list of members with their addresses and a classified index of products with the names of manufacturers.

The Association is a joint sponsor of the International Chemical and Petroleum Engineering Exhibition, held in London every four years, and organizes joint ventures with financial support from the Board of Trade at the ACHEMA, the triennial German chemical plant exhibition.

It supplies a range of technical services, including answering a large number of 'where to buy' enquiries by post and telephone. It is an important channel of information between members and their customers, offering unbiased advice on the plant and services available from the British chemical engineering industry. It has sponsored nine research projects in chemical engineering at several universities since 1962, paid for by interested member firms. It is concerned with standardization of chemical plant and is represented on some sixty technical committees of the British Standards Institution.

The Association is in close contact with the Ministry of Technology, which is the sponsoring department for the chemical plant industry, and the National Economic Development Committee. It keeps in touch with customer industry associations and those covering kindred areas of the engineering industry, and with appropriate professional and learned societies. It is a founder member of the European Committee of Chemical Plant Manufacturers.

These comments and descriptions are largely factual and not likely to be disputed, and fairly easy to unravel. But we were anxious to obtain a more meaningful and active picture of the Association than could be gleaned from a study of documents. We began with a series of discussions with the permanent officials and seven visits were devoted to this purpose. An eighth visit sought evidence of activities by a review of samples of correspondence with members as indicated from certain files of the Association. In addition we requested assistance in visiting member firms who were selected at random by the Secretary. Three organizations were visited in order to find out what their views were on the Association.

In 1966 four members of the Association left and established the British Chemical Engineering Contractors' Association and a visit was made to the director of that Association. It is on the basis of these discussions that we began to formulate the following appreciation.

The Association exists as part of an elaborate network of sources of aid and users of aid. Above the Association is the Confederation of British Industry and the British Mechanical Engineering Federation (now Confederation). Somewhere separate from it, perhaps parallel to it, is the Chemical Industries' Association and the new British Chemical Engineering Contractors' Association. Surrounding it are numerous other associations of related industries and many of its member firms will also be members of one or more of these other associations.

As with most trade associations, relations with government are important and take up a great deal of time and effort. Considerable controversy has been going on since 1965 about the relative efficiency of the process plant industry in view of the large fluctuations in demand and supply and the consequent long periods of delay in meeting orders in boom periods. As a result, the government believes that imports of chemical plant are excessive and due primarily to domestic delays in meeting orders. It is also suggested that British process plant exports could be much greater.

There has been considerable pressure on the industry to increase its rate of investment but the plant manufacturers are somewhat sceptical about the advice they receive. They believe that in the past three years they have made considerable progress and that they should now be able to cope satisfactorily with another boom.

It is not necessary to enter into the technicalities of this controversy except as it affects the working of B.C.P.M.A. and its members. Apart from the work involved within its offices and for its officers and officials, the Association is much concerned with the work of the Process Plant Working Party, set up under the aegis of the National Economic

Development Office in July 1966 'for the purpose of studying the imbalance between demand and supply of process plant, to advise on necessary action, and to stimulate it'. It consists of representatives of four trade associations, two trade unions, four government departments, the Gas Council, and NEDO. It has published three reports on investment by the process industries and is now attempting to establish how far UK plant manufacturing capacity is adequate to meet the demand. These reports were not intended to be a substitute for market research by individual equipment manufacturers but they have provided useful guidelines.

The Ministry of Technology has also set up an Expert Committee on Process Plant with the following terms of reference: 'To consider, in consultation with the Process Plant Working Party, the further measures necessary to promote co-ordination of the process industries and process plant suppliers; to define objectives for the future development of plant suppliers; to make detailed recommendations designed to promote the efficiency and competitiveness of plant suppliers; and to advise on the adequacy or otherwise for these purposes of the finance available to them from their own resources or other existing sources of finance.' The setting up of this committee is a matter for regret by the Association though it is composed of individuals, serving in their personal capacities and chosen, in some cases, as a result of suggestions put forward by B.C.P.M.A., who are well qualified to advise the Ministry about the problems facing chemical plant manufacturers.

The future prosperity of the Association's members is of course intimately bound up with these problems but much of the Association's concern must be defensive and political, concerned to protect its members against unjust accusation and unwanted interference. Whatever the merits of the committees, it is doubtful whether they have achieved a great deal and the only short-term outcome of government concern is likely to be yet one more official body to exhort the industry to do something about the present demand and supply situation. If that does happen, B.C.P.M.A. members may well wonder what the Association has achieved, other than avoid the almost certain direct government intervention that would have occurred without the Association's activities.

Whilst members' attitudes may be positive or negative towards the Association without greatly influencing its existence, the crucial problem for the British Chemical Plant Manufacturers' Association is the use that its members make of it. In our discussions with three member firms (not necessarily representative of the total membership) we were surprised to find that they were relatively uninformed about the Association's activities and were not very impressed with what they had found out. However, none of them had any clear idea of what more the Association ought to be doing and it is notoriously easy to criticize another organization and yet leave undefined the role that the critics believe it ought to follow. The interesting and important point that came out from two of these discussions was that the firms would be willing to pay a much higher membership subscription if they were able to obtain better individual services and more detailed information on certain points than they were now receiving. That criticism appears to be primarily directed towards exporting and the implication was that the Association ought to be doing much more to find out about market opportunities and to negotiate contracts, particularly where they involved manufacturers from a number of different industries.

The critics were not anxious to play a more active role in the Association themselves and it could have been said that we were faced with merely another example of the dilemma of democracy—the system did not work perfectly but the elector was not willing to do anything about changing the system. On the other hand, the analogy is misleading because a trade association is not representative of every firm in the industry nor is total membership needed before useful work can be achieved. If associations were run entirely by their elected members, apathy or non-participation would be a crucial democratic difficulty. But the officials who are appointed to carry out policies (or to help form them) have created a different situation. Their existence implies a high degree of professionalism and of speedy commercial action. One of the members interviewed would have preferred much greater power being given to the permanent officials and suggested that council members should not become involved in the details of association policy or practice. Criticisms were naturally made about the officers and it was felt that a shorter term in office would be desirable. That was coupled with the view that more specialist groups or committees should be set up to consider in detail the special problems of particular segments of the industry.

The lack of specialist sector committees may have been a contributing factor to the decision of four very large chemical engineering contractors to break away from the Association to form the British Chemical Engineering Contractors' Association. They have very little in common with the majority of the Association's members, some of whom are very small firms manufacturing specialized equipment; the membership as a whole appears to reflect the pattern of the engineering industry in general and includes small, medium and large companies. The contractors, on the other hand, are giant firms able to handle contracts worth several million pounds and undertake to erect complete oil refineries and similar mammoth enterprises. The four firms have been joined by two others, and any other British firm able to construct an entire chemical plant anywhere in the world would be eligible for membership. There appear to be a few firms verging on eligibility and there are a number of much smaller firms that might in time grow large enough to qualify. In addition there are at least nine large American firms with companies established in this country who ought to be eligible but by friendly agreement are not members. This is due to the fact that there is fierce competition abroad between the two national groups and there is no likelihood of their collaborating in one British association. The anti-trust legislation in the United States may be a complicating factor. The main function of the Contractors' Association is to represent its members in the normal way but with particular concern for tax, customs duty, and E.C.G.D. policies that affect overseas construction jobs. As its membership is so small its formalities are minimal and its monthly meetings are attended by the managing director or an immediately subordinate director of its member firms. On the face of it, there seems to be no need for separate associations because there are examples of other trade associations representing a very wide range of firms all broadly linked to one particular technology or type of customer.

In this complicated situation it is extremely difficult to reach any satisfactory assessment of the adequacy and necessity of the plant manufacturers' association. Its existence for nearly fifty years suggests that it has performed a useful function. The changing nature of the requirements of its members should bring about new activities and they will be associated with the reforms coming from the C.B.I. report on mechanical engineering trade associations.

The C.B.I. were asked by the British Mechanical Engineering

Federation to help in undertaking a review of the trade associations in the industry. The report was produced after many discussions and enquiries over several years.[1]

The Council of B.C.P.M.A. considered the report at a special meeting in January 1967 and its majority view was that a central body would be of benefit to the industry and to the Association. A conference organized by the C.B.I. in June 1967 reviewed reactions to the report and examined some of the detailed changes that would be needed to carry it out. The meeting agreed, although not unanimously, to proceed with the matter and a steering committee was set up to draft a constitution for the central body that would be considered by a further conference. An interim report was published in February 1968.

A more popular version of the report was issued in July 1968 and announced that positive action had been taken to set up the new central organization. It stressed that its purpose was to seek support from companies in the mechanical engineering industry for a new central organization and to ask them to encourage their sector associations to join and support the new organization. The main reasons for the new organization were given as: increasing foreign competition and increasing government intervention, heavier costs, and taxation. 'If the industry is to counter these trends it must speak and act as a united and powerful force in dealing with Government and others when the interests and future prosperity of the industry are at stake.' The booklet points out that the government has neither the time nor the inclination to listen to a large number of trade associations in an industry but that it does consider the views of large associations representing an entire industry.

The new association will 'studiously avoid duplicating work that can be done better by sector associations or the C.B.I.' It will be located in the same building as that occupied by the British Electrical and Allied Manufacturers' Association who will supply accommodation and services on favourable terms. Four officials are to be appointed initially and will start work whilst a constitution is being worked out and members recruited. Financial support is promised by a group of large companies in the industry.

The Association has emphasized that while supporting a central organization, it believes that its success will depend on continued sup-

[1] See page 33.

76

port for specialist associations. 'This problem underlines the need for rationalization of the sectional associations and the Chairman has had informal talks with a number of associations with interests similar to B.C.P.M.A. While these talks revealed a desire for rationalization they also demonstrated that associations do not want to lose their identity. The Executive Committee feels that the technological links between associations in the process plant field are so strong that rationalization could provide better and more effective service for members and that loss of identity could well be more apparent than real. The Committee will be examining this matter in greater detail in 1968.' [1]

The British Mechanical Engineering Confederation is now in existence and B.C.P.M.A. is one of its ten founder members.

We have learned enough about B.C.P.M.A. to know that we would not be able to make any reliable comments about it without much more detailed study. It would require at least one year to obtain a comprehensive understanding of its activities and to make recommendations for possibly desirable changes. It was not the intention of this study to make such a detailed study nor to act as consultants. Our aim was to obtain an appreciation of the activities and problems of a trade association so as to be aware of the nature of one of the major sources of aid to management. Any later comments about trade associations may or may not apply to B.C.P.M.A. but are intended to be relevant to trade associations as aids to management in general.

[1] Annual Report for year ended December 31, 1967.

Chapter 4

The Research Association

The research association that accepted our request for co-operation was the British Launderers' Research Association. Its premises are at Hillview Gardens, Hendon, N.W.4.

It was difficult to determine the best methods for studying this organization, which embraces a large number of members and committees and carries out a wide range of scientific research, most of it in specialized fields that we were not qualified to assess. It also was necessary to find out what the members of the association thought about it, and we believed that it would be important to know the views of firms in the laundry industry that did not belong to it. In order to understand the functions and achievements of the association, it was clearly necessary also to consider the services provided by other organizations in that and related industries. In addition, we had to consider the role of the Ministry of Technology in B.L.R.A. activities. We decided to attempt a superficial look at most of these secondary issues but to concentrate our attention on the central activities of the association. Apart from learning about its premises and activities and talking to its officials, the best method of obtaining an understanding of its total functions over a period of time seemed to be through attending meetings of its Council of members and the main committees of the Council. This was readily agreed to. Thus what follows is based on the following sources of information:

(a) six visits to Council meetings between May 1966 and May 1968;
(b) two meetings of the Finance and General Purposes Committee of the Council;
(c) four meetings of the Programme and Research Sub-Committee of the Council;

(d) visits to the Association's laboratories and talks with the Director and Secretary on February 15, 1966, November 2, 1966, and December 5, 1967;

(e) attendance at the Annual General Meeting on March 16, 1967, with about 200 people present;

(f) visits to two member firms;

(g) visits to two non-member firms;

(h) one visit to the Association of British Launderers and Cleaners, the trade association of the industry;

(i) visit to the International Laundry, Dry Cleaning and Allied Trades Exhibition at Olympia, July 1966;

(j) interview with the retiring chairman of the Association, Mr McKinney, on March 15, 1968, and interview with his successor, Mr R. Le Poidevin, September 15, 1968;

(k) meeting with the Director to review the work of the Association and to discuss the functions of the Committee of Directors of Research Associations, July 13, 1967.

The Association was founded on July 23, 1920. The registered number of members at that time was 300. The aims of the Association (which was registered as a limited company with licence to omit the word 'limited') was stated as follows:

'(a) to promote research and other scientific work in connection with the laundry and cleaning trades or industries, and for that purpose to establish, form equipment and maintain laboratories, workshops, or factories, and conduct and carry on experiments, and to provide funds for such work, and for payment to any person or persons engaged in research work, whether in such laboratories or elsewhere, and to encourage and improve the education of persons who are engaged in or are likely to be engaged in the said industries;

(b) to prepare, edit, print, publish, issue, acquire and circulate books, papers, periodicals, gazettes, circulars and other literary matter treating of or bearing upon the laundry and cleaning trades or industries, and to establish, form and maintain a library;

(c) to retain and employ skilled professional or technical advisers or workers in connection with the objects of the Association;

(d) to encourage the discovery of, and investigate and make known the nature and merits of inventions, improvements, processes, and materials.'

By 1946 the membership had risen to 1,500 and in 1968 it was 1,200. This decline is mainly due to mergers within the industry and does not appear to indicate any lack of support. In 1968, two member firms on average closed down every week.

The premises at Hendon comprise offices, laboratories, and a fully equipped laundry that used to function on adjoining premises, was bought in 1965 by the Association and has been equipped with considerable help from the manufacturers of laundry equipment.

In 1967 the Association's balance sheet showed that it had assets of just under £100,000. Its current liabilities amounted to £38,457. The income from subscriptions was £97,000 and grants from the Ministry of Technology amounted to £52,000. Income from the sale of publications and sundries was £1,480, income from technical advice to members £5,374 and other miscellaneous receipts of about £10,000.

The Association is managed by a Council, now consisting of twenty-six members. One of them is appointed by the Ministry of Health to represent the National Hospital Service, two members represent manufacturing and distributing firms, one member represents co-operative laundries, two members represent the Ministry of Technology, and one member is a visitor appointed by the Ministry of Technology with special responsibility for ensuring a high level of scientific work. The Director of Research of the Association is Mr J. Leicester who is the chief executive, and he is universally accepted as the major dynamic force in building up and securing the work and status of the Association. The administration of the Association is in the hands of the Secretary, Mr W. H. J. Parker.

Ordinary members pay a membership fee based on turnover at the rate of 2s 1d per £100 on the first £200,000 of turnover, 1s 7d per £100 on the next £400,000 of turnover, and 1s per £100 on all turnover above £600,000, subject to a minimum subscription of £20 per laundry.

Apart from ordinary members, there can be industrial members who are concerned with everything other than running a laundry that is relevant to a laundry, and the rate there is at a minimum of £50 per annum. The Co-operative Laundry and Allied Trades Association pays on the same basis as ordinary members. The subscription of associate members who are delegates of other associations is fixed by negotiation. Representatives of ministries, or laundries of public and hospital organizations, pay at the rate of £3 4s 0d per 1,000 pieces per week on the first 200,000 pieces and lower rates thereafter with a minimum rate of £31 10s 0d per laundry. There are other categories of membership but these are the main ones.

The Council has two main sub-committees, one dealing with finance and general purposes, and the other with programme and research. The Association is listed as being a member of about thirty different committees outside of its own organization, including the Committee of Directors of Research Associations of which Mr Leicester was the chairman in 1968. The other main organizations to which it sends representatives are the Committee of Directors of Textile Research Associations, the British Scientific Instrument Research Association, the Society of the Chemical Industry, the International Scientific and Technical Committee on Laundry, the Confederation of British Industry Technical Committees, the Association of British Launderers and Cleaners, the Laundry Industry Board of Examiners, the Dyers and Cleaners Research Organization, the Textile Institute, and the British Standards Institution.

The Association employs a staff of about seventy, most of whom are scientists and technologists of some distinction in their own field as judged by their publications and attendances at appropriate conferences. The scientific status of the work is particularly the concern of the two visitors appointed by the Ministry of Technology, one of whom is an independent academic with relevant knowledge and experience, whilst the other has appropriate industrial experience.

It is impossible to provide a satisfactory layman's account of the research that the Association undertakes. It may be adequate for the present purpose to list some of the main topics recorded in the 1967 annual report. There is a section on soiling and soil removal that involves microscopical studies, radio isotope techniques, soiled test piece techniques, bleaching, and soil removal from polyester fabrics. Then follows a section on microbiological studies concerned mainly with disinfection of wool and disinfection in dry cleaning. A third section deals with washing processes involving, for example, stain removal treatments. The fourth section deals with drying, and within that section there is a report on the use of heat transfer fluids, closed circuit tumbler dryers, and drying in dry cleaning machines. The fifth section deals with distillation, filtration and sludge removal.

These are part of the traditional areas of research involving both the basic physical sciences and their application. Perhaps more interesting because it is more generally understandable are the matters dealt with under the heading of 'Mechanization and Automation Studies'. The main study is concerned with continuous flat work processing and that involves the effect of using certain fibre and belt constructions with the commercial running of the prototype commercial machines installed in two laundries. Another project is concerned with the continuous processing of shaped articles, such as shirts. The third section is concerned with auto-racking and packing, and that is mainly a study of the 'Rackerjack' automatic racking unit. The Rackerjack is described by the manufacturers as 'a machine for racking finished articles into customer bundles, then presenting each bundle in a predetermined order convenient for packing. It is so versatile that launderers handling from 25,000 articles per week upwards can beneficially utilize it. It is circular with a diameter of 19 feet. It comprises sixty customer bins arranged in two tiers, one above the other and mounted in a rotatable ring.' The installation and use of this machine involves considerable changes in the pattern of flow of work through the laundry if maximum benefit is to be achieved. The Anne Shaw consultancy firm has been used for work study trials during the initial phase of proving the machine in a commercial laundry.

The other main development in this field is the installation of a computer. In the 1966 annual report it is stated that automation in the sorting room will inevitably affect office routines. 'Visits to a number of laundries have been made to study their office methods and to determine what basic routine must be carried out in all laundry offices and what routines are specific to a particular laundry. From this collated information the first stage will be an attempt to design a customer control card that would be filled in by the customer, checked and punched in the sorting room, used by the automatic reading equipment to produce van lists, receipts, accounts etc. and finally forwarded to the packing room for control of the auto-racking equipment.' It was first intended to have a small computer specially built for this purpose but the estimates showed that that would be excessively expensive.

Instead it was decided to buy a small technical computer, the Elliot 903, because it could be used for the research project and would then be available as a permanent technical computer unit for use on other work in the research laboratories. The Ministry of Technology favoured this proposal and provided 50 per cent of the cost with an earmarked grant.

One of the technical officers of the Association makes one half-day visit to each member firm per year, partly to discuss anything of interest to the laundry, partly to give technical advice on specific matters. In 1967 900 such visits were carried out. In one visit, on the basis of the advice given, the laundry was enabled to save £4,000 a year in its pressing department. As a result of the popularity of these visits, one technical officer now undertakes consultancy visits on a fee basis for assignments taking longer time than the half-day visit to which each member is entitled. The demand for his services is increasing.

Finally, the Association has an extensive programme of education, conferences and information and library services. Many of these activities bring the Launderers' Association into contact with other research associations and also with similar bodies abroad.

This is in no way a complete description of the work of the British Launderers' Research Association and it is not the intention of this report to be comprehensive in that sense. Enough has been said, however, to give a picture of its activities so that the reasons for joining or not joining the Association can be better understood. The two laundries that we visited who were not members had sensible grounds for not joining. One managing director thought that there would be too small a return on his subscription to make it worth while. He did not appear to have a great deal of evidence on which to base this calculation. He is, however, the secretary of his local branch of the trade association and presumably obtains considerable information from that source. Furthermore, the firm had no ambitions to continue in existence after the present generation of management and had therefore no plans to develop nor expand. Thus its attitude to research is understandably negative. The other firm that we visited had a special relationship with a group of hotels and seemed to be satisfied with the technical knowledge it obtained through other associations and through the trade press.

We obtained introductions to two member firms from B.L.R.A. They were enthusiastic about the Association and its benefits. One manager pointed out that the cost of employing his own research officer would be at least £1,500 a year and his annual subscription was considerably less. He found that there were particular advantages in the regular bulletins and the special technical publications that were issued, especially those reporting on research projects. He also found that the information being obtained about new machinery by the Association was valuable enough to lead him to install one continuous washing machine in his own laundry. The other major advantage was the use of testing techniques that enabled him to check on the efficiency of equipment with the assistance of the Association. The other member visited was a former chairman of the Association and thus was very well informed of its activities and facilities. He found that the visits of technical officers were extremely valuable, as were the other facilities that enabled him to obtain solutions to technical queries.

In the course of conversation with other members, particularly of the Council, it appeared that there are a number of less tangible influences in determining membership. There is a certain prestige associated with membership of the Council, particularly within the industry, and that is reinforced with the benefits that can be derived from the informal contacts made at Council meetings. Membership of the Council certainly enables individual launderers to be fully informed of association activities and of the opportunities available to members. Most members are partially influenced in their decision to join the Council by the feeling that they are fulfilling a duty to the organization. Most members, particularly Council members, have a genuine interest in the scientific and technological aspects of the research taking place. So far as can be judged, the Association appears to be democratic: it has an elected Council, and any member may visit the Association at any time and can be in close contact with its work if he so wishes.

In the period of our project the laundry industry faced a number of serious problems. The introduction of the Selective Employment Tax hit the industry hard, and the first statutory order under the original Prices and Incomes Act regulating price increases was made against the laundry industry. In his 1967 annual report the Director of the Association stated: 'My chairman has already made reference to the vicious financial conditions imposed upon an essential service indus-

try. This has inevitably had a serious effect upon the research association's intensive efforts in the field of mechanization and automation.
Successes outlined in my report last year have been rendered sterile by
the financial burden pressed upon the industry. Market surveys on the
potential sales of new equipment have been rendered useless, and as a
result of the financial inability of laundries to re-equip with this new
machinery, engineering members developing and building the new
generation of laundry machines have found that a stable home market
no longer exists. What is even more disturbing to the country's balance
of payments is that this machinery cannot be proven before the manufacturers can enter a lucrative export market.'

There is an increasing awareness in the Launderers' Association (and
in most other associations) of the serious problem of disseminating the
knowledge acquired through research to member firms and in enabling
them to apply it. In an interesting article on this problem Dr John
Weston, Director of the Building Research Station, stated: 'Whilst I
would be the last to argue that the construction industry does not need
more research, its crying need is to improve the processes by which
new ideas get into practice and to shorten the lag between idea and
action. It used to be thought that good research brought its own reward,
not only in the Ph.D. for the participant but in the automatic recognition by a waiting industry of the value of the new process, or material,
or what have you. The naïvety of this view has come increasingly to be
recognized in the construction industry by those engaged on research
and by those engaged in practice whether in design or in construction.
The research workers have come to realize that they must understand
the industry, not only technically in terms of the physical and chemical
properties of materials but also operationally in terms of the methods
of manufacture, stocking, delivery and assembly. And in the end they
need awareness of the economic and social forces which shape the
industry itself.'[1]

THE PROBLEMS OF B.L.R.A.

B.L.R.A.'s traditional problem of selecting the right problems to
investigate and obtaining the money necessary for research have been
solved, provided that the laundry industry continues to be prosperous.
It seems that the perennial problem of the application of research find-

[1] *The Financial Times*, November 13, 1967.

ings is now handicapped by some government policies that adversely affect the contemporary laundry industry. If research is not applied, the industry's prosperity will suffer, and its willingness to contribute to research will be lessened. However, it would appear that the laundry industry needs marketing research at least as much as any other type of research.[1]

On the other hand, the effect of government policies and economic development is likely to lead to a laundry industry consisting mainly of large firms with more automated processes involving heavier capital investment. That may be linked to an enhanced concern with research, if only to increase the return on capital through better methods.

The need will thus remain to 'sell' research through demonstrating the advantages of applying it. The main problem of B.L.R.A., as defined by the chairman and the director in 1968, was to find ways of increasing contacts with members. The solution may emerge from extending the work of the technical officers, and the annual free half-day visit to each member firm should in time expand into a comprehensive, paid consultancy service. That should focus attention on management problems in general and on marketing in particular. That would take the research association into part of the field covered now by the industry's trade association, so that co-ordination leading to eventual unification should eventually occur.

None of these developments would necessarily increase the number of firms interested in research. Nor will they automatically ensure greater efficiency and effectiveness. The incompetent and complacent firm will not become involved in these developments and there is no guarantee that it will die. The research association should help the good to get better but can now do nothing for those most in need of aid.

One opportunity for influencing the less able firm could be through training, and B.L.R.A. has achieved a great deal here. But the main course in laundry technology is now being run by the Derby College of Technology, and an industrial training board will in time take over the rest of training. The training of management is likely to be the last concern of most training boards, and that function might well be adopted by the research association; it is linked to the problem of

[1] See *What's Next?* by E. W. Swetman, ABLC Journal (Association of British Launderers and Cleaners), March 1968, pp. 126-130.

disseminating research and it may increase contacts with the non-member firm needing management aid.

The laymen cannot estimate the likelihood of a permanent need for research in the laundry industry. It may be that existing problems will be solved before long, and future problems might be dealt with by manufacturers of laundry equipment and detergents, or by their research associations, although no such research resources appear to exist at present. No independent assessment is now made about the long-term research needs of an industry. If support from the industry declined, the Ministry of Technology might eventually withdraw its grant. It is unlikely that a proposal to abolish an association would come from the staff.

Chapter 5

The National Agricultural Advisory Service

The National Agricultural Advisory Service exists to give farmers and horticulturalists in England and Wales free scientific and practical advice on any aspect of farming and horticulture. It is the biggest single employer of agricultural graduates in Britain; the Service provides farmers with expert and unbiased opinion based on knowledge derived from both research and practice. The farmer must have confidence in the advisers if he is to ask for help and to accept the advice given. N.A.A.S. expects its staff to have a high standard of technical knowledge combined with the ability to deal with people so that they will understand and adopt better methods. N.A.A.S. is a branch of the Ministry of Agriculture, Fisheries and Food. It was set up in 1946 and has its origins in the provincial university advisory departments, the pre-war County Agricultural Organizers of the County Councils, and the wartime county agricultural executive committees. The committees exercised strong powers to compel farmers to achieve the highest possible standards of output.

N.A.A.S. officers make about 400,000 visits to farms and small-holdings every year to discuss problems on the spot. Many other methods are used to stimulate interest and new ideas, such as conferences, demonstrations, small farmhouse meetings, and other group methods. 'A neighbour's example is often the most effective way of persuading a farmer to try out something new. The experienced adviser will be the first to admit how much he can learn from his more progressive farmers and he will try to use their holdings as demonstration sites and will certainly invite them to speak at meetings and conferences.'[1]

N.A.A.S. is organized from a central headquarters in London

[1] *A Career in the N.A.A.S.*, Ministry of Agriculture, 1967, p. 1.

through eight regions, with a unit in each county. It has about 1,500 advisory staff, and its total budget is £4 million. The director and the deputy director, with a number of senior advisers and specialist heads, are located in London. Each of the eight regional directors has a regional centre with laboratories and specialist officers dealing with a number of applied sciences, husbandry, horticulture, and farm and horticulture management (including work study). The county agricultural adviser is in charge of each county unit and usually is a general agriculturist. He is assisted by a deputy county agricultural adviser and by specialist advisers in livestock husbandry, poultry husbandry, dairy husbandry, mechanization, and horticulture. Each county is divided into a number of districts, each under a district agricultural adviser who is in regular contact with the farmer. Each district has about 500 farms over 15 acres in size. Through the district adviser all the other specialist services within N.A.A.S. can be integrated and mobilised to assist the farmer.

To support its work, the National Agricultural Advisory Service maintains twelve experimental husbandry farms and nine experimental horticultural stations. They conduct long-term crop and livestock experiments which could not be tackled on the ordinary commercial farm.[1] With the help of interested farmers, N.A.A.S. also carries out many experiments and trials on commercial holdings in the country. The results of this work are circulated to every member of N.A.A.S. to guide his advice to farmers. All staff are encouraged to keep their knowledge up to date and to maintain contact with colleagues and with research workers in universities and research institutes.

Although N.A.A.S. is part of the Ministry of Agriculture, it emphasizes its independence of government agricultural policy. 'All members of the N.A.A.S. have full freedom to give technical and economic advice which they think best suited to the circumstances of the particular farm or holding. The only consideration in the adviser's mind is what would benefit the farmer. He must be able to look at each farm as a unit, to weigh up all the factors and resources which can influence the general plan of working and to give the farmer or grower the best advice he can on increasing the profitability of the holding.'[2]

[1] This work is separate from the activities of the Agricultural Research Council, with nearly fifty establishments, and a budget of £13 millions; it operates under the surveillance of the Department of Education and Science.

[2] *A Career in the N.A.A.S.*, p. 5.

However, N.A.A.S. is increasingly involved in the activities of the Ministry of Agriculture, and its officers have to give advice and opinions on a number of grant-aid schemes. There can be little doubt that the average farmer associates the Service with the Ministry. In recent years they have been much concerned with a farm business recording scheme that provides grants for farmers who maintain specified financial records. Some farmers are rumoured to be suspicious of N.A.A.S. and believe it to be linked to the Inland Revenue as well as the Ministry of Agriculture. Its somewhat dictatorial wartime ancestry has not been forgotten by some older farmers. Other farmers look on it as largely a technical service that is not very well qualified to cope with the financial and business aspects of farming. At the other extreme, a few farmers depend on N.A.A.S. for help on every problem that they face.

As we could not hope to make a thorough study of the whole of N.A.A.S., we decided to concentrate on the work carried out by the county office in Surrey, located at Guildford. We made eleven visits to six members of county staff over the three years of the project, four visits to regional headquarters and one visit to national headquarters for an interview with the Director of N.A.A.S., Mr W. R. Smith. We decided that we ought to examine the reaction of farmers to the Service, and with the co-operation of N.A.A.S. we were able to meet three farmers, two of them for a second interview. Lastly, we had to remember that there were a number of other sources of aid available to farmers and we interviewed representatives of four of them—the British Oil and Cake Mills Company Limited, the Surrey Farm Institute, Messrs. Lugg and Gould (management consultants specializing in farming), and the Milk Marketing Board and one of its customers.

The three farmers visited in the company of N.A.A.S. advisory officers were as follows:

Farm A. This is a farm of about 150 acres widely dispersed. The farmer has been a tenant for about sixteen years. He is a graduate in agriculture and had previously been employed by N.A.A.S. He told us that N.A.A.S. originally confined itself to technical advice and he was impressed by the way in which newer management techniques have been used to give him the advice he sought. On the first visit in December 1966, the aim of the visit was to give advice about the construction for new buildings for housing cattle and for a milking parlour. The farmer did not have enough capital to undertake the building himself and he was dependent on his landlord to provide the £2,000 needed and to obtain the necessary planning permission. Proposals from a building contractor had already been obtained and the N.A.A.S. officers were invited to give their opinion on this. A detailed discussion ensued and the farmer seemed satisfied with the guidance he obtained during the one and a half hour's visit. The N.A.A.S. officer, in discussion after the visit, said that he had four aims in mind for that visit. First, he wanted to give the farmer knowledge about costs of building, advice on looking after cattle and crops, and guidance on planning his activities. Second, he wanted to persuade him that his present plans for building were too grandiose and would be uneconomic as the farmer's rent would be increased to cover the cost of the new building. Third, he wished to encourage the farmer to make use of the adviser's skills that have been developed by continuous problem solving tasks. Fourth, he hoped to help the farmer consider long-term opportunities and difficulties over the next ten to fifteen years.

A second visit was paid to the farm in March 1967 in company with a N.A.A.S. adviser. The purpose of the visit was to discuss the detailed implications of planning to expand his herd of dairy cattle from fifty to eighty. The farmer was proposing to develop both the raising of cattle for beef and for milk. N.A.A.S. advised him to concentrate on milk production and their guidance was based on costing and market forecasting. The farmer accepted their advice. An appropriate form of building was also advised which would be eligible for a Ministry of Agriculture grant.

Farm B is about 350 acres in size and primarily concerned with rearing dairy cattle, numbering between eighty and 100. The owner farmer had had some six years' experience of farming. The purpose of the visit was to work out the advantages and disadvantages of beginning to keep pigs at the farm. The N.A.A.S. adviser obtained a general knowledge of the farm and the farmer's competence. He discussed several possibilities with the farmer but gave no final advice on the spot. Later, he told the farmer that his costing showed that keeping pigs would not be sensible as the farmer had grossly overestimated the income that he would obtain. It appeared that the farmer had been tempted to rush in on a new enterprise because of a period of bad luck, mainly arising through illness among his cows. The N.A.A.S. advice helped him make an objective analysis of the situation. He appeared to be a cautious man by temperament and was able to accept the independent opinion of N.A.A.S.

Farm C covered a total of about 600 acres, part of which was owned by the farmer and part of which was rented. He grew a number of crops and had especially developed the sale of potatoes in recent years, having set up outlets among local retailers. On the basis of that distribution system, he was considering the introduction of poultry and the sale of eggs and he wanted advice from N.A.A.S. about the advantages and disadvantages of such an enterprise. The farmer had an opportunity to buy secondhand the necessary sheds and other equipment for about £1,000. The plant would be housed in a concrete-floored barn on the farm where a lease was held, and the N.A.A.S. poultry adviser examined this barn very carefully. He suggested bringing in a colleague who was a specialist in chicken accommodation. The poultry adviser made it clear that the final decision about the breeds of chickens to be stocked would have to be the farmer's and N.A.A.S. would simply point out the relative advantages and disadvantages of the different breeds. He could tell the farmer which strains of chicken gave the best returns and the number of staff needed for flocks of different breeds.

The primary concern of the N.A.A.S. officers was the problem of the existence of an appropriate market. He was very doubtful about the potential benefits arising from the existing retail distribution of potatoes and pointed out that there was a considerable difference between the attractions of fortnightly deliveries of potatoes and daily deliveries of fresh eggs.

The chicken accommodation expert later visited the farm. In the end, the farmer, having received a detailed written report with estimates of income and expenditure, decided not to proceed with the introduction of chickens.

We were not qualified to assess the scientific and technical advice given by N.A.A.S., but there is no evidence of dissatisfaction with it. Much more difficult to assess is their business and economic advice. One of our informants was critical of their conservatism and timidity towards large capital investment and another was very grateful to N.A.A.S. for helping him save on a projected silo.

The standard N.A.A.S. procedure when asked for advice on farm business management is to prepare a Farm Management Report on an annual basis. It depends on a schedule of information that the farmer completes on a trading account and/or gross margin basis. The trading account schedule begins with a valuation of the farm's livestock ('at realistic values'), crops, tillages, and bought stores as at the beginning of the year. The second section summarizes expenses under the headings of: (1) purchases of livestock, feed, seeds, and fertilizers; (2) wages and National Insurance, including casual labour and payments for work to the farmer's wife; (3) power and machinery; (4) sundries; (5) rent and rates; (6) other charges and owner occupier's expenses; (7) other information, such as value of unpaid manual labour, including the farmer's. The third section records all receipts, including subsidies, grants, and rental value of house. The fourth section gives closing valuation at the end of the year. Finally, a calculation is made of the value of invested capital.

Additional information 'required for business analysis' covers (a) acreage devoted to particular crops, (b) livestock and other stock in numbers and age groups, (c) transfers between dairy herd and other cattle, (d) milk production in gallons for each month, and (e) allocation of bought feed and farm grain.

This information, covering four printed foolscap pages, is then analysed by N.A.A.S. to produce a 'gross margin analysis', covering each main crop and each type of livestock, and a 'whole farm analysis', showing each type of fixed cost and gross margins on each crop or livestock.

The Farm Management Report comprises a contemporary comparative analysis of the information obtained with average and premium standards for farms of similar size and enterprise combinations in the region.[1] N.A.A.S. deal with this information in such strict confidence that only a code number appears on the report.

The Farm Management Report would normally be discussed by the farmer and the N.A.A.S. officer, but some private study by the farmer is necessary. It would be interesting to know how many farmers are sufficiently experienced and sophisticated to interpret such a report. Extensive 'observations' may be added and are usually helpful, but in

[1] 'Enterprise' means each major activity on the farm—keeping pigs, poultry for egg sales, etc.

one that we were shown by a farmer, the comments seemed somewhat lengthy and indicated the inevitable limitations of the statistical presentation. That report and the observations are assessments of previous performance and may give no positive guidance to the farmer about desirable changes or opportunities. Technical and financial advice will normally be given in the discussion, and its depth varies with the farmer's objectives. The advice may include full or partial budgets.

The farmer may be involved in a great deal of other office work, particularly in connection with applications for subsidies and grants. Some of them are:

(i) Claims for agricultural investment grants on fixed equipment (six pages plus twelve pages of explanation);

(ii) Application for grants for grubbing orchards (one page plus two pages of explanation);

(iii) Application for horticultural business grant (one page plus four pages of explanation);

(iv) Horticulture improvement scheme (four pages plus eight pages of explanation);

(v) Application for grant under farm water supply scheme (four pages plus three pages of explanation).

There are other application forms for field drainage grants, calf subsidies, grants for new tractors, beef cow subsidy, and rabbit scrub clearance grants—thirty-six separate grants and subsidies in 1968.

These grants and subsidies are the concern of the Ministry of Agriculture, not of N.A.A.S. But N.A.A.S. officers are directly concerned with the technical aspects of certain of the business management type schemes and can be asked for advice by Ministry colleagues on their appraisal of certain other schemes. In Surrey at least, the Ministry and N.A.A.S. operate from the same address. This association with administrative and bureaucratic complexities is not necessarily detrimental to the farmer's attitude to N.A.A.S.—most of the forms lead to money for the farmer in the end—but it provides more grounds for the suspicious farmer to doubt the independence of N.A.A.S. and the objectivity of its advice.

Sixteen thousand civil servants look after 200,000 farmers in England and Wales. National expenditure on agriculture, including £128 million on grants and subsidies and £146 million on price guarantees, totalled £380 million in 1968.[1]

It is not surprising that the Ministry of Agriculture recognised the need to help farmers maintain improved business records. A grant of £70 per annum for three years, or £100 if the N.A.A.S. 'gross margin summary' is also compiled, is payable to most farmers who make 'a record keeping business, whose services are generally available to farmers for a fee, responsible for keeping your records', including accountants and farmers' co-operatives. The farmer begins the process of application by sending a form to the divisional office of the Ministry and if he is found to be eligible 'a N.A.A.S. officer will discuss with you what information has to be recorded for you to get the grant for the first year and the date from which recording should start.'[2]

Another and more unusual project is the Ministry's 'Small Farm (Business Management) Scheme'. The scheme offers grants 'to certain small farmers who are prepared to keep farm records and to improve their business with the advice of the N.A.A.S.'. Broadly speaking, farms between 20 and 125 acres are eligible. In order to qualify for a grant, a farmer must 'carry out an approved three-year farm management programme designed to improve the profitability of your business. The programme for your farm will be drawn up in discussion with the Advisory Officer and may include any activities or changes in farm management that may be necessary to improve your business. There is, however, one essential rule: *you must keep proper farm records for each of the three years for which the programme runs.*'[3]

The amount of grant payable at the end of each year is in the first year £50 plus £2 for each acre of crops and grass, for the second year £50 plus £3 10s 0d for each acre, and for the third year £50 plus £3 for each acre. The maximum area which can qualify for the acreage payment is 100 acres giving a maximum grant for any business of £1,000.

The aim of the scheme is to increase the profitability of the farm, so that if the programme of improvement is successful, the farmer will earn increased profits as well as receiving his grant.

The Advisory Service does not of course exist to fill in forms. It is

[1] *The Civil Service Land Army*, John Cherrington.
The Financial Times, July 31, 1968.
[2] Ministry of Agriculture Form FBR.1 (Rev. July 1967), p. 2.
[3] Ministry of Agriculture leaflet SFM1, p. 1.

concerned with an overall view of a farm when giving advice on individual enquiries. The advice may be about anything and it could be continuous and general. But N.A.A.S. does not deal with veterinary matters, and cannot offer a day-to-day management service. Its interests are in farm planning and management and the provision of technical information and advice. It has no enforcement powers, nor can it make a farmer seek advice, nor use it when he has obtained it.

The Service must be one of the few suppliers of aid that keeps detailed records of staff activities. Each advisory officer compiles a quarterly return analysing all visits and activities. This information is sent to the regional offices. It is not clear what use is made of this information in administering the service.

In trying to assess the value of N.A.A.S. to farmers, it must be remembered that a number of other sources of help are available and most of them duplicate some N.A.A.S. services. However, the outstanding difference between N.A.A.S. and other sources of aid is that the farmer has to pay for many of the others. The aid may be provided by a statutory organization like the Milk Marketing Board which is particularly anxious to encourage farmers to maintain a proper record of individual milk yields and enterprise costings. Some manufacturers of products used by farmers also supply aid. The British Oil and Cake Mills Ltd. has an advisory service that was started in 1927 and now numbers some 100 poultry advisers and 100 agricultural advisers, with a few specialists on pigs. Most of the advisers are graduates or possess other appropriate qualifications. The main function of the advisory service is to see that the feedstuffs sold by the company are used correctly on the farm. The advisers may help farmers with many of the day-to-day problems of keeping livestock. Annual refresher courses are held for the advisory staff, and technical literature is provided. The company trains its advisers in business techniques and communication. The company also has departments of farm business and farm buildings to supply further help if needed.

Several firms of private consultants now exist to help farmers. They compile reports about the farm and propose a plan for its future development, together with a budget. They offer to come back and compare actual performance against budget. Several of these companies also offer special accountancy services and deal with taxation.

The Milk Marketing Board provides a number of services to farmers in addition to their basic function of buying milk and selling it to distributors and manufacturers. Their primary interest in the services they provide is to raise the level of productivity of milk farmers and to assist them in managing and feeding their dairy cows so as to maintain the highest possible qualities. They have an extensive artificial insemination service and their twenty-three centres are responsible for two-thirds of the cattle bred in this country.

To keep farmers abreast of new developments the Board run advisory services with qualified field staff. Their 'low cost production service' provides a costing and advisory service for milk producers. For a set fee, the members receive a monthly visit from the Board's consulting officers who compile costings, give short-term advice to the farmer, and later provide a more detailed review and suggestions on his system of husbandry. In some areas of the country the low cost production service is incorporated in the total farm business service which was initiated in 1965 under the Ministry of Agriculture's Farm Business Recording Scheme.

To keep dairy farmers up-to-date with farm management details, the Board runs advisory services staffed by a team of qualified Consulting Officers. The Low Cost Production Service is used by 3,000 milk producers. In the Basic Dairy Business Service, members receive a monthly visit from the Consulting Officer Service to spot check current herd profitability, compare results under confidential code number with other group members, and advise on any aspect of dairy management. The monthly visit also means information about the previous month's costs, and returns can be collected to produce an annual summary to help the dairy farmer make long-term management decisions.

Low Cost Production has now been expanded to cost the whole farm. The total Farm Business Service provides the comprehensive analysis of the dairy herd and all the features of the Basic Dairy Business Service, together with a gross margin analysis of each other farm enterprise and a trading account for the whole farm. L.C.P. Small Farm Business Service is also available for small farmers receiving a grant under the Ministry of Agriculture Small Farm (Business Management) Scheme.

In addition, the Board operates its own commercial enterprises such as creameries and transport fleets which give the Board first-hand knowledge of commercial practices and technical developments. The creameries provide an outlet for milk not required for liquid consumption.

N.A.A.S. DIFFICULTIES

The advisory services of many kinds that are available to farmers cannot be readily evaluated. Farming is subject to many influences that affect performance and not all can be improved by advice and aid. But aid will be less productive if the suppliers of aid have problems of their own.

N.A.A.S., like all public services, faces problems caused by its limited budget and its inability to increase income through earnings. All its services are supplied free of charge to the farmer and most of them are very valuable. But there is no talk of charges for these services, even when public expenditure is under severe restraint. Such charges could be beneficial as people often respect services more highly when they have to pay for them.

The ability to earn an income might help to establish some criteria for assessing N.A.A.S.'s achievements and failures. N.A.A.S. does not provide any public account of its achievements and it is not subject to any kind of inspection apart from auditing. It is somewhat incongruous that a public service concerned with improving performance and encouraging productivity does not evaluate its own performance. It would be extremely difficult to set up an adequate assessment system, but a number of procedures could be examined and if appropriate they could be introduced gradually within an experimental programme.

'Profit earnings' would not be adequate indicators, particularly as N.A.A.S. has an expensive responsibility to help the incompetent farmer. Making contact with such farmers that are most in need of their services is difficult. Some special effort to raise the standards of the least efficient farmer is needed and he will not necessarily be a smallholder. Compulsory inspection would be undesirable and ineffective. An unconventional approach and perhaps a separate organisation may be necessary.

N.A.A.S. has done little to deal with the suspicion of government that is traditional among farmers and perhaps even more widespread today than it was when N.A.A.S. was founded in 1946. That suspicion is not necessarily rational and seems entirely unjustified in view of many benefits that the farmer derives from government policies. But the authoritarian image presented by a government agency, even when its front line is so closely in touch with the population it serves, must hinder that agency's achievements. Perhaps even closer links are needed between farmers and N.A.A.S. so that it becomes much more fully integrated into the working and social life of the farming community.

An appropriate structure would be difficult to devise but an agricultural advisory service ought to be integrated into the network of voluntary associations in farming. Perhaps N.A.A.S. should be the scientific and technical secretariat of the agricultural community. But there are dangers—instead of being run by civil servants it might be controlled by officials of trade associations and professional institutes, and there might be no significant improvement in status. On the other hand, a simple, flexible arrangement, perhaps beginning with informal consultations based on a randomly chosen group of farmers, rather than the 'establishment' of farmers' leaders, might be possible. Whatever scheme might emerge, there are signs of an unnecessary barrier between N.A.A.S. and those farmers who could benefit most from comprehensive and long-term advice on their future policies.

The relationship of N.A.A.S. with the Ministry of Agriculture, and with government in general, may be a serious handicap, at least for the farmer who might be persuaded to use its services if it were entirely independent. N.A.A.S.'s close and increasing participation in numerous ministry activities is unfortunate, and the independence of the service should be demonstrated, protected, and extended.

If N.A.A.S. became more a partner of the farmer instead of his adviser and (in relation to grants and subsidies) almost an inspector, the situation would be very different. N.A.A.S. could earn at least part of its income by sharing the profits that could be related to the systematic advice provided. There would be a regular, continuing relationship between N.A.A.S. and farmers. More importantly, N.A.A.S. could create a permanent link with the farm, presumably the ultimate concern of N.A.A.S., given the scarcity of agricultural land, and not only the temporary tenant or owner. N.A.A.S. could do much to ensure such permanent links.

Fortunately, N.A.A.S. already carries out its advisory work informally. The farmer receives fairly prompt service, although an advisory officer can seldom appear immediately he is summoned. The basic business management documents compiled about each farm with the co-operation of the farmer, enable an objective assessment to be made of the farm in comparison with national and local studies of similar farms. Each adviser has considerable freedom in organizing his work and morale is good. An adviser would expect to carry out a maximum of six visits a day on technical matters and also spend an hour or so in his office. On the more complex business management advisory work, no more than one or possibly two visits per day are possible.

The size of N.A.A.S. and its regions cannot be easily judged. The South-East Region employs 200 staff and the regional director believes that he could not adequately supervise a larger number. No systematic investigation has been made to determine whether that size of staff, in relation to the number and type of farmers in the area, is right. A much larger or much smaller number of advisers may be needed. As the Service is available to any farmer in the country, there are problems in ensuring appropriate facilities. There may be places in which some demanding farmers exploit their opportunities to the disadvantage of others. The undemanding farmer may simply avoid using N.A.A.S., possibly because he has been disappointed in the past at the speed, frequency or extent of the service. The effectiveness of N.A.A.S. cannot be judged by the opinions of the staff or of the farmers now using it—much more important would be a survey of the views of farmers who do not use it or who have used it previously but have ceased to do so now. Such a survey, however, would only be part of a proper evaluation process.

Any unnecessary duplication of facilities between N.A.A.S. and private firms or other public services would be absurd. No adequate review of the total situation has been carried out and such a study is necessary and potentially valuable. A collaborative system could be devised whereby individual firms and consultants could be drawn into a partnership, formal or informal, with N.A.A.S., on a more rational basis than may in fact happen now, so as to ensure that special skills are fully used. Most agricultural advisory work is undertaken by N.A.A.S. and there is no need to exaggerate the problem of duplication. But the relative scarcity of skilled men suggests that a fully co-ordinated scheme, covering public employees and private individuals and firms, would be preferable to all concerned.

100

PART B

The Users of Aid

Foreword

The following four chapters describe what we discovered about the seventeen firms that collaborated on this project and their use of external aid. The methods used to obtain information are described in Appendix 2. But it has been difficult to find the best method for reporting and assessing the information obtained. It was neither possible nor desirable to repeat every item of information. Instead, we drew up a schedule of basic information that should be included in the account of each firm, and it has been used as the basis for each of the following reports. The information is presented in the form that seems appropriate for each firm and is not in the same systematic sequence for all firms. As we were unable to obtain all the information for every firm, I have made it clear when estimates were used because the facts did not exist or were not provided.

The schedule comprised the following parts:

(i) *Technology and organization.* What the organization does and how it does it—(a) physical size, output, products; (b) formal organization structure; (c) informal processes observed; (d) assessment of general soundness or weakness of organization.

(ii) *Finance.* Capital, income, expenditure, surplus or profit for at least one recent year, preferably 1966. Sources of income. Investment policy during the three years of project with actual figures where available.

(iii) *Employees.* Numbers, type of work, qualifications, salaries, labour turnover, absenteeism, morale assessment, promotion policies, attitude to external aids of each informant.

(iv) *Legal status.* Private limited liability or public company, official body etc.

(v) *Membership of external aid organizations.* i.e. trade associations, research associations etc. Dates of membership, fees paid, participation —e.g. (a) attendance at annual general meeting, (b) membership of committees etc., (c) attendance at other meetings, (d) use made of services available—observed and reported.

(vi) *Use of other external aid.* In particular management and technical consultants. Public services—e.g. Export Services Department of the Board of Trade. Frequency, type of problem, firm's assessment of value, investigator's assessment of benefit derived.

(vii) *Routine use of external aids observed.* Description of the use of external aids used in the normal course of the major routine activities of the organization as observed by the research assistant on his visits.

(viii) *New projects and the use of external aids.* A description for each new activity begun during the project and observed on visits. The following information was sought: (a) description of project—aim, size, resources used, assumed major difficulties at origin, other difficulties discovered, date begun, date of planned completion, date completed; (b) personnel of organization involved; (c) observed and reported use of external aid in course of project; (d) research assistant's views on (1) problems and benefits of the use of external aids, (2) other possible external aids that could have been used with advantage; (e) assessment of attitude to external aids of all main employees involved.

(ix) *Efficiency.* An assessment of the firm's efficiency was made in 1967 and reviewed in 1968. The research assistant was to examine which problems of the organization had remained unsolved and to indicate whether other external aids were needed.

(x) *The influence of the chief executive.* Brief description of his personality, education, and social class. Goals and 'philosophy', attitude to external aid, his influence on the external aid attitude of other members of the organization.

(xi) *General impression.* (a) of the organization, (b) of the executive system, and (c) of the use of external aid.

It will be clear from the accounts that follow that we have in no way aimed to provide a comprehensive history or description of the organizations studied. We were primarily concerned with the organization's external relationships and particularly those that appeared to be a source of aid, and thus we selected many of the activities of the organization for particular study and ignored others. However, in order to understand the organization and its problems we had to seek at least a superficial knowledge of its structure and performance. The choice of information and thoroughness with which it was studied and analysed clearly depended on the judgment of the research team and mistakes could have been made.

As previously explained, these reports are intended to be entirely factual and objective. They have all been written in collaboration with the informants and they have confirmed the correctness of the facts. Opinions and assessments have been confined to later chapters reviewing our findings and the firms are not responsible for those views and have not been consulted about them in all cases.

This degree of collaboration is perhaps unusual, but it seems sensible in order to improve accuracy and relevance. Each firm was invited to suggest additions and deletions, and the first drafts sent to them were deliberately provocative in order to stimulate an emphatic reaction on matters of judgment. I believed it desirable to use the names of the firms and aid organizations, and it was essential to offer a right of scrutiny and comment in return. Four of the twenty-one organizations chose anonymity but their reasons did not involve any dispute over relevant facts.

The reports on the farmers, the builders, and the distributors are preceded by brief descriptions of their industry and economic sector. The manufacturers were not sufficiently homogeneous to make such an introduction possible.

Paragraphs in the reports on firms have been numbered to facilitate discussion between readers.

An analysis of known external contacts during one year has been summarized in each firm's report. As some contacts could be placed in several categories, the section totals sometimes exceed the total number of contacts.

Chapter 6

The Farmers

Some elementary description of British agriculture may be found useful in considering the reports on the four farms that follow and in appreciating the work of the National Agricultural Advisory Service. Nothing more than some basic facts can be provided which will almost certainly be found inadequate by the experts. However, some framework is necessary to place the farms in their national context.

One initial problem is to decide how a farm can best be measured. It could be by the value of the output or the net income received by the farmer or by the amount of capital employed. The Ministry of Agriculture now prefer to measure 'the standard labour requirements for the cropping and stocking of a farm, using as the unit of measurement the standard man day'. This is defined as the annual requirements of manual labour needed on average for the production of crops and livestock with an addition for essential maintenance and other necessary tasks. The requirements are expressed in terms of 'standard man days' (per acre of crops or per head of livestock) which represent eight hours manual work for an adult male worker under average conditions. 275 standard man days is taken to be the equivalent of a year's work for one man. Thus a holding with 275 standard man days represents a one-man business.

There are about 450,000 agricultural holdings in the United Kingdom, giving an average size of almost 100 acres. Slightly over half are part-time holdings, the occupiers of which generally have another source of income besides farming. An official survey in 1965 showed that there are about 220,000 full-time holdings and that about half of the industry's total output comes from the 42,000 holdings classified as large commercial farm businesses. A further 66,000 are classified as small commercial farm businesses which are able to operate as viable enterprises. Of the remaining 112,000 full-time farms many provide sufficient livelihood for their occupants, and others could do so with improvement or through co-operation or better business management. Many offer too restricted a scope for economic progress, and amalgamation into larger units is being officially encouraged. The average size of full-time holdings in England and Wales is between 135 and 140 acres of crops and grass.

The large holdings constitute 10 per cent of all holdings, cover 40 per cent of the total acreage of crops and grass, and employ more than 50 per cent of full-time male agricultural workers. Their average size is 300 acres.

The medium size holdings cover 30 per cent of all acreage devoted to crops and grass with an average size of 130 acres. They employ 25 per cent of full-time workers.

The small holdings employing one to two men represent about one quarter of all holdings in the United Kingdom. They cover about 20 per cent of the total acreage, with an average size of 62 acres, and produce about 20 per cent of the total output of the agricultural industry. Both these and the medium size holdings depend mainly on dairy and livestock farming. They employ about 15 per cent of all workers.

The very small holdings, with an average size of 16 acres, number about 200,000 and cover only 10 per cent of the total acreage and supply 8 per cent of the industry's total output. They are mainly concerned with pigs, poultry, beef, cows and sheep. They employ 5 per cent of full-time workers.

There were 388,000 full-time agricultural workers in the United Kingdom in June 1965, nearly all of whom were males. The average earnings was just under £14 a week and the average working week was about 50 hours.

The value of all United Kingdom agricultural output at farm gate prices in 1967 was £1,917 m. The cost of our foreign food imports was £1,425m.

This country is virtually self-sufficient for liquid milk, poultry, meat, eggs, and most potatoes.

In the financial year 1965-6 the following main outputs were achieved: wheat 4 million tons, barley 8 million tons, oats 1,200,000 tons, potatoes 7,500,000 tons, milk 2,739 million tons, hen and duck eggs 1,220 million dozen.

In 1966 it was estimated that there were the following numbers of livestock in the United Kingdom: dairy cows 3,200,000, other cattle 9 million, sheep and lambs 30 million, pigs 7 million, poultry 119 million.

The net income of all farmers amounted to £472 million in 1966-7. The total number engaged in agriculture is about 800,000 representing 3 per cent of the total employed labour force and provides 3 per cent of the gross national product. Since the 1939-45 war considerable efforts have been made to provide a secure income for farmers and a range of government policies have been established over the past twenty years to this effect.

The most important policy concerns the annual review of prices carried out in accordance with the Agriculture Act 1947. The ministers primarily concerned discuss with representatives of farmers (in practice the three farmers' unions in the United Kingdom) and consider production trends, market requirements, world market prospects, the cost of subsidies, the trend of profits in the industry as a whole, the increasing efficiency of the industry, etc. In the light of their discussions the ministers determine guaranteed prices for fat cattle, fat sheep, fat pigs, eggs, wool, milk, cereals, potatoes, and sugar beet. These guarantees apply for the ensuing twelve months. Various grants in aid of particular kinds of production are also considered and may be changed. The final decisions on changes in guaranteed prices and in production grants are published in an annual White Paper. Cost of government support to the industry in 1966-7 was about £234m. and the estimate for 1967-8 was £287m.

Governments since the war have preferred to help farmers by allowing the ordinary channels of trade to flow freely. When market prices are below the guaranteed prices, the government makes deficiency payments to the farmers to cover the differences between the average market price realized and the guaranteed price for output eligible for the guarantee.

It is of course extremely difficult to assess the efficiency of farming in the United Kingdom. There has been a considerable reduction in labour employed and a considerable rise in output in the last twenty years. One of the major indicators of productivity is the increase in mechanization. Probably the best single measure of that is the rate at which horses have been replaced by tractors. In 1939 there were

649,000 farmhorses. By 1965 that had dropped to 21,000. The number of tractors in 1942 was 117,000 and 480,000 in 1966. Britain now has one of the heaviest tractor densities in the world—one to every 36 acres of arable land. 63,000 combine harvesters were in use in 1966. A wide variety of machines for harvesting and preservation of grass are used; milking machines are installed on all except the smallest farms; and over 90 per cent of the farms in Britain have an electricity supply and accompanying equipment. There are about 1,300 farmers' machinery syndicates through which farmers have the use of expensive equipment without tying up their own capital.

The range of profit between individual farms is very wide as may be expected from the variety of land and crops and the ability of the occupier. Nearly all farms show average profits in recent years of between £5 and £15 per acre. There is a marked tendency for small farms to show higher profits primarily because of the higher proportion of profit represented by personal work on the small farm.[1]

Organization F1: Highway Model Farm

1. Mr P. Skinner is an ambitious entrepreneur who farms several hundred acres in Surrey, and buys and sells land as a business venture. Although only thirty years of age, he had five years' business experience in publishing before taking up farming as his career in 1962. He inherited Highway Model Farm from his mother, and his brother is also a farmer. Many of his policies in recent years have been dictated by problems connected with death duties, and it is very difficult to assess his success by any normal criteria because of the complex inter-relationships of his activities and the need for financial transfers to reduce tax liabilities and increase capital value. Our interpretation of the financial information that we have been able to obtain is given in Table A, but it is an over-simplification of a complicated situation.

2. In 1968, Mr Skinner farmed between 500 and 600 acres. He owns about 100 acres. He has a right to participate in 10 per cent of any profits if the rented land is sold for building purposes. That is unlikely to happen under existing town and country planning legislation. About 370 acres are devoted to barley and about 500 acres are under cultiva-

---

[1] The information reported here is taken from *The Structure of Agriculture*, Ministry of Agriculture, H.M.S.O. 1966, *Agriculture in Britain*, Central Office of Information, H.M.S.O. 1967, and 'Bringing the Food Bill into Balance', George Huckle, *The Times* September 11th, 1968.

tion altogether. He has a contract to sell 21 pigs a month through the Fatstock Marketing Corporation. He has 25 pedigree Jersey cows and plans to increase his herd to 40 ultimately. He sells turf and he is developing woodlands by planting poplars. He is building up a herd of bullocks and now has about 80, aiming at 200 eventually. He is developing a trout pond of 4 acres and has fifteen clients each willing to pay £50 a year for fishing rights. Mr Skinner has a very successful farm shop which adjoins a busy road and deals with a large number of customers throughout the year, selling farm produce and an increasing range of groceries.

3. Mr Skinner is his own general manager as well as being the owner and acting as an entrepreneur. He now employs two men, one is a qualified herdsman and the other is a tractor driver. There are two women assistants serving in the shop, under the supervision of Mrs Skinner. Until recently Mr Skinner employed a firm of contractors who supplied all his labour requirements for a fee of £58 a week. As a result of his policy to invest extensively in farm machinery, he has discontinued his contract with the contractors but calls them in from time to time.

4. It seems that capital assets of about £38,000 are employed in the business, and annual profits earned but not withdrawn are now about £3,000. Mr Skinner expects to need twelve years to build up a satisfactory farming business, earning profits of about £6,000.

5. As we were primarily interested in his external contacts we noted in the course of our visits that the following external aids were mentioned:

The Fatstock Marketing Corporation;
The Milk Marketing Board;
The Ministry of Agriculture;
A veterinary surgeon;
An accountant;
The National Agricultural Advisory Service;
Various suppliers of equipment.

6. His accountant and his bank are extremely important for financial reasons and indirectly influence the level of performance of the farm.
7. Mr Skinner is a member of the National Farmers' Union but plays

110

no active part in its activities. He believes that the Union serves a useful purpose, primarily in the annual price negotiations.

8. Mr Skinner once asked N.A.A.S. for advice about buying an expensive corn dryer for £5,200. He was dissatisfied with their information and guidance and they appeared to lack relevant experience. They tried to convert him to an entirely different approach to his problem. He has not used N.A.A.S. again for any purpose although he would do so if he felt it necessary.

9. He reads *The Stockbreeder* and *Farmers' Weekly*.

10. Mr Skinner is a very confident and independent person who has taught himself a great deal about farming and has applied his knowledge gained from commerce to farming and made it a financial success. He enjoys farming and chose it because he likes country life and self-employment. He has a great deal of drive and initiative and considerable ability. Mr Skinner had a good education at a minor public school and has no qualifications or higher education. He comes from a 'good' family. He married in 1966.

11. He is sceptical about specialists and the providers of external aid, he prefers using his intuition, supported by the informal and indirect learning that he has absorbed through his family and through his contacts with neighbouring farmers. He may suffer from failing to use technical aid but he is compensated by the expertise of friends and relations, together with his own acute business sense. However, he would almost certainly benefit from a professional assessment of his farm and from a costing analysis, whether provided by N.A.A.S. or the Milk Marketing Board or private consultants. He appears to have made occasional mistakes in his planting decisions, and in buying cattle, through lack of experience.

TABLE A. *Highway Model Farm*

INCOME, EXPENDITURE AND CAPITAL

A. *INCOME*

	1964	1965	1966	1967
From crops	5,830	8,105	8,817	8,365
From other sources	2,000	2,000	2,000	2,000 approx.
	7,830	10,105	10,817	10,365

B. *WAGES*

Fees to contractors	£14 per acre—corn			
	£4 per acre—grass	884	1,406	

111

ASSOCIATIONS AND CONSULTANTS

C. *CAPITAL INVESTMENT*

	6,184	2,575	800	2,000

D. *PROFITS* *

After living expenses paid	−887	−173	150	600

E. *CAPITAL VALUE*

Excluding land owned	8,756	8,894	12,148	14,548

* Excludes cost of Mr Skinners' services.

ANALYSIS OF EXTERNAL CONTACTS
July 1, 1967 – June 30, 1968

NAME OF ORGANIZATION	HIGHWAY MODEL FARM
CONTACTS OBSERVED	2
CONTACTS REPORTED	0
TOTAL CONTACTS ANALYZED	2

A. *Type of contact:* 1. Normal 'business' 2   2. Unusual 'business'
                       3. Aid—deliberate   4. Aid—indirect

B. *With whom*

1.	Supplier	2.	Management Consultant	3.	Technical Consultant
4.	Research Association	5.	Trade Association	6.	Public Body
7.	Competitor	8.	Training Board	9.	Customer 1
10.	National Economic Committee	11.	Building Contractor	12.	Local government authority
13.	Professional practice	14.	Government department	15.	Foreign organization
16.	Employment agency	17.	Professional Institute	18.	Head Office
19.	College	20.	Research organization	21.	Bank
22.	Trade Union	23.	International official body	24.	Wholesaler
25.	Retailer	26	Sub-Contractor 1	27.	
28.		29.		30.	

C. *Purpose*

1.	Give information—general	7.	Give advice—general
2.	Give information—technical	8.	Give advice—technical
3.	Give information—commercial	9.	Give advice—commercial
4.	Seek information—general	10.	Seek advice—general
5.	Seek information—technical	11.	Seek advice—technical
6.	Seek information—commercial	12.	Seek advice—commercial

13. Buying operations
15. Research and development operations
17. Financial operations
19. Production operations 1

14. Selling operations 1
16. General management operations
18. Personnel operations
20. Other

D. *Duration of Contact*
  1. Up to one hour continuously
  2. Up to one day continuously 1
  3. Up to one week continuously 1
  4. Up to one month continuously
  5. Up to three months continuously
  6. Up to six months continuously
  7. Up to nine months continuously
  8. Up to twelve months continuously
  9. Over twelve months continuously
  10. From time to time irregularly

E. *Cost to Organization*
  1. Free 1
  2. Unassessed
  3. By annual subscription (give amount if possible)
  4. £...........................
  5. By professional scale— estimated at £..................
  6. As % of main contract— estimated at £..................
  7. Under £25 1
  8. £26 – £50
  9. £51 – £100
  10. £101 – £1,000

F. *Nature of evidence*
  1. Observation by researcher 2
  2. Verbal report 1
  3. Correspondence seen
  4. Minutes of meetings
  5. Technical reports
  6. Financial statement
  7. Organization's statistics
  8. Special report for researcher
  9. Information from outsider
  10. Other (specify)

G. *Implications for Firm* (or other type of organization)
  1. Contact is likely to effect firm's current performance. 2
  2. Contact is not likely to effect firm's current performance.
  3. Contact is likely to effect structure of firm's organization. 2
  4. Contact is not likely to effect structure of firm's organization.
  5. Contact is likely to increase profit or surplus. 2
  6. Contact is not likely to increase profit or surplus.
  7. Contact does extend firm's network of external relationships. 2
  8. Contact does not extend firm's network of external relationships.
  9. Contact is likely to increase firm's efficiency. 2
  10. Contact is not likely to increase firm's efficiency.

Organization F2: Horringdon Farm

1. Horringdon Farm is Crown property and the life tenant is Mr John Blake. His brother has a farm about two miles away. Mr Blake is thirty-seven years of age. He has farmed there for many years and comes of a farming family. In 1966 he was concerned about the effect of a possible new road that would take away some of his farm. After careful consideration he decided to stay where he was instead of seeking another Crown farm elsewhere.

2. The farm consists of 240 acres divided into a few large fields and is suitable for dairy farming and arable crops. There is a comfortable farmhouse in the centre of the farm. In October 1967 there were 127 Redpoll cows and two bulls. These were divided into two herds, one regarded as a milk herd and the other regarded as a replacement herd.

3. Mr Blake concentrates at present on producing barley, but he also has root crops, clover, and some corn. He operates a seven-year rotation system which is modified to suit the chemical needs of the land and market conditions, in the context of government subsidy policy in any year. In 1966 he sold cattle valued at £1,000 to Rumania.

4. Mr Blake employs one skilled cowman and two young assistants. He plays a very active part in the work of the farm and has no other business interests. He tends to concentrate on the maintenance work, apart from his duties of farm manager and foreman. The cowman is treated as almost a partner within his specialized activities. Mr Blake and the cowman usually meet every day to discuss any farm problem.

5. The farm suffers from a lack of capital but Mr Blake is following a policy that will gradually improve the assets available. He is keen to avoid increasing his overdraft commitments and will, for example, buy second-hand farm equipment where it would be uneconomic to buy new. The balance sheet value of the capital employed in the farm was £16,443 in 1966. He made a net profit of £2,000 in 1966, £750 of which was invested in machinery. Total income from sales was £10,904 of which milk represented two-thirds. He had an overdraft of about £3,000 and owed about another £4,000.

6. Mr Blake is a member and Area Officer of the Redpoll Society. He is a member of the National Farmers' Union and chairman of one of the local branch committees. He is a member of the Surrey Grasslands Association. Mr Blake possesses sufficient expertise and reputation to be used as judge in the meetings of the Redpoll Society and clearly obtains a great deal of knowledge from these social-scientific meetings. He uses the Artificial Insemination Service of the Milk Marketing Board and its Milk Recording Service. He consults N.A.A.S. periodically but does not always follow their recommendations.

7. An important source of guidance and information is obtained from a number of suppliers, such as David Brown Tractors Ltd. and Bibbys, and the auction prices of cattle reported by an auctioneer affect Mr Blake's policies. He is guided in his sales decisions by his corn mer-

chants, and tries to find the best time for putting his cattle on the market. Mr Blake also seems to find considerable help from *The Stockbreeder* magazine.

8.   He has been for some years a member of the Kingston Area Productivity Association. He attended a course on work study for farmers held at Kingston College of Technology in 1965. The course included a project on the planning of a new milking parlour, and Mr Blake's farm was used as the basis of the project.

9.   Mr Blake's accountant provides historical financial information but does not appear to play any other part in dealing with the problems of the farm nor with advising on future development. For example, his policy of buying cheap secondhand equipment involves him in extra maintenance work, although he believes it to be uneconomic to buy a new combine harvester for such a small acreage of arable crop. It would clearly involve complex calculations to prove that he was right.

10.   Voluntary sources of aid that are under the control of farmers are preferred to those provided by professional experts and official bodies, some of which charge fees that Mr Blake considers high. This reflects his slightly suspicious personality and his belief that only farmers really understand farming problems. He does not feel that there may be advantages in using experts, at least in formulating long-term strategy. He is a quiet, reserved man but fully aware of his competence to manage the farm properly.

11.   So far as we could judge, the farm should be able to produce better results than those currently obtained. The plan for cattle-rearing and milk production offers opportunities for better performances. Mr Blake may have failed to achieve the best results because he does not attempt to measure his performance against objective yardsticks. He does not know whether he needs aid. Clearly his desire for independence influences his attitudes and that may be a major obstacle to his further progress. He has had no formal training in farming and thus his knowledge is limited to his experience, however extensive that may now be.

12.   He believes that the root of his problems is undoubtedly lack of capital, and that shortage is unlikely to be overcome by careful husbanding of his current resources and annual profits. He has not explored sources of finance that should enable him to retain his independence. As a result, he undertakes very difficult tasks on his own for which outside help is needed. For example, he began to build a

storage barn in August 1966 and he had got no further than digging out the holes and erecting support posts by October 1967. That delay was primarily due to uncertainty about the proposed new road. Mr Blake says that he wanted to avoid unnecessary capital investment.

13. It is interesting to note that Mr Blake is a member of Surrey Farmers Ltd., a co-operative society of about one thousand farmers, each of whom subscribes a minimum of £10 capital. They are encouraged to leave their annual dividend in the society and are permitted to hold up to £1,000 worth of shares. This organization employs professional staff, sells a wide range of products, and obtains supplies for its members at optimum prices. In 1965 their gross sales amounted to £834,000 and they ended up with a net trading profit of £2,000. The low return meant that no dividend could be paid that year, and the situation is thought to be due to the effects of the Selective Employment Tax. The society employs four representatives. 75 per cent of orders come by telephone or post and that is possibly due to the visits of the representatives. Representatives visit farms every two or three weeks to build up contacts and to ensure that the goods supplied to farmers are satisfactory. The company is a kind of hybrid between a friendly society of farmers and a bureaucratic business.

14. During this project we have noted several steps taken to improve the efficiency of the farm and to increase output. There can be no doubt of Mr Blake's competence to maintain the farm at its current level of achievement. What seems to be in doubt is his ability to raise productivity considerably and to extend his size of operations, should he wish to do so. It may therefore be that the ultimate criterion of his performance is his ability to improve standards and to plan long-term survival. Financial difficulties may limit opportunities and some expert help might be welcomed, provided Mr Blake's personal viewpoint was fully considered before proposals were submitted to him.

ANALYSIS OF EXTERNAL CONTACTS
July 1, 1967 – June 30, 1968

NAME OF ORGANIZATION	HORRINGDON FARM
CONTACTS OBSERVED	5
CONTACTS REPORTED	—
TOTAL CONTACTS ANALYZED	5

A. *Type of contact:* 1. Normal 'business' 4   2. Unusual 'business' 1
3. Aid—deliberate   4. Aid—indirect

B. *With whom*

1. Supplier 3	2. Management Consultant	3. Technical Consultant
4. Research Association	5. Trade Association	6. Public Body 1
7. Competitor	8. Training Board	9. Customer 1
10. National Economic Committee	11. Building Contractor	12. Local government authority
13. Professional practice	14. Government department	15. Foreign organization
16. Employment agency	17. Professional institute	18. Head Office
19. College	20. Research organization	21. Bank
22. Trade Union	23. International official body	24. Wholesaler 1
25. Retailer	26.	27.
28.	29.	30.

C. *Purpose*

1. Give information—general	7. Give advice—general
2. Give information—technical	8. Give advice—technical
3. Give information—commercial	9. Give advice—commercial
4. Seek information—general	10. Seek advice—general
5. Seek information—technical	11. Seek advice—technical 1
6. Seek information—commercial	12. Seek advice—commercial 1
13. Buying operations	14. Selling operations 3
15. Research and development operations	16. General management operations
17. Financial operations	18. Personnel operations
19. Production operations 3	20. Other

D. *Duration of Contact*

1. Up to one hour continuously 3	6. Up to six months continuously
2. Up to one day continuously 1	7. Up to nine months continuously
3. Up to one week continuously	8. Up to twelve months continuously
4. Up to one month continuously	9. Over twelve months continuously 1
5. Up to three months continuously	10. From time to time irregularly

E. *Cost to Organization*

1. Free 4	6. As % of main contact— estimated at £..................
2. Unassessed 1	
3. By annual subscription (give amount if possible)	7. Under £25
	8. £26 – £50
4. £.....................	
5. By professional scale— estimated at £.................	9. £51 – £100
	10. £101 – £1,000

F *Nature of evidence*

1. Observation by researcher 5	6. Financial statement
2. Verbal report 5	7. Organization's statistics
3. Correspondence seen	8. Special report for researcher
4. Minutes of meetings	9. Information from outsider
5. Technical reports	10. Other (specify)

117

G. *Implications for Firm* (or other type of organization)
   1. Contact is likely to effect firm's current performance. 5
   2. Contact is not likely to effect firm's current performance.
   3. Contact is likely to effect structure of firm's organization. 5
   4. Contact is not likely to effect structure of firm's organization.
   5. Contact is likely to increase profit or surplus. 5
   6. Contact is not likely to increase profit or surplus.
   7. Contact does extend firm's network of external relationships. 4
   8. Contact does not extend firm's network of external relationships. 1
   9. Contact is likely to increase firm's efficiency. 4
   10. Contact is not likely to increase firm's efficiency. 1

Organization F3: Anonymous

1. This is a farm of 70 acres and in 1967 it supported 83 Jersey cows. They yield about 180 gallons of milk a day and most of this is sold to the Milk Marketing Board. Kale is the only crop grown. Income in 1967 amounted to £13,500, £8,000 of which was obtained from the sale of milk and the rest from the sale of cream.

2. The owner of the farm does not live there and it is run by a resident manager who occupies the farmhouse with his wife and three children. The manager of another of the owner's farms a few miles away has some indefinite supervisory responsibility. The present manager is helped by a very competent cowman, another young man working there for two years before going to agricultural college, and a schoolboy who works at weekends. The manager's wife is in charge of the sale of cream which she delivers daily. Labour is in short supply and little help has come from the Ministry of Labour or the Youth Employment Service. The youngsters that have been employed have been recruited through introductions from friends and neighbours.

3. The manager has been anxious to increase the sale of cream during the course of the project, and on one occasion telephoned to ask for help in finding new customers. I hesitated to make suggestions in case a consultancy situation might complicate our research role. However, he seemed satisfied with some general advice about marketing and advertising and followed up my proposals. It clearly is difficult for the manager's wife to cope with deliveries to local restaurants and shops as well as dealing with her domestic tasks.

4. In 1967 the price of milk in the summer was 2s 1d and 4s 3d in the winter, plus a premium or bonus that varied between 1d and 10d per gallon. Skimmed milk brought in between 1d and 3d per gallon. Milk prices are changed from time to time by the Milk Marketing Board in accordance with the market situation. Cream on the other

hand can yield *between 7s 9d and 9s 6d per pint,* depending on the quantity sold at one time. Thus ten gallons of milk in the winter would earn about £2 for the farmer, and one gallon of cream about £4. Ten gallons of milk are needed to produce one gallon of cream.

5. The demand for cream is very high for short periods, such as at Christmas. In 1966 the manager could not make enough cream and bought extra milk from a neighbour.

6. The Milk Marketing Board sells cream produced at its own creameries and thus only pays farmers the relevant milk price that covers its purchases of milk for use in its creameries.

7. Neither the owner of the farm nor the senior manager was present at any of our visits. The owner is a businessman and he had invested enough to equip the farm adequately when the present manager took over in 1965. The farm is very productive and the manager runs it efficiently. As laymen, we could find no grounds for faulting the farm's performance.

8. The manager is an active and enthusiastic member of the National Farmers' Union. In addition to his interests in the N.F.U.'s normal functions, he is particularly interested in the opportunities it provides for meeting other farmers, such as at clay-pigeon shooting, at the Annual Dinner, and at visits to other farms on 'farm walks'. He depends very much on informal contacts and sources of information to guide his management of the farm. His friends and neighbours also provide practical help in times of illness or other difficulty.

9. The farm owner is a member of the Jersey Society which records the characteristics of all pedigree cattle of this type. It also issues licences permitting the use of the word Jersey in selling cream. It gives advice on all matters concerning these pedigree herds.

10. The Milk Marketing Board, as the farm's major customer, is of course an important external contact. They provide a 'low cost production' analysis service at a fee of £72 a year but the manager believes it unnecessary to subscribe as he received a very similar service without charge from the British Oil and Cake Mills Company Limited who supply him with feeding stuffs. Their recording system enables him to compare the yield from his cows with other similar cows and with other similar farms. However, information under the B.O.C.M. scheme is not available until after the end of the particular financial year.

11. The manager was invited by his veterinary surgeon to attend a

meeting of the Surrey and Middlesex Animal Health Study Group, consisting of veterinary surgeons and farmers who are particularly interested in new knowledge about the health of cattle. The local officers of the Ministry of Agriculture and of the National Agricultural Advisory Service also support its activities. At the meeting he attended in October 1966, a member of the Cattle Breeding Centre at Reading spoke of 'Cattle Fertility'. There was an active discussion and the manager appeared to derive benefit from the knowledge acquired and from meeting the people present.

12. The manager had a critical opinion of the National Agricultural Advisory Service. On one occasion he asked for their help to overcome poor yields from five acres of grassland. No adviser was able to call for ten days by which time he had discovered, with the help of neighbours, that slugs were the cause of his problem. Recently, there was milk fever on the farm and his vet contacted a nutritional chemist within N.A.A.S. who was not able to be of much assistance. The vet charged a fee of £7 for his attendance when the N.A.A.S. officer visited the farm. The milk fever problem has not yet been overcome, but with the help of B.O.C.M., feeds will be modified to make good any mineral deficiencies in the soil. The manager feels that the chief fault of N.A.A.S. lies in its range of specialists, each of whom has a different approach to the farm and none seems to appreciate fully the farmer's practical difficulties.

13. Underlying his attitude to N.A.A.S. is his belief that farming problems are too subtle to be solved by technicalities alone. For example, he knows that a careful selection of feeding stuffs will reduce costs and maintain nourishment. But if the mixture is unpalatable to the cows it will lead to a reduction in yield.

14. The veterinary surgeon is very important at a farm devoted to milk production from a very good pedigree herd. He attends regularly and is usually available at very short notice. Of course he charges fees and the manager believes them to be high. Perhaps those fees are a necessary cost, like buying cattle feed, rather than an external aid, but there are indications that veterinary advice extends beyond the immediate purpose of any visit and a broader consultancy relationship has been built up. The vet maintains careful records for each cow at the farm. Productivity of the farm depends very much on keeping the cows in milk for the maximum period. Thus proper insemination at

the right time is important, and their health must be preserved, and on both these matters the vet is of vital importance.

15. Every farm nowadays obtains numerous supplies from firms, and there is some evidence that advice and aid is involved with many purchases. The manager of this farm prefers to deal with one or two suppliers whom he knows and trusts, rather than searching for goods at a low price. Fortunately, prices for top quality feeds and other goods are reduced when bought under a long-term contract.

16. The farm manager left school at the age of fourteen and has spent all his life in farming, gradually working his way up until he obtained the management of this farm. He is now in his late thirties and sees his present job as a major career achievement, for it has enabled him to join the ranks of the owners and managers instead of simply being an ordinary employee or farm labourer. That has not stopped him from taking an active part in all farm work. He has no formal qualifications in agriculture but he is currently studying for the examinations of the City and Guilds of London Institute Diploma in Farm Management.

ANALYSIS OF EXTERNAL CONTACTS
July 1, 1967 – June 30, 1968

NAME OF ORGANIZATION	F3 ANONYMOUS
CONTACTS OBSERVED	10
CONTACTS REPORTED	17
TOTAL CONTACTS ANALYZED	27

A. *Type of contact:*

1.	Normal 'business' 12	2.	Unusual 'business'	
3.	Aid—deliberate 10	4.	Aid—indirect 5	

B. *With whom*

1. Supplier 12	2. Management Consultant	3. Technical Consultant 2
4. Research Association	5. Trade Association 1	6. Public Body 4
7. Competitor 1	8. Training Board	9. Customer 3
10. National Economic Committee	11. Building Contractor	12. Local government authority
13. Professional practice 2	14. Government department	15. Foreign organization
16. Employment agency	17. Professional institute	18. Head Office
19. College	20. Research organization	21. Bank
22. Trade Union	23. International official body	24. Wholesaler
25. Retailer	26. Agricultural Show 2	27.
28.	29.	30.

C. *Purpose*
1. Give information—general
2. Give information—technical
3. Give information—commercial
4. Seek information—general
5. Seek information—technical 8
6. Seek information—commercial 2
13. Buying operations 4
15. Research and development operations
17. Financial operations 1
19. Production operations 14

7. Give advice—general
8. Give advice—technical
9. Give advice—commercial
10. Seek advice—general 1
11. Seek advice—technical 7
12. Seek advice—commercial 3
14. Selling operations 3
16. General management operations 4
18. Personnel operations 1
20. Other

D. *Duration on Contact*
1. Up to one hour continuously 13
2. Up to one day continuously 7
3. Up to one week continuously
4. Up to one month continuously 1
5. Up to three months continuously

6. Up to six months continuously
7. Up to nine months continuously
8. Up to twelve months continuously
9. Over twelve months continuously 1
10. From time to time irregularly 5

E. *Cost to Organization*
1. Free 16
2. Unassessed
3. By annual subscription 1 give amount if possible)
4. £..................
5. By professional scale— estimated at £..................

6. As % of man contract— estimated at £..................
7. Under £25 6
8. £26 – £50
9. £51 – £100
10. £101 – £1,000

F. *Nature of evidence*
1. Observation by researcher 10
2. Verbal report 27
3. Correspondence seen 1
4. Minutes of meetings
5. Technical reports

6. Financial statement
7. Organization's statistics
8. Special report for researcher
9. Information from outsider
10. Other (specify)

G. *Implications for Firm* (or other type of organization)
1. Contact is likely to effect firm's current performance. 27
2. Contact is not likely to effect firm's current performance.
3. Contact is likely to effect structure of firm's organization. 16
4. Contact is not likely to effect structure of firm's organization. 11
5. Contact is likely to increase profit or surplus. 24
6. Contact is not likely to increase profit or surplus. 3
7. Contact does extend firm's network of external relationships. 27
8. Contact does not extend firm's network of external relationships.
9. Contact is likely to increase firm's efficiency. 27
10. Contact is not likely to increase firm's efficiency.

Organization F4: Anonymous

1. This is a mixed milk and arable farm covering 726 acres. It is run by a family partnership and is leased in the name of the senior partner.

2. The farm employs about eight staff, including two foremen; it appears to be the most efficient of the four farms in this project.

3. The senior partner is a graduate in agriculture of Oxford University, now in his seventies, and he has spent half of his adult life in farming. Farming is a way of life for him and his family. He has been the tenant of this farm since 1939 and pays a rent of £5 per acre.

4. This farmer has given us a great deal of statistical information, including a copy of his annual accounts for the year ending September 30, 1965, and a N.A.A.S. farm management report for the year ending September 29, 1964. He is thus the most informative of the farmers in our sample.

5. Of the farm's 726 acres, 60 acres were given over in 1965 to wheat, 158 acres to barley, 12 acres to arable silage, 10 acres to potatoes, 255 acres to grass grazed only, and 231 acres to grass cut.

Yield/acre of arable crops

Wheat	26	cwt/acre
Barley	25	cwt/acre
Arable silage	7	cwt/acre
Potatoes	10	tons/acre

Livestock—grazing stock

Dairy cows	161	
Beef cows	3	
Other cattle over two years	42	⎫
Other cattle one to two years	67	⎬ replacements for dairy herd
Other cattle under one year	45	⎭
Greyface ewes from Scotland	104	
Other sheep over six months	20	
Sows	46	
Pigs over two months	209	

Finance 1965

Partner's capital accounts:

Senior partner	£14,080
His wife	£3,946
His son-in-law	£6,421
His daughter	£9,789
giving a total of £34,236	

Fixed assets

Tenants' improvements	£2,837
Machinery and Implements	£3,865
Combine Harvester	£580
Motors and lorries	£658
Tractors	£922
	£8,862

Income 1964:   each partner received £1,119
       1965:   each partner received £905

A figure of £280 appears in the accounts for each year as 'Partner's Private Consumption' for each partner.

Expenditure

Purchases:		
	Sheep	£1,114
	Feeding Stuffs	£6,148
	Seeds	£1,388
	Fertilizers and sprays	£4,765
	Wages and National Insurance	£10,770
	Services hired	£1,222
	Rent and rates	£3,758
	Petrol and oil and machinery repairs	£2.478
	Repairs and renewals to buildings	£1,838
		£33,481

Surplus or Profit

Net profit for the year September 30, 1965   £3,621

Sources of Income

By Sales and Services

Cattle (non-herd)	£486
Pigs	£6,296
Sheep	£873
Milk	£29,989
Corn	£1,765
Cereal deficiency payments	£1,419
Potatoes	£1,392
	£42,220

6. The farm uses the National Agricultural Advisory Service regularly and N.A.A.S. officers believe that the farm is well managed. In June 1965 they reported that the pig food cost per hundred pounds of pig output was above average and needed closer investigation. Towards the end of the next year the partners decided to give up pig breeding. They also gave up growing potatoes as a result of the unprofitable results revealed by the N.A.A.S. farm management analysis.

7. The farm was an early user of the farm management accounting subsidy provided via N.A.A.S., and a clerk from the partners' accountant attends once a week to pay all bills and note all income received.

The farm office is generally a major focal point of the farm and is well run. Extensive records and charts are maintained and used.

8. The senior partner is a member of the English Guernsey Cattle Society used primarily for registering pedigree cattle in the herd book. It also negotiates on behalf of quality milk producers with the Milk Marketing Board to obtain a satisfactory premium.

9. One of the partners takes an active interest in the National Farmers' Union, and all the partners appreciate the Union's activities in representing the farming community and in supplying a number of services, such as legal advice. The N.F.U. is likely to be used on all non-technical matters. The senior partner in particular is a continuing student of agriculture and active use is made of agricultural research reports and relevant academic journals. A weekly farming paper is read. The Ministry of Agriculture's Veterinary Services Laboratory had been used, especially when one of the sheep produced a dead lamb a month before it was due. The farmers were anxious to find out whether their flock had been infected by worms.

10. In addition to these special external aids, extensive use is made of the farm's accountant, and also local farming societies, partly for social pleasures and partly for technical problems.

11. Suppliers are also important but the fund of specialized knowledge possessed by the partners makes them independent of much of the casual information that seems important to the other farmers in this study.

12. The partnership has had a long struggle to build up sufficient capital to equip the farm properly, and the senior partner believes that the battle is still continuing because replacements cost so much more than the original machines.

13. The future of the farm presents an important problem to the partners, as the farm is leased to the senior partner and need not be made available to the others after his death. If it were, it would certainly be at a much higher rent in view of the considerable increase in the value of land since the tenancy began. It may be that the rent would almost be beyond a price that would permit farming to continue on an economic basis.

14. A number of steps have been taken to reduce the problem of death duties and capital gains, but there does seem to be a need for specialized advice that would ensure the continuity of efficient farming.

Although lawyers can give such advice in general terms, the particular farming complications would seem to require a more subtle advisory service.

ANALYSIS OF EXTERNAL CONTACTS

July 1, 1967 – June 30, 1968

NAME OF ORGANIZATION	ANONYMOUS F4
CONTACTS OBSERVED	9
CONTACTS REPORTED	1
TOTAL CONTACTS ANALYZED	10

A. *Type of contact:* 1. Normal 'business' 4 2. Unusual 'business'
   3. Aid—deliberate 3 4. Aid—indirect 3

B. *With whom*

1. Supplier 2	2. Management Consultant	3. Technical Consultant
4. Research Association	5. Trade Association	6. Public Body
7. Competitor	8. Training Board	9. Customer 1
10. National Economic Committee	11. Building Contractor 1	12. Local government authority 1
13. Professional practice	14. Government department 1	15. Foreign organization
16. Employment agency	17. Professional institute	18. Head Office
19. College	20. Research organization 2	21. Bank
22. Trade Union	23. International official body	24. Wholesaler
25. Retailer	26. Other farmer 2	27.
28.	29.	30.

C. *Purpose*

1. Give information—general	7. Give advice—general
2. Give information—technical	8. Give advice—technical
3. Give information—commercial	9. Give advice—commercial
4. Seek information—general 2	10. Seek advice—general 2
5. Seek information—technical 3	11. Seek advice—technical 2
6. Seek information—commercial	12. Seek advice—commercial
13. Buying operations 2	14. Selling operations 1
15. Research and development operations 2	16. General management operations
17. Financial operations	18. Personnel operations
19. Production operations 8	20. Other

D. *Duration on Contact*
1. Up to one hour continuously 2
2. Up to one day continuously
3. Up to one week continuously 3
4. Up to one month continuously
5. Up to three months continuously
6. Up to six months continuously
7. Up to nine months continuously
8. Up to twelve months continuously
9. Over twelve months continuously 1
10. From time to time irregularly 4

E. *Cost to Organization*
1. Free 4
2. Unassessed
3. By annual subscription 1 (give amount if possible)
4. £..................
5. By professional scale— estimated at £..................
6. As % of main contract— estimated at £..................
7. Under £25 2
8. £26 – £50 1
9. £51 – £100
10. £101 – £1,000

F. *Nature of evidence*
1. Observation by researcher 9
2. Verbal report 8
3. Correspondence seen
4. Minutes of meetings
5. Technical reports 1
6. Financial statement
7. Organization's statistics
8. Special report for researcher
9. Information from outsider 1
10. Other (specify)

G. *Implications for Firm* (or other type of organization)
1. Contact is likely to effect firm's current performance. 8
2. Contact is not likely to effect firm's current performance. 2
3. Contact is likely to effect structure of firm's organization. 4
4. Contact is not likely to effect structure of firm's organization. 6
5. Contact is likely to increase profit or surplus. 7
6. Contact is not likely to increase profit or surplus. 3
7. Contact does extend firm's network of external relationships. 10
8. Contact does not extend firm's network of external relationships.
9. Contact is likely to increase firm's efficiency. 8
10. Contact is not likely to increase firm's efficiency. 2

Chapter 7

The Builders

There are about 90,000 firms in the building industry and in civil engineering, some employing 40,000, many one-man businesses. The gross output of building and civil engineering was about £4,000m. in 1967, including £1,100m. of repair and maintenance work. The construction industry employs about 1,700,000 people, and there are another 300,000 people employed in the construction materials industries. Several professions are involved in construction, particularly architects, several specialist types of engineers, and quantity surveyors. There are numerous trade unions, some overlapping but making efforts to integrate. Finally, there is a range of clients, some with very great experience of construction, most involved in building only once in their lives.

The problems of the construction industry are aggravated by rapid change. Changes are taking place in the building contract, in the use of new materials, in the management of the building site, and in the types of work being carried out.

Building work absorbs about half the nation's capital investment each year. Building employees represent over 7 per cent of the total working population. New housing accounts for just over a quarter of building output, with approximately one half under public authorities and one half being built for private clients. The annual rate of house building is about 400,000 new houses per year and it would seem necessary to increase this to about 500,000 if the standard of housing is to be improved. The Ministry of Public Building have estimated that about two million existing houses are unsuitable for habitation.

The volume of building output increased on average by 7 per cent a year from 1956 to 1961 and by nearly 5 per cent from 1961 to 1966, and the number of workers has fallen. Since that date, the industry has been held back through government policy and economic uncertainty. Informed opinion expects the growth rate will be about 3 per cent in 1968 and 1969.

The rate of technical change is difficult to assess. 'System' building has been largely confined to local authority housing; in the first nine months of 1967 30 per cent of their dwellings used one of these 'prefabricated' methods. The techniques used by the construction industry are continually changing and that trend has important consequences for producers of materials and components. The output of bricks has remained virtually static in recent years while the output of lightweight building blocks, cement, and concrete has moved ahead. Clay roofing tiles have been replaced by concrete tiles. There have been sharp rises in the use of precast and prestressed concrete, ready-mixed concrete, concrete pipes for drainage, copper tubes for central heating, aluminium window frames, window fittings and door furniture, and plastic rainwater and soil goods. This trend towards new materials and components will almost certainly continue with a wider use of plastics and possibly aluminium.

There is no need to describe in more detail the nature of the building industry and the many problems that confront it. There have been a series of studies in recent years that demonstrate only too clearly the enormous demands that are made on one of the oldest industries in this country, and the complexities of modernization have been described. Perhaps the most significant change is reflected in the growing popularity of the term 'the construction industry' in place of the more traditional separation of building from civil engineering. Whilst the traditional differences remain, links between the two activities are increasing.

The main sections of the Emerson Report entitled *Survey of Problems before the Construction Industries,* prepared for the Minister of Works and published in 1962, indicate the industry's difficulties:

1. Confidence and Continuity;
2. Building Materials—Supply and Distribution;
3. Building Operations and Civil Engineering;
4. Relations between the building owner, professions, and contractor;

5. The placing and management of contracts;
6. Apprenticeship and training;
7. Research;
8. The public interest in increased efficiency.

There are many organizations offering aid to all branches of the construction industry. First, the Ministry of Public Building and Works has an active and extending programme of research, development, management training, and consultancy. It is promoting new methods, industrialized building, information and research, and the better co-ordination of activities between the numerous people involved in a building project. For the individual building firm, the Ministry is primarily useful as a source of information and statistics, and possibly of free consultancy. There is a very small consultancy unit at the Ministry, but that has been mainly concerned to date with the building problems of local authorities.

Second, there are trade associations for the building materials manufacturer, the building contractor, the building merchant, and all the ancillary sub-contractors needed to complete a modern building. Many of these bodies, and particularly the National Federation of Building Trades' Employers, offer assistance to builders. The chart on page 131, taken from the evidence submitted to the Royal Commission on Trade Unions and Employers' Associations by the Federation, indicates the complex network of organizations that now exist within the building industry.

There are several sources of new knowledge and research. The Building Research Station is maintained by the Ministry of Technology. It studies building materials and methods, and the needs of those who use buildings. Recently the Construction Industry Information and Research Association has been established. It evolved out of the Construction Industry Research Association, and its change of function and organization reflect to some extent an inadequacy in the original scheme. The Agrément Institute was recently set up, to conduct detailed investigations into industrialized and prefabricated building systems in order to offer guidance to the industry and to public authorities on the advantages and limitations of each of the many systems now available. The Institute of Builders is a professional

130

Chart 1

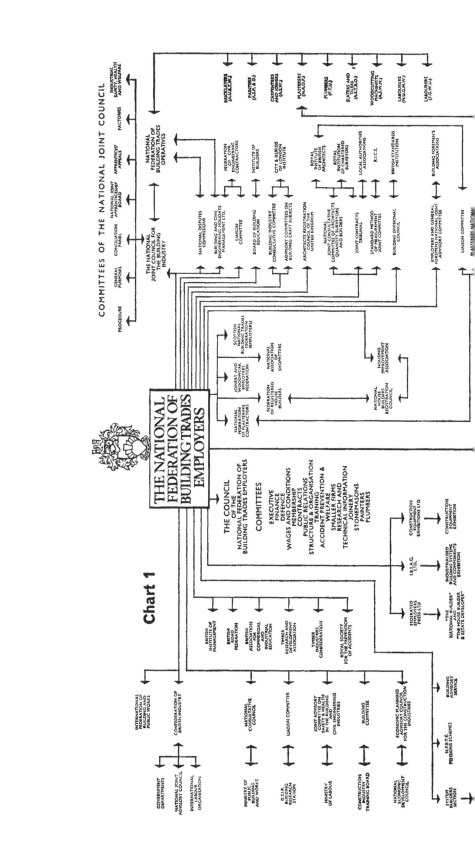

COMMITTEES OF THE NATIONAL JOINT COUNCIL

THE NATIONAL FEDERATION OF BUILDING TRADES EMPLOYERS

institute providing a scheme of studies for those wishing to acquire a comprehensive technical and management knowledge of building.

In recent years there has been some research into the human problems associated with building. The Tavistock Institute has carried out studies on behalf of a committee representing both the contractors and the professions involved in building. Two books have been published but little more has been done than to sketch out the nature of the problem and to indicate some of the opportunities that exist for changes that would be of advantage to all concerned. The research programme originally sponsored by the industry ceased through lack of funds.[1]

The National Economic Development Council has set up economic development committees for (a) building, (b) civil engineering, and (c) construction materials. The primary task of the committees is to decide what is wrong with these industries and to devise and recommend ways of putting it right. 'The Economic Development Committees represent a new dimension in government/industry relations. They provide the first instance where departments, management and trade unions have been brought together for frequent and regular discussion in the context of particular industries and about the whole range of their problems.'[2]

The building committee has been concerned with the import and export of building materials and with demand and output forecasts. It is exploring the possibility of a study of the structure of the industry, and examining most of the problems concerned with manpower, including the supply and the optimum use of building workers. It has ensured that the Banwell Report on *The Placing and Management of Contracts for Building and Civil Engineering Work* is not forgotten and that as many as possible of its recommendations are carried out. It is sponsoring inter-firm comparisons in the industry in co-operation with the Construction Industry Training Board — rapidly becoming another major source of aid for the building industry.

There are extensive educational and training facilities that directly and indirectly provide aid to the building industry. The colleges of building undertake the basic training of craftsmen and managers in the industry. They are now supplemented by the courses provided by the

---

[1] *Communications in the Building Industry*, G. Higgin and N. Jessop, Tavistock Publications, 1965, describes the project.

[2] 'Economic Development Committees—A New Dimension in Government/Industry Relations', T. C. Fraser, Journal of Management Studies, May 1967, p. 165.

Construction Industry Training Board. Each of the professions associated with building has its own extensive educational network and many of these provide post-graduate courses and services that occasionally involve the builder. Special courses for the building industry have been provided by Urwick, Orr & Partners Limited, a major management consultancy firm, for many years.

Finally, there are informal and indirect sources of aid, such as the advice and information provided by building suppliers and builders' merchants. There are informal discussions between builders in many places and with varying degrees of formality.

Perhaps the casual employment of labour helps to distribute knowledge when workers move from one contractor to others within a particular area or throughout the country.

Two aid organizations in particular are worth noting:

The Advisory Service for the Building Industry was created by a trade association and now functions as a consultancy firm. The Advisory Service was set up in 1954 by the National Federation of Building Trade Employers and has become accepted as an important source of training and consultancy. In 1967 it planned to carry out 110 courses in twenty-seven different fields. It has carried out over 1,000 consultancy assignments.

The funds make available under the post-war Marshall Aid Scheme from the USA helped to establish the Service. It has a management committee composed almost entirely of members of the Building Trade Employers, but 60 per cent of its activities involve firms that are not members of the Federation. It charges £40 per day per man for most assignments, plus £40 per week for the services of a supervising consultant. There are now 22 consultants, all of whom have had experience in the industry and possess professional qualifications. The consultants work in teams of six or seven under a supervisor. Assignments usually begin with a free one-day survey. Then agreement is reached with the client about the work that should be carried out. The Service arranges short-term attendance at clients' firms, and the director of the Service favours frequent return visits to firms instead of very long continuous assignments. In 1967 the director received two complaints about his consultants, and he regarded that figure as rather high.

There are both residential and non-residential courses. Some are open to all, some are specially prepared to meet the needs of one firm. The number of courses has increased from eighty in 1965 to 110 in 1967, presumably reflecting the growing influence of the Construction Industry Training Board's grants for approved training courses. Since the Service's training programme started, over 10,000 people from all branches of the construction industry have attended courses. The Service publishes leaflets on the application of management techniques to the building industry.

The National Housebuilders Registration Council has been used by several of the firms in our survey. It is an independent, non-political, non-profit-making body approved by successive governments. Its members include representatives of the Building Societies' Association, the Royal Institute of British Architects, the Royal Institute of Chartered Surveyors, a number of women's organizations, local authority organizations, owner-occupiers, building employers, and building trade unions, together with government observers. Building employers are the largest single group but only constitute one-third of the Council's membership. All members of the Council are distinguished leaders in their own field. These Council members are unpaid, but their policies are carried out by paid staff, including over 120 technical field staff stationed throughout the country.

The aim of the Council is to ensure that no purchaser of a new house need be out of pocket through major defects in construction. In the long term, the aim is to contribute towards a gradual improvement in standards and to a better understanding between housebuilders and purchasers.

In 1966 the Building Societies' Association recommended to its members that mortgage facilities should be made available only to registered housebuilders. Since then, more housebuilders have applied to join the register than did in the first twenty-five years of the Council's history. While the full number of builders is not yet known, it seemed that by the end of 1966 the Council was dealing with between 60 and 70 per cent of all private enterprise houses for sale, and the proportion was rising rapidly.

The Council obtains its finance by levying a fee of six guineas for every house built by a registered builder. It spends that money on unscheduled inspections of such houses, unless the construction has been supervised by an architect or surveyor employed by the purchaser. In addition the Council has insurance policies that can provide a two-year warranty up to £5,000 per house. The Council will compensate any purchaser who has defects in a certified house which an independent arbitrator judges to be due to non-compliance with the Council's standards and which the builder has not remedied. A further warranty from the third to the tenth year after the house is certified enables payment up to £2,500 to be paid against the cost of making good damage due to a major structural defect. In addition some insurance protection is provided against the bankruptcy of the builder in most circumstances before and after completion.

The Council works through two main committees. One is concerned with registration, and admits builders to the register provided they conform to a number of requirements. The other committee is concerned with drafting standard specifications with which all registered builders must comply. The new specification adopted in 1966 has three main elements: the first covers matters of workmanship and finish which are outside the scope of building regulations laid down by the Ministry of Housing; the second element covers matters of design which affect the comfort and convenience of the owner or occupiers and these again are outside building regulations; the third element covers some matters within the building regulations because it seemed right to provide the builder with a comprehensive document that would define in some detail what he had to build, and inform the purchaser in some detail what he was buying. These latest standards cover garages and central heating but exclude extras that individual purchasers may order. The Council's main aim is to ensure a sound standard of workmanship and of material in the basic construction and finish of the house.

Clearly the success of the scheme depends on the attitude of builders and on the Council's inspection service, and although this can never be so extensive as to ensure that mistakes never happen, there can be no doubt of the successful growth of this scheme particularly in view of the recent attitude of the building societies. As is clear from some of our firms, the conscientious builder welcomes the positive role of the Council and the somewhat negative policeman aura does not seem to bother the good builder. In any case, the extensive insurance programme of the council presumably makes good the deficiencies of both the builder and the Council's inspection system.

Organization B5: Anonymous

1. A private business established in the 1930s as a builder and contractor, it now comprises five companies: one specializing in general building (the parent company), one building mainly flats and houses, two buying land, and one acting as a sales organization for the buildings erected speculatively. There are four directors and three other senior executives. The managing director is the founder of the business. We have not been able to obtain detailed financial information about the business but it is believed that annual turnover is approximately £250,000.

2. The number of employees of the group varies in relation to the amount of building operations in hand but does not appear to rise above forty. This usually includes three site foremen, ten office personnel, and about twenty-five other employees, mainly labourers, lorry drivers, plant operatives, and maintenance men. The firm make extensive use of specialist sub-contractors particularly in relation to excavating, concreting, bricklaying, carpentry, roofing, electrical and plumbing installations, and decorating. Thus the practical dimensions of the organization far exceed its legal employees, and this phenomenon of sub-contracting is a major problem—and boon—of the construction industries.

3. There is usually one major estate and one or two smaller estates being built by the head office staff, and another under the control of the main subsidiary company, situated some ten miles away. The sales of these houses is undertaken by the third main component of the business, in association with a large firm of estate agents.

4. The firm makes extensive use of external contacts, many of whom are external aids. They can be usefully divided into the following categories:

(a) *Trade associations.* The parent company is a member of the Federation of Master Builders. It has also shown a nominal interest in other bodies indirectly through the individual and professional interests of its staff, such as the Institute of Quantity Surveyors. It is a member of the National House Builders' Registration Council. One of the managers is a keen member of the British Institute of Management.

(b) *Suppliers and sub-contractors.* This category includes a very wide range of professions and trades, embracing 'labour only' sub-contractors for building, suppliers of bricks and other building materials, prefabricated complete housing systems (particularly exemplified by Trusteel Limited), and several architects and solicitors that are used for particular contracts and sales.

(c) *Finance.* Commercial Banks are used as sources of funds for buying land on which houses and flats are then to be built, and building societies and local authorities are used as a source of funds for people who wish to buy houses from the firm. A regular source of financial help is a prominent firm of merchant bankers which supplies money in the form of mortgages and loans in relation to a major project, such as a block of flats.

(d) *Sales.* The firm makes extensive use of one major local firm of estate agents but has recently established its own subsidiary solely concerned with sales as it has been dissatisfied with the services provided by estate agents. A firm of advertising agents has been used to prepare brochures and public relations material needed for the sale of property.

(e) *Public Bodies.* The firm has numerous contacts with local planning and building authorities, and frequently is involved with a number of authorities at different levels in relation to one particular project. Occasionally, the authorities disagree with one another as to the desirability of a development or of the particular characteristics of the buildings that are acceptable. These negotiations can be long drawn out and involve considerable expenditure, particularly when a planning application rejected by the appropriate local authority is submitted on appeal to the Ministry of Housing. Another aspect of the positive role of local authorities is the work of the building inspectors, who at first sight may appear to be obstacles to quick building but can prove to be valuable advisers and prevent the accidental inclusion of sub-standard work within new buildings. The company is familiar with the work of the Building Research Station but no direct use has been made of its services during the course of this research project. Finally, two members of the organization are involved with a local technical college for technical training.

(f) *Miscellaneous aids.* These include (i) trade and technical journals which are of considerable importance and are closely and systematically studied by the senior executive in charge of one major subsidiary, and (ii) the Youth Employment Service in relation to recruitment of young office staff for training.

5. The business derives considerable benefit from the personal abilities

of the chief executive who devotes most of his time to its operation. He is well informed about building but is able to delegate a great deal of work to subordinates with clear responsibilities and terms of reference. He is concerned with finance and with the general growth of the company. He has a target for growth of about 20 per cent per year but is satisfied when he achieves 10 per cent in difficult years, and subscribes to the view that planned and determined growth each year is essential.

6. The most interesting external relationship and aid that was observed during our investigation was the use made of the products of Trusteel Limited. The aim of the particular development was to erect ninety-five different houses in nine different designs over a three-year period. The first stage began in 1967 when twelve houses were erected. Despite poor economic conditions, the houses were selling well towards the end of the year, with six of them sold by November 28th.

7. The method of building is comparatively fast and simple. The manufacturers supply a steel frame and details of the construction system, and the components can be ordered from usual suppliers as and when required, thus avoiding the need to hold expensive stocks. The buildings can be erected more quickly than by traditional methods so that when sales are moving fast, finance is tied up for shorter periods.

8. The development of the site is the responsibility of the builders with a site foreman in charge of local daily activities. Trusteel Limited provided the services of a technical representative with expert knowledge and he was able to train the firm's employees within a few days, since the special requirements of the system presented few problems. After that initial period spent on the site, the representative makes occasional visits and will attend when required.

9. The system works well because of the prompt delivery of parts on demand, it enables building to be carried out more quickly with fewer men, the need for plastering (one of the major causes of delay in house completion) is reduced, there is less money tied up in the building of a house, there is less time lost through bad weather, and there is easier site control. There are also some probable advantages to the finished building, particularly thermal insulation and lack of shrinkage cracks.

10. The firm appears to be well above average in efficiency in all major activities. It is outstanding for the building industry in that it has tackled the marketing problems seriously and with some success. It is alert to new opportunities in industrialized building materials, and

it has satisfactory financial resources. It has found the land needed for its development and appears to be growing at a satisfactory rate. It is difficult to identify the exact influence of any particular external aid on the activities of this successful organization. The overall picture is clearly one of a network of external relationships, each contributing to the overall performance. Each of these external relationships is involved in turn in its own network of relationships and appropriate external aids. The success of this company may well be due much to its willingness to make use of the many independent sources of supplies available to the smaller building firm, so that the role of aid is intricately built into the normal functioning of the business.

11. The firm's only weakness is the absence of concern with the best possible performance. The managing director has said that he is not personally opposed to the use of management consultants but he does not believe that the staff would welcome them. Probably consultants are not needed but some concern with assessment of achievement would be useful. Thus although the managing director aims to expand at the rate of 20 per cent per annum he is satisfied with 10 per cent when economic conditions are unsatisfactory. Perhaps that indicates a lack of appreciation of opportunities for corporate planning and suggests a rough-and-ready attitude that might not be satisfactory if business conditions were really bad. The firm operates in a prosperous area of South-East England, with a rising population, and thus the demand for new accommodation is very considerable and is only interrupted from time to time by economic policy involving a reduction in available credit.

ANALYSIS OF EXTERNAL CONTACTS
July 1, 1967 — June 30, 1968

NAME OF ORGANIZATION	ANONYMOUS B5
CONTACTS OBSERVED	5
CNTACTS REPORTED	3
TOTAL CONTACTS ANALYZED	8

A. *Type of contact:*   1. Normal 'business' 5   2. Unusual 'business'
   3. Aid—deliberate 3   4. Aid—indirect 1

B. *With whom*
   1. Supplier 1   2. Management Consultant   3. Technical Consultant 1

139

4.	Research Association	5.	Trade Association 2	6.	Public Body
7.	Competitor	8.	Training Board	9.	Customer 1
10.	National Economic Committee	11.	Building Contractor	12.	Local government authority
13.	Professional practice 2	14.	Government department	15.	Foreign organization
16.	Employment agency	17.	Professional institute	18.	Head Office
19.	College	20.	Research organization	21.	Bank
22.	Trade Union	23.	International official body	24.	Wholesaler
25.	Retailer	26.	Estate Agent 2	27.	
28.		29.		30.	

C. *Purpose*

1. Give information—general 1
2. Give information—technical 1
3. Give information—commercial
4. Seek information—general 1
5. Seek information—technical 3
6. Seek information—commercial 1
13. Buying operations
15. Research and development operations 2
17. Financial operations
19. Production operations 2

7. Give advice—general
8. Give advice—technical
9. Give advice—commercial
10. Seek advice—general
11. Seek advice—technical 1
12. Seek advice—commercial
14. Selling operations 3
16. General management operations 2
18. Personnel operations
20. Other 1

D. *Duration of Contact*

1. Up to one hour continuously 1
2. Up to one day continuously 1
3. Up to one week continuously
4. Up to one month continuously

5. Up to three months continuously

6. Up to six months continuously
7. Up to nine months continuously
8. Up to twelve months continuously
9. Over twelve months continuously 1
10. From time to time irregularly 5

E. *Cost to Organization*

1. Free 3
2. Unassessed
3. By annual subscription 2
   (give amount if possible)
4. £.....................
5. By professional scale— estimated at £.................

6. As % of main contract— estimated at £.................. 1
7. Under £25
8. £26 – £50
9. £51 – £100
10. £101 – £1,000

F. *Nature of evidence*

1. Observation by researcher 5
2. Verbal report 8
3. Correspondence seen
4. Minutes of meetings
5. Technical reports

6. Financial statement
7. Organization's statistics
8. Special report for researcher
9. Information from outsider
10. Other (specify)

140

G. *Implications for Firm* (or other type of organization)
1. Contact is likely to effect firm's current performance. 7
2. Contact is not likely to effect firm's current performance. 1
3. Contact is likely to effect structure of firm's organization. 4
4. Contact is not likely to effect structure of firm's organization. 4
5. Contact is likely to increase profit or surplus. 6
6. Contact is not likely to increase profit or surplus. 2
7. Contact does extend firm's network of external relationships. 6
8. Contact does not extend firm's network of external relationships. 2
9. Contact is likely to increase firm's efficiency. 3
10. Contact is not likely to increase firm's efficiency. 3

Organization B6: Anonymous

1. This is a small family firm of general builders and decorators. The business was founded in 1929 by two working builders and has grown to its present position through considerable effort of four active directors. The original two partners are still working but some of the major building projects were under the care of the son of one of the founders. He joined them in 1957. The business became a company in 1961. In November 1967 he left the employment of the company and took up a position on the staff of the Construction Industry Training Board. All the shares are held by five directors.

2. The firm operates primarily in South London but now has a branch producing joinery, in a South Coast town, which was established in 1961. Total numbers employed has not exceeded seventy, including about nine head office staff. The activities of the firm can be divided into (a) a few large contracts, valued at several thousand pounds each, (b) a large number of smaller jobs, possibly thirty at one time, primarily concerned with house repairs, decorations, and small developments, and (c) the joinery business.

3. The performance of the business over the years 1964 to 1967 can be seen from the attached table:

	1964 £	1965 £	1966 £	1967 £
Turnover	139,788	183,976	161,976	175,411
Wages and salaries paid	56,941	53,293	57,495	58,551
Employees	67	65	65	53
Capital invested	13,081	13,951	13,225	9,553
Profits	597	4,196	3,351	269 [1]
Assumed fixed assets	5,462	7,833	7,798	6,380

[1] Excluding bad debts and Construction Industry Training Board levy and grant.

4. Taking turnover as equal to 100 in 1964, it rose to 131 in 1965, fell to 115 in 1966, and rose to 125 in 1967.

5. Bearing in mind that prices were rising by about 15 per cent over this period, the 1967 turnover probably represents a real increase over 1964 of about 10 per cent. It has been achieved with a reduction in staff of about 20 per cent.

6. It should be stressed that the company, being primarily a family business, can best be judged by the standards of living of the owners rather than the profit figures alone. The amount recorded for wages and salaries does not include the remuneration of the directors.

7. The work of the firm is organized with clear divisions of responsibilities between the directors and the head office staff, and there is usually a site foreman on each of their main building jobs. In many ways the division of responsibilities is excessive as there does not appear to be any deliberate machinery for consultation between the directors. Board meetings are not held to plan and review work.

8. This absence of company planning is a serious disadvantage in periods of bad business, and the building industry has been subjected to a number of such periods in recent years. We were asked during the course of one visit whether some advice could be given on how to find additional customers, and a meeting was arranged at Kingston College of Technology between the junior director and a group of students attending an advanced management course. He provided a description of the business and its activities, and received the following suggestions for marketing and advertising activities:

'1. A programme of "desk research" is likely to be useful. This would primarily consist of an analysis of work done in the past year or two so that the company can have a clear picture of (a) the types of work that it has been doing with percentages of total income for each major category; (b) the profitability of the different types of work, particularly the commercial work; (c) the history of a sample of small customers to see whether they evolve from the "changing the washer" category into commissioning a major project.

2. The firm should consider whether there are advantages in specializing in particular types of work such as central heating installation or the conversion of bungalow lofts.

3. Special attention should be paid to the use made by local residents of improvement grants for older houses. It may well be that this is a field where a small specialist staff could be built up and a particular

142

sales campaign undertaken. It is believed that when one house in a street obtains a grant for, say, the installation of a bathroom, there is every chance that the building firm concerned would obtain additional orders from neighbours.

4.   Every effort should be made to contact former clients to invite their further business. Where it is known that they have in fact undertaken further building but given contracts to other firms, enquiries should be made as to how and why the other builders were selected.

5.   Detailed investigation should be made of every competitive tender applied for but not granted, to ensure that the company is in a competitive state.

6.   ADVERTISING

(a) Unless much more money is to be spent on calendars it was felt that they are not sufficiently attractive to command respect from the recipients;

(b) The use of the more expensive diaries for special customers was commended but it did not seem that there was much value in sending out ordinary diaries when so many are nowadays given out as Christmas presents by industry;

(c) With the money saved and perhaps with the additional expenditure of £100 a carefully prepared brochure illustrating work that has been completed in the past year or two, should be introduced and sent out to past and prospective customers;

(d) An advertising policy in relation to local newspapers ought to be very carefully considered. If it can be afforded, the advertisements ought to describe particular types of work, such as central heating installation, and indicate the likely cost wherever possible. Such specific advertising ought also to help solve the problem of evaluating advertising but there is no certain way of measuring precisely the benefit obtainable from advertising.'

9.   Two of these proposals were carried out; the insertion of one advertisement in a local newspaper and the introduction of a new calendar.

10.   The other proposals may have been considered unsound. The firm's progress has depended on extensive relationships with many individuals and firms, partly through the personal contacts of the directors, partly through active participation in the activities of local political, com-

munity, and trade organizations, such as the National Federation of Building Trade Employers. There may have been some resistance to the introduction of more modern, albeit elementary, marketing procedures because it may have seemed unwise to change the image of the business that had been built up, particularly in recent years. Unfortunately, there is no evidence that any conscious decision was taken on this matter.

11. The financial acumen of the company is no more than average, and its success in tendering for larger contracts has been slightly disappointing in recent years.

12. A considerable effort is put into submitting tenders for available building contracts, particularly in the 1966 recession. In one case, they understood that their tender was undercut by three other bids. The company were at the time working on another contract for the same organization, apparently to their satisfaction.

13. Although none of this evidence is conclusive, there seems to be opportunities for more effective operations and better performance. Probably there were difficulties in achieving change through the difference in the ages of the three senior and the junior director.

14. The junior director made considerable efforts to qualify himself for his present and future career. He studied for qualifications from the Institute of Building and during the project he attended and completed successfully a four-year part-time course for the National Diploma in Management Studies at Croydon Technical College. He is a licentiate of the Institute of Building and an associate member of the British Institute of Management. He is about thirty-five. He attended a direct grant school, leaving at sixteen. He is married with two children.

15. The firm's customers include a few large organizations and the largest contract they were involved in during the course of this project was worth £35,000.

16. In addition they have done some house building for local authorities, and office building and decorating for other public bodies. They have built some private houses up to a value of £10,000, and they have numerous individual customers for painting, decorating and repair work.

17. The joinery company occupies a former stable and employs about ten men. It is under the management of an experienced joiner who is independent of head office for all normal activities. There have been

periods of anxiety since the works were set up in 1961, but progress has been satisfactory on the whole.

18. Part of the work is concerned with joinery required for the firm's building contracts, part comprises separate orders obtained locally through the initiative of the manager. That may involve relatively unskilled work, such as the repair of wooden pallets, or skilled work such as the making of counters for a bank.

19. Although employees do not appear to be well paid, labour turnover is low and morale among staff is good. There is a pension scheme for the directors only. The firm has for many years had apprentices and trainees, and it has benefited from the grants available through the Construction Industry Training Board, receiving in 1967 six times the value of the levy they paid to the Board.

20. Most members of the firm have numerous external contacts. The nature of the work brings them into contact with many sub-contractors, members of the professions serving the construction industry, and a range of clients. They have made use of aid organizations available to the building trade, including the National Federation of Building Trades Employers, the National Building Agency, the Building Research Station, the Building Centre, the Advisory Service for the Building Industry, the Construction Industry Training Board, Croydon Technical College, Kingston College of Technology, and a wide range of general and specialist publications supplying information that is both of specific technical importance and in some cases generally helpful.

21. One case where an external aid was not of value concerned the Export Services Branch of the Board of Trade. The Board was approached for advice about opportunities for exporting joinery products but nothing happened and nothing was done by the firm to begin exporting.

22. There are some intriguing problems about this firm in relation to the use of external aids. The organization appears to be active and reasonably efficient because it has survived for forty years. The directors appear to be regularly in touch with most sources of information and advice, and lack of knowledge was never a problem. Yet the firm's prosperity is precarious, resembling many small building firms. Its own premises are somewhat dilapidated and in need of painting. A great deal of energy is devoted to the search for customers but only within conventional limits.

23. Membership of local organizations was justified because of the opportunities they presented for obtaining new business. They may have done so but they were at least as important in meeting a need for social contact and social status. The existence of aid organizations and local business associations do not in themselves lead to improved standards of management and performance.

24. At one site meeting attended by the junior director, the architect was present, accompanied by the electrical contractor and the heating engineer. The contract was for building offices. At this meeting the architect was concerned with preventing problems emerging and hence was a protective influence benefiting all the others involved in the construction of the building. This building firm could be successful by meeting the wishes of the architect, who of course is paid by the client, and by leaving complicated and specialized tasks to specialists selected with the approval of the architect.

25. Clearly, some considerable aid must have been obtained from the architects, surveyors, contractors, and sub-contractors that the firm are involved with in the course of their work, particularly on their larger contracts. There is an extensive network of relationships involved in building construction, extending to a number of public officials such as the building inspector and the fire officer. Some of these appear to have punitive functions but each person in the network supports the others, or at least is necessary to the completion of the work of the others. This literal inter-dependence creates crises and rows when one of the individuals in the network fails to perform properly, but on balance the contribution of each profession and trade compensates for the ignorance and the incompetence of others.

26. Such networks of inter-dependence exist throughout modern economies, but the one described in the construction industry is deliberately organized, however inadequately, and is a potent source of aid.

ANALYSIS OF EXTERNAL CONTACTS
July 1, 1967 – June 30, 1968

NAME OF ORGANIZATION	ANONYMOUS B6
CONTACTS OBSERVED	22
CONTACTS REPORTED	1
TOTAL CONTACTS ANALYZED	23

A. *Type of contact:* 1. Normal 'business' 17   2. Unusual 'business' 1
                  3. Aid—deliberate 4   4. Aid—indirect 1

B. *With whom*

1. Supplier 5	2. Management Consultant	3. Technical Consultant
4. Research Association	5. Trade Association 1	6. Public Body 3
7. Competitor	8. Training Board 1	9. Customer 5
10. National Economic Committee	11. Building Contractor	12. Local government authority
13. Professional practice	14. Government department 1	15 Foreign organization
16. Employment agency	17. Professional institute	18. Head Office 1
19. College 2	20. Research organization	21. Bank
22. Trade Union	23. International official body	24. Wholesaler
25. Retailer	26. Sub-Contractor 1	27. Architect 1
28. Possible employee 1	29.	30.

C. *Purpose*

1. Give information—general	7. Give advice—general
2. Give information—technical	8. Give advice—technical
3. Give information—commercial	9. Give advice—commercial
4. Seek information—general 7	10. Seek advice—general 2
5. Seek information—technical 6	11. Seek advice—technical 2
6. Seek information—commercial 4	12. Seek advice—commercial 2
13 Buying operations 2	14. Selling operations 6
15. Research and development operations 1	16. General management operations 3
17. Financial operations 2	18. Personnel operations 5
19. Production operations 12	20. Other: Transport 1

D. *Duration of Contact*

1. Up to one hour continuously 9	6. Up to six months continuously
2. Up to one day continuously 1	7. Up to nine months continuously
3. Up to one week continuously	8. Up to twelve months continuously
4. Up to one month continuously 1	9. Over twelve months continuously 2
5. Up to three months continuously	10. From time to time irregularly 6

E. *Cost to Organization*

1. Free 13	6. As % of main contract— estimated at £..................
2. Unassessed 1	
3. By annual subscription 3 (give amount if possible)	7. Under £25 1
	8. £26 – £50 1
4. £..................	
5. By professional scale— estimated at £..................	9. £51 – £100
	10. £101 – £1,000 1

147

F. *Nature of evidence*

1. Observation by researcher 22	6. Financial statement
2. Verbal report 21	7. Organization's statistics
3. Correspondence seen 3	8. Special report for researcher
6. Minutes of meetings	9. Information from outsider
5. Technical reports	10. Other (specify) 3 (not specified)

G. *Implications for Firm* (or other type of organization)

1. Contact is likely to effect firm's current performance. 19
2. Contact is not likely to effect firm's current performance. 4
3. Contact is likely to effect structure of firm's organization. 13
4. Contact is not likely to effect structure of firm's organization. 10
5. Contact is likely to increase profit or surplus. 18
6. Contact is not likely to increase profit or surplus. 5
7. Contact does extend firm's network of external relationships. 22
8. Contact does not extend firm's network of external relationships. 1
9. Contact is likely to increase firm's efficiency. 17
10. Contact is not likely to increase firm's efficiency. 6

Organization B7: W. H. Gaze & Sons Limited

1. W. H. Gaze & Sons Limited is the parent company of a group of construction companies. The firm was established as a family business in 1879 and it remains a private company, with several members of the Gaze family as directors. The chairman is Mr R. W. H. Gaze and his brother Mr Douglas E. Gaze is the Deputy Chairman and joint-managing director. The firm occupied new head offices and building yards on the Portsmouth Road, Thames Ditton, Surrey in 1965.

2. Some idea of its range of activities can be obtained from a list of the companies and their activities. Gazes of Kingston Limited is responsible for the larger building contracts, such as the Customs House at London Airport and the halls of residence at the University of East Anglia. Gazes of Surbiton Limited deals with smaller and more conventional building projects. Gazes Electrical Services Limited, Mould & Blaydon Limited, and Metal Engineering Services Limited provide specialist services for the other Gaze companies and for customers. Gazes Hard Courts Limited build tennis courts and sports grounds. Gazes Public Works Limited carry out numerous contracts for local authorities. Home Decor Limited is a retail business concerned with the sale of wallpaper and paint. Gazeway Plant Hire Company Limited hires out building plant to other Gaze companies and to other building contractors when possible. Project Control Limited carries out planning for local authorities. Gazelle Swimming Pools Limited was recently

established to construct swimming pools for the private home and built at the rate of one per week in 1967. Three specialized concrete companies have been established or bought up in recent years—Formcrete Limited, Diespeker Concrete Company Limited, and Kleine Reinforced Concrete Company Limited. Finally, there are a number of autonomous overseas companies in South Africa.

3. The Group now has a conventional range of central services for all its companies but until about 1965 there was considerably more independence in accounting and planning. The Group has made use of outside computer services and has been considering buying its own computer.

4. We have not been provided with any information about the Group's finances. I would guess that its turnover is about £4,500,000 per year and that its level of efficiency probably enables it to earn a profit of 5 per cent of turnover before tax.

5. Gazes were one of the firms that we interviewed in the pilot survey, and we asked them to collaborate in the major project when other building firms would not help us. They agreed readily. We made six visits to their head office to interview the managing director, another director, the company secretary, and several senior executives. We also interviewed the executives in charge of six subsidiary companies, we made six visits to two of the company's building projects, and we interviewed the architects and the clients. Gazes have been clients of Associated Industrial Consultants Limited and we interviewed them to obtain their views of their association with the company.

6. The Group now employs about 1,200 people, although the number fluctuates with the state of business. In addition they make use of a large number of sub-contractors. One of the consultant's reports in 1963 pointed out that the length of service of many staff spoke well of the company as employers but that the age level was high, with 54 per cent of male staff being over fifty-seven years of age. The consultants recommended the appointment of a Group Staff Officer but no such senior personnel appointment has been made. The average age is now lower.

7. A group of companies of this size has a very wide range of external contacts and has made use of numerous external aids. The managing director of the parent company is a member of the National Federation of Building Trades Employers and the Company is a member of the National Contractors Group of the National Federation. Mr D. Gaze

was Vice-Chairman of the South-West London area of the N.F.B.T.E. in 1967 and Chairman in 1968.

8. Another director and now joint-managing director was President of the Builders' Conference in 1968 and he attends these conferences four times a year. He is also a member of the Royal Institute of Chartered Surveyors and of the British Institute of Management.

9. A highly qualified engineer was appointed a director with responsibility for the engineering companies in 1968. A young management accountant was appointed in August 1967.

10. Other specialist executives are usually members of the appropriate specialist institute. These institutes were not used for dealing with any current problem during this project.

11. The Building Research Station is used to obtain advice on problems arising from new processes.

12. The company have made use of Associated Industrial Consultants Limited on a number of occasions since 1960. (In 1938 the firm had built a house for one of A.I.C.'s directors). The original discussions with A.I.C. were related to the idea of becoming a public company. When that proposal was dropped, the relationship between the company and A.I.C. was maintained and has involved a number of assignments. The first one, in 1962, was a general review of the organization, and led to proposals for an integrated structure. The most important proposal was the setting up of a new holding company which would take over most administrative and accounting functions.

13. The second main investigation that A.I.C. carried out, in 1963, concerned the layout of a new headquarters for the Gaze Group of Companies, consisting of an office block, workshops, and a yard for storing building equipment. Their proposals have been followed in detail.

14. A number of other reports followed in 1963 and 1964, concerned with data processing, costing, inventory control, and management accounting, and it would appear that many of these recommendations have been carried out. But A.I.C. have not been concerned with implementing their proposals.

15. A.I.C. have not been required to investigate in detail the Group's financial or marketing policies. As many building firms, Gazes have suffered periods of bad business, primarily through changes in national economic policy. The latest of these occurred in 1967 and the com-

150

pany's turnover and profits dropped. But we received no evidence of active concern with marketing problems, nor with opportunities for stabilizing demand.[1]

16. Thus the role of A.I.C. has been to give advice and information when requested to do so. They only do what they are asked to do and have not achieved a comprehensive advisory role, and that may have preserved the past neglect of finance and marketing. The financial situation has probably improved with the appointment of a non-executive financial director who is a member of the family on the board of a city merchant bank; that appointment was recommended by the consultants.

17. The consultants have accepted an episodic relationship that occasionally has matured into a specific assignment. It might be to the advantage of both parties if the relationship was more stable and if regular reviews and advice were proferred, whether or not it appeared to be relevant or convenient to the directors of the company at that time. The consultants, and Gazes, might benefit if A.I.C. were told which of their proposals were adopted and the reasons for rejecting others.

18. We made a number of visits to two of the firm's major building projects during our investigation. The first was a new building for Her Majesty's Customs at London Airport, and the second was a new school for educationally subnormal children for the Borough of Richmond. At both projects we spoke to the Clerk of Works, the sub-contractors, the architect, and representatives of the client.

19. All our information showed that the company had a high reputation for craftsmanship and efficiency. The situation at London Airport was more complex than at the school because of the need to deal with the Commandant of London Airport, the British Airport Authority and with the Customs, as well as numerous sub-contractors. The blending of these relationships with the development of the building seemed to work smoothly and the central role of the architect as co-ordinator was very apparent in the London Airport project.

20. So far as the school was concerned, the architect was on the staff of the client, Richmond Borough Council, and that reduced the size of the communication network. Modern construction materials were used, and the building went up on time. We obtained some idea of the exter-

[1] However, we now understand that the firm is moving into civil engineering and is considering property development. It is also exploring the possibility of establishing itself in the North-East of England.

151

TABLE A   *Site Population*   GAZES OF KINGSTON LTD. — SCHOOL SITE

Week	Work	Gazes' Employees									Sub-Contractors					Richmond Borough			
		Carpenter	Labourer	Ganger	Machine Driver	Bricklayer	Pipelayer	Carpenter	Drainlayer	Site Foreman	Labourers	Bricklayers	'Prefabrication' Erectors	Erectors	Electricians	Borough Architect	Clerk of Works	Borough Engineer	Total
Sept. 2, 1967	Erection of offices. Alteration to entrance and children's walkway to Carlisle School. Demolitions. Site clearance and carting rubbish away.	1	2	1	2					1									7
Sept. 9, 1967	Erection of canteen, and dividing partition into store and drying room. Excavations on roadway. Site clearance and carting rubbish away.	1	2	1	2					1							1		8
Sept. 16, 1967	Three labourers in C. Springer soil connection. Reduced site levels, erection of profiles and letting out. Excavation of roadway. Carted away hardcore to roadway. Excavations for soil and surface water connections in Hanworth Road.	1	2	1	1					1	3					1		1	11
Sept. 23, 1967	Three labourers Messrs C. Springer. Connections to water main one week behind (awaiting completion of drain connections before this can be made).	2	4	1	1					1	3							1	13

152

Date	Notes										Total
Sept. 30, 1967	Three labourers Messrs C. Springer. Connections to water main two weeks behind (awaiting completion of drain connection before this can be made).	4	6	1	1	1	1	3	1	1	19
Oct. 7, 1967	Two labourers Messrs C. Springer. Connections to water main three weeks behind, awaiting now for the in valve **B**.	4	7	1	1	2	1	2			18
Oct. 14. 1967	Two bricklayers + one labourer. Hardcore to oversite now one week behind schedule, due to lack of information required to complete soil connections inside building areas. Awaiting clarification of fence time to rear of No 17 Hanworth Road.	4	6	1		1	2	1	1	2	19
Oct. 21, 1967	One bricklayer, one labourer. Hardcore to oversite now two weeks behind due to lack of information required to complete soil connections.	5	6	1		2	1	1	1	1	19
Oct. 28, 1967	Three bricklayers, one labourer. Messrs Edwards.	7	5	1	2		1	1	3	1 1	20
Nov. 4, 1967	Three bricklayers, one labourer. Messrs Edwards.	7	6	1		2	1	1	2		20
Nov. 11. 1967	No sub-contractors.	7	6	1		2	1	1	2	1	18

nal contacts involved in such a project by studying the weekly records maintained on the site, and Table B is a summary of the main working groups and visitors to the site during the first thirteen weeks of building. In addition, there was a considerable flow of deliveries.

21. The school was estimated to cost about £95,000 and was planned to last between seventy and eighty years. Most of the outside walls were prefabricated and delivered to the site ready to be erected. That was done quickly.

22. The plans for the school were drawn up by the Borough Architect's Department, after consultation with the Greater London Council who had had considerable experience in this type of school. A number of special features needed for an educationally subnormal school were introduced, such as special assembly points outside each classroom, a second exit from each room, and girls' and boys' toilets for nearly each classroom. All accommodation was to be on the ground floor. A special outbuilding for pets was provided.

23. The site foreman reported no difficulties. The plans had been satisfactory, although the architect in charge had been changed during the course of building. There was a resident clerk of works to represent the client and the architect and he looked after several jobs on different sites. A monthly site meeting of all concerned was held to control the construction programme.

24. By most criteria the Gaze Group of companies operates efficiently and so far as we can judge without financial and statistical information, it maintains an adequate standard of performance in all its activities. It has shown a remarkable adaptability in the post-war years and has slowly evolved from a small family business to a large modern firm of building contractors, endeavouring to set up a coherent and varied structure of related activities. It has invested wisely in the development of concrete and has bought up specialist firms that were leaders in that field. It has recognized the opportunities presented by rising living standards and set up a separate company specializing in the construction of swimming pools.

25. Since Mr Douglas Gaze took over as managing director in 1961 he has ensured that the advantages of a traditional business are being reinforced by necessary modernization. He has not hesitated to bring in competent people from outside the family, including directors, and has made use of management consultants.

26. The final assessment of its overall efficiency must be based partly on the ambitions and goals that Mr Gaze has set for the organization. There is perhaps some uncertainty here. If he wants to grow into a large national contracting organization, as it appears, it is surprising that growth has not been more deliberate and planned—some of the specialized developments mentioned earlier have come through approaches made to Gazes rather than within a deliberate long-term planned expansion (e.g. the swimming pool company). But even proposals offered to a firm have to be assessed, and we were not aware of any major error of judgment. Perhaps the pace of development has been slow and cautious, but it has been definite, particularly during the past five years.

27. The company has no need for additional external aids in the main, although from the longest perspectives benefit might be gained from aids concerned with organization, development planning, and marketing.

ANALYSIS OF EXTERNAL CONTACTS
July 1, 1967 – June 30, 1968

NAME OF ORGANIZATION	W. H. GAZE
CONTACTS OBSERVED	20
CONTACTS REPORTED	2
TOTAL CONTACTS ANALYZED	22

A. *Type of contact:* 1. Normal 'business' 21 2. Unusual 'business'
3. Aid—deliberate 4. Aid—indirect 1

B. *With whom*

1. Supplier 7	2. Management Consultant	3. Technical Consultant
4. Research Association	5. Trade Association	6. Public Body 1
7. Competitor	8. Training Board	9. Customer 5
10. National Economic Committee	11. Building Contractor 1	12. Local government authority 7
13. Professional practice 2	14. Government department	15. Foreign organization
16. Employment agency	17. Professional institute	18. Head Office 3
19. College	20. Research organization	21. Bank 1
22. Trade Union	23. International official body	24. Wholesaler
25. Retailer	26. Sub-contractor 3	27.
28.	29.	30.

155

C. *Purpose*
1. Give information—general
2. Give information—technical
3. Give information—commercial
4. Seek information—general 6
5. Seek information—technical 8
6. Seek information—commercial 2
13. Buying operations
15. Research and development operations
17. Financial operations
19. Production operations 19

7. Give advice—general 1
8. Give advice—technical 2
9. Give advice—commercial
10. Seek advice—general 2
11. Seek advice—technical 2
12. Seek advice—commercial
14. Selling operations
16. General management operations 3
18. Personnel operations 2
20. Other

D. *Duration of Contact*
1. Up to one hour continuously 9
2. Up to one day continuously 3
3. Up to one week continuously 1
4. Up to one month continuously 4

5. Up to three months continuously 3

6. Up to six months continuously 2
7. Up to nine months continuously
8. Up to twelve months continuously
9. Over twelve months continuously 1
10. From time to time irregularly

E. *Cost to Organization*
1. Free 10
2. Unassessed 9
3. By annual subscription (give amount if possible)
4. £..................
5. By professional scale— estimated at £..................

6. As % of main contract— estimated at £..................
7. Under £25 1
8. £26 – £50
9. £51 – £100
10. £101 – £1,000

F. *Nature of evidence*
1. Observation by researcher 20
2. Verbal report 20
3. Correspondence seen 1
4. Minutes of meetings
5. Technical reports

6. Financial statement
7. Organization's statistics
8. Special report for researcher
9. Information from outsider
10. Other (specify)

G. *Implications for Firm* (or other type of organization)
1. Contact is likely to effect firm's current performance. 20
2. Contact is not likely to effect firm's current performance. 3
3. Contact is likely to effect structure of firm's organization. 8
4. Contact is not likely to effect structure of firm's organization. 13
5. Contact is likely to increase profit or surplus. 14
6. Contact is not likely to increase profit or surplus. 8
7. Contact does extend firm's network of external relationships. 20
8. Contact does not extend firm's network of external relationships. 2
9. Contact is likely to increase firm's efficiency. 15
10. Contact is not likely to increase firm's efficiency. 7

Organization B8: Sibson Developments Limited

1. This small company of speculative housebuilders concentrates on developing estates in the areas from Southampton to Brighton and Croydon to Dartford. It was started in the 1950's and incorporated in

156

1961. In that year it built twenty-six houses, and in 1967 expected to complete forty-five, a reduction on the estimate of seventy made in 1966.

2. The business employs four executives only. Mr G. W. Sibson is the managing director, concerned with the planning of the business, the acquisition of sites, and the sale of houses. He is a quantity surveyor by profession, now in his early forties. He has a contracts manager who is concerned with all the detailed practical problems of building and visits the building sites regularly. There is a costs department at the company's headquarters run by Mr Sibson's father. There is normally in addition a site agent for each site under construction, but at the end of 1967 there was only one site agent although three sites were in hand —the other two were dealt with by the manager. At the beginning of that year two site agents were dismissed as a result of low house sales, and building progress slowed down.

3. The firm makes extensive use of sub-contractors, including 'labour only' sub-contractors, many of them on a semi-permanent basis. A great deal of information and guidance is obtained from suppliers of materials and internal finishings, through direct representation and technical data sheets. This extensive use of other organizations is part of Mr Sibson's deliberate policy of remaining a small firm and he has no ambitions to grow too large. He has appreciated the additional costs arising from the creation of the Land Commission and took all necessary steps prior to the relevant dates to begin construction as required by law so as to avoid the Commission's levy. As a result, the company has in hand sufficient land and houses to keep it busy for two years, to the end of 1969—and by that time Mr Sibson believes that the economic effects of the Land Commission's activities should have been clarified, thus enabling better decisions to be made about the future.

4. The efficiency of the business can be assessed in part by the amount of net profit before tax as compared with the assets employed, and the following figures for the years 1964-1967 have been supplied by the company's auditors:

	Net Profit before tax	Balance Sheet value of Total Assets	Profit % of Capital
	£	£	
1964	5,802	35,667	16
1965	5,910	36,804	16
1966	9,356	43,613	21
1967	6,359	49,705	13

5. It will be obvious that this firm has numerous external relationships and some of them qualify as external aids. In most cases, however, there is a typical supplier-customer relationship but it would seem that there is a widespread tendency to supply advice and information as well as the purchased goods and services. Mr Sibson finds the National House-builders Registration Council valuable and their inspectors are welcomed because of their help in avoiding complaints at a later date from purchasers. Similarly, the local authority building inspectors are accepted in a positive sense and there is no resentment at their activities.

6. Mr Sibson uses architects, particularly in relation to planning applications, but will make do with competent draughtsmen where that is possible. Estate agents are most important as advisers on the nature of a proposed estate, as well as in their more obvious role of salesmen. As large numbers of houses are involved, the firm negotiates special reduced charges with the agents. A particular agent is given an exclusive agency for a limited period and receives a lower commission on sales during that period. Mr Sibson is a partner in one of the estate agencies that he deals with.

7. The complicated relationships that can exist are exemplified in the problems associated with planning permission in one estate at Polegate. Detailed permission for development had already been obtained when the land was bought but Mr. Sibson wanted an improvement on the permitted development. He revised his plans and his architect, in conjunction with the architect who advised East Sussex County Council, slowly worked out a scheme that was acceptable both to Sibson and to the Council. Mr Sibson's new plan would have included a service road adjacent to the main trunk road to service the site. Eventually it was agreed that instead of building rows of town houses, the firm should build bungalows and chalets which are believed to be much more popular among older people likely to retire to these properties. This extensive and skilled negotiation lasted over a period of eighteen months. Only some of the proposals of Mr Sibson and the County Architect were acceptable to the local council but at least a considerable economic advantage had been obtained through the combined use of professional advice and legal rights. This incident suggests that government authorities are not necessarily enemies of enterprising businessmen.

8. Capital for the business was initially obtained from some of Mr

Sibson's own money and from mortgages from banks on purchased land. Since 1965 the services of merchant bankers have been used, at a higher rate of interest than is payable to joint-stock banks.

9. One major influence on the success of the business is the chief executive. Mr Sibson is not only qualified to deal with housing professionally but is also a shrewd businessman with a keen appreciation of financial requirements and market opportunities. He appears to be a calm, relaxed, and incisive person, able to delegate a great deal of work to his subordinates and interferes very infrequently with their activities. The number of decisions taken by the subordinates and the importance of them may on occasions almost suggest excessive delegation, but the effort and time that Mr Sibson has devoted to selecting, training and building up relationships with his small staff has ensured that there is confidence on both sides and an understanding of areas of freedom to act.

10. Mr Sibson has a very positive appreciation of the value of using other people and other organizations outside of his employ and that in turn reduces the amount of finance that he must command in order to achieve success. This awareness of external resources is shared by his contract manager and site manager who devote considerable efforts to finding and retaining good suppliers and sub-contractors.

ANALYSIS OF EXTERNAL CONTACTS

July 1, 1967 – June 30, 1968

NAME OF ORGANIZATION	SIBSON DEVELOPMENTS LTD
CONTACTS OBSERVED	10
CONTACTS REPORTED	1
TOTAL CONTACTS ANALYZED	11

A. *Type of contact:*   1. Normal 'business' 8   2. Unusual 'business'
3. Aid—deliberate 2   4. Aid—indirect 1

B. *With whom*

1. Supplier 3	2. Management Consultant	3. Technical Consultant 1
4. Research Association	5. Trade Association	6. Public Body 1
7. Competitor	8. Training Board	9. Customer
10. National Economic Committee	11. Building Contractor 1	12. Local government authority 1
13. Professional practice	14. Government department	15. Foreign organization

16. Employment agency	17. Professional institute	18. Head Office
19. College	20. Research organization	21. Bank 1
22. Trade Union	23. International official body	24. Wholesaler
25. Retailer	26. Estate Agent 1	27. Sub-contractor 1
28.	29.	30.

C. *Purpose*

1. Give information—general 1
2. Give information—technical 2
3. Give information—commercial 1
4. Seek information—general 1
5. Seek information—technical 2
6. Seek information—commercial 2
13. Buying operations 2
15. Research and development operations
17. Financial operations
19. Production operations 9

7. Give advice—general 1
8. Give advice—technical 3
9. Give advice—commercial 2
10. Seek advice—general
11. Seek advice—technical
12. Seek advice—commercial
14. Selling operations 1
16. General management operations 1
18. Personnel operations
20. Other

D. *Duration of Contact*

1. Up to one hour continuously 4
2. Up to one day continuously
3. Up to one week continuously 1
4. Up to one month continuously

5. Up to three months continuously

6. Up to six months continuously
7. Up to nine months continuously
8. Up to twelve months continuously
9. Over twelve months continuously 5
10. From time to time irregularly

E. *Cost to Organization*

1. Free 4
2. Unassessed
3. By annual subscription 1 (give amount if possible)
4. £.................
5. By professional scale— estimated at £..................

6. As % of main contract— estimated at £..................
7. Under £25
8. £26 – £50

9. £51 – £100
10. £101 – £1,000

F. *Nature of evidence*

1. Observation by researcher 10
2. Verbal report 9
3. Correspondence seen
4. Minutes of meetings
5. Technical reports

6. Financial statement
7. Organization's statistics
8. Special report for researcher
9. Information from outsider
10. Other (specify)

G. *Implications for Firm* (or other type of organization)

1. Contact is likely to effect firm's current performance. 10
2. Contact is not likely to effect firm's current performance. 1
3. Contact is likely to effect structure of firm's organization. 7
4. Contact is not likely to effect structure of firm's organization. 4
5. Contact is likely to increase profit or surplus. 10
6. Contact is not likely to increase profit or surplus. 1
7. Contact does extend firm's network of external relationships. 1
8. Contact does not extend firm's network of external relationships.
9. Contact is likely to increase firm's efficiency. 11
10. Contact is not likely to increase firm's efficiency.

Chapter 8

The Manufacturers

Organization M9: Osway Limited

1. Osway Limited is a private company founded in 1954. There are two working directors—Mr O. C. Otterway, the managing director and major shareholder, and Mr F. W. J. Austin, production director. The capital for the business has come entirely from Mr Otterway and there are no outside shareholders, mortgages, overdrafts, or any other source of outside capital. We have not, however, been given annual accounts. From a number of indicators it would seem that the company's turnover in 1966 was about £70,000 and its labour costs about £15,000.

2. The company manufactures a range of inexpensive whitewood furniture, and its main customers are multiple stores and department stores. At the beginning of 1966 it employed two salesmen, but by September there was only one. They have about one hundred customers. Production is usually in batches of twenty-four or forty-eight units.

3. Mr Otterway is a man of about fifty with numerous business interests. He was originally a builder before he established this firm. He is a member of the Institute of Directors. He is a well-to-do man and he is not primarily concerned with creating a large business. He keeps in close touch with all aspects of the business but is primarily concerned with finance, sales, and purchasing. Mrs Otterway has been in charge of the office since August 1967.

4. When we first interviewed him in January 1966 Mr Otterway complained about the restricted space available at his factory in Egham, Surrey, and he has talked on a number of occasions about the problems of finding a larger factory. He had sought a licence from the Board of Trade to extend his premises but because of the policy of restricting development in the South-East, he was refused building permission. He

complained of the difficulty of finding an appropriate site elsewhere without losing his labour force, consisting of about twenty-two people, most of whom were semi-skilled. Numerous sites were considered over a period of two years. It seemed curious that despite the frequent talk of moving nothing seemed to happen, and I mistakenly believed that the failure to find a suitable new factory was due to a lack of initiative. Mr Otterway believed that no hint of a move should be given to anyone because of the risk of losing employees. However, we discovered on August 23, 1967, that he had sold his factory in Egham and moved to a site outside Chichester, Sussex, in the interval between two of our quarterly visits. The new building had been a factory for making dog biscuits, and was originally a large mill, on the outskirts of the town, near Goodwood racecourse. Mr Otterway financed this move by selling his old premises, his home, and the farm that he owned, and within a few weeks was manufacturing, though with difficulty, at the new premises.

5. The present factory is large enough to permit a more rational manufacturing system. Stocks can now be stored and a more continuous flow of production is possible in advance of orders. The machinery was moved from the old factory.

6. In October 1967 a daily average of 55.5 units of furniture were produced and 42.5 units were finished. By May 1968 output had increased to 80.6 units and finishing to 66 units. The aim is to manufacture 100 units daily.

7. Four of the Egham employees moved down to Chichester (although twelve had originally agreed to move) and the rest of the 1967 total of thirty were locally recruited. Many recruits came to enquire about jobs, and only a few were sent by the Ministry of Labour. Thus an important problem for the firm now is the training of unskilled labour, some of whom were agricultural workers and drivers. The firm is covered by the Furniture and Timber Industry Training Board, and at his previous factory Mr Otterway said that he was unworried about the need to pay a levy of 0.9 per cent of his wages bill and he did not intend to undertake any apprenticeships. Shortly after his move, however, he was glad to receive visits from the Training Board's staff, and he has agreed to send some of his workers, particularly a boy apprentice, to appropriate classes for which he will be able to claim back from the Training Board the cost of the fees and expenses.

8. When Mr Otterway was first visited, he appeared to be totally unconcerned with the extensive network of external aids that exist in the furniture industry and made no direct use of them. He received a wide range of publications about the industry and about those organizations, and read them carefully. He was very much influenced, however, by the work of competitors, as perceived by their catalogues, market assessments, and his sales. When he moved to Chichester, he began to make use of the consultancy facilities of the Furniture Development Council, and they designed his new production system for a fee of 150 guineas. He also began to appreciate the need for training, and became much more concerned with the industry's training board.

9. Despite his previous efforts to locate a suitable new factory, it seems that he only discovered the Chichester site accidentally through his solicitor hearing of its availability.

10. The company expects considerable expansion of its sales in the coming years and looks forward to an early turnover of £100,000, eventually reaching £250,000. Mr Otterway is now considering the possibilities of exporting and of taking part in a trade mission to the USA.

11. Clearly a major reconsideration of policy emerged with the acquisition of the new factory and it is not altogether clear whether the desire to move and to grow came from a predetermined decision, or whether, having found the new premises, the relevant changes in organization and outlook began to appear from necessity. Whatever the answer may be—and it is unlikely to be a simple one-way answer—the new burdens and opportunities have led to a much more positive use of external aids that are so considerable in the furniture industry.

12. It is relevant to note that the furniture industry has a complex network of trade organizations. There is the Furniture Development Council, set up by the Industrial Organization and Development Act 1947 with the objective of increasing furniture production and efficiency. All firms in the industry have to pay a statutory levy to the Council of 9s 2d per £1,000 of turnover. Without further charge, each firm registered with the Development Council can become a member of the Furniture Industry Research Association. The Development Council's main task is to give information and provide consultancy services about management and production problems, such as the improvement of plant and factory layout, improved manpower utiliza-

tion, and costing and control systems. Much of the Council's work pays for itself and therefore the bulk of the industrial levy of about £75,000 annually can be used for the work of the Research Association. The Research Association also receives a grant from the Ministry of Technology.

13. The Furniture Industry Research Association exists to give information on technical aspects of furniture and bedding production. It carries out a number of basic, long term investigations and the results are published and circulated to members. In addition, like most research associations, the F.I.R.A. undertakes paid sponsored investigations for individual firms on a confidential basis.

14. The Furniture Development Council and the Furniture Industry Research Association now share the same building in Stevenage, Hertfordshire. This is a modern building specially built with the needs of the two organizations in mind, and they have a joint director.

15. The turnover of the industry is about £140 million and more than half its output comes from factories in London and High Wycombe. As a result of this concentration, it is believed that its overheads, primarily distribution, are high and getting higher, accounting for nearly 7s in each pound paid by the retailer for a piece of furniture. Materials are estimated to account for about 9s in the pound, and labour, estimated to account for 3s in each pound, is the third highest item of cost. Productivity per man employed has been increasing—since 1958 the industry's output has risen 7 per cent while the numbers employed have gone down slightly to just under 60,000. In the same period, hourly earnings have gone up by a quarter, so the efficient and economical use of manpower is of prime importance, and much of the work of the two bodies is devoted to this aspect. In giving these facts, a publication of the two bodies adds: 'F.D.C. also does a lot to keep industry in touch with what goes on in the world outside, by liaison with such bodies as the Forest Products Research Laboratory, the research associations concerned with timber, textiles, glue, plastics and metals, other research organizations and technical colleges.' It concludes: 'The basis of the furniture industry has, in a short period, changed from that of craft to that of technology. Inevitably many firms have difficulty in keeping up to date with new methods, processes and materials. Technological growth has in many instances outpaced the supply of fully qualified staff. Adequate testing and research facilities would be uneconomic if

installed by each individual firm. F.I.R.A./F.D.C. tries to meet these needs on behalf of all its members.'

16. In addition to these official bodies the furniture industry has a lively and extensive network of trade associations. The national body is the British Furniture Manufacturers' Federated Association. It was formed in 1944 and is composed of eleven regional manufacturers' associations and two specialist national bodies. It has about 950 members, representing 95 per cent of the furniture industry's production capacity. One important activity of the Federation is to conduct the annual furniture exhibition at Earl's Court which replaces the large number of small exhibitions that existed before the Second World War, at considerable cost to the industry and with no particular advantage, it is claimed, to the consumer. However, some provincial exhibitions are still held.

17. In addition to the Development Council, the research association, and the trade association, the furniture industry has its own joint industrial council that establishes minimum wages and working conditions. It is also interesting to note that there is the Worshipful Company of Furniture Makers, and unlike many other city livery companies it was only founded a few years ago—in 1952.

18. The object of the Company is: 'To foster the ancient craft of furniture making in the United Kingdom in such a manner as is calculated to advance the standard of design and technical knowledge of those in the craft and generally to direct the design of furniture to the benefit of the community.' The Company is essentially a charitable organization and membership is by election.

ANALYSIS OF EXTERNAL CONTACTS
July 1, 1967 – June 30, 1968

NAME OF ORGANIZATION	OSWAY LTD
CONTACTS OBSERVED	5
CONTACTS REPORTED	1
TOTAL CONTACTS ANALYZED	6

A. *Type of contact:* 1. Normal 'business' 4   2. Unusual 'business' 1
3. Aid—deliberate   4. Aid—indirect 1

B. *With whom*
1. Supplier 2   2. Management Consultant   3. Technical Consultant

165

4.	Research Association	5.	Trade Association	6.	Public Body 2
7.	Competitor	8.	Training Board 1	9.	Customer
10.	National Economic Committee	11.	Building Contractor 1	12.	Local government authority
13.	Professional practice	14.	Government department	15.	Foreign organization
16.	Employment agency	17.	Professional institute	18.	Head Office
19.	College	20.	Research organization	21.	Bank
22.	Trade Union	23.	International official body	24.	Wholesaler
25.	Retailer	26.		27.	
28.		29.		30.	

C. *Purpose*

1. Give information—general
2. Give information—technical
3. Give information—commercial
4. Seek information—general 1
5. Seek information—technical 2
6. Seek information—commercial
13. Buying operations 1
15. Research and development operations 1
17. Financial operations
19. Production operations 4

7. Give advice—general
8. Give advice—technical
9. Give advice—commercial
10. Seek advice—general 1
11. Seek advice—technical 2
12. Seek advice—commercial
14. Selling operations
16. General management operations
18. Personnel operations
20. Other

D. *Duration of Contact*

1. Up to one hour continuously 1
2. Up to one day continuously 2
3. Up to one week continuously 1
4. Up to one month continuously
5. Up to three months continuously 1

6. Up to six months continuously
7. Up to nine months continuously
8. Up to twelve months continuously
9. Over twelve months continuously
10. From time to time irregularly 1

E. *Cost to Organization*

1. Free 2
2. Unassessed
3. By annual subscription 2
   (give amount if possible)
4. £.................
5. By professional scale—
   estimated at £.................

6. As % of main contract—
   estimated at £.................
7. Under £25
8. £26 – £50
9. £51 – £100
10. £101 – £1,000

F. *Nature of evidence*

1. Observation by researcher 3
2. Verbal report 4
3. Correspondence seen
4. Minutes of meetings
5. Technical reports

6. Financial statement
7. Organization's statistics
8. Special report for researcher
9. Information from outsider
10. Other (specify)

166

G. *Implications for Firm* (or other type of organization)
   1. Contact is likely to effect firm's current performance. 5
   2. Contact is not likely to effect firm's current performance. 1
   3. Contact is likely to effect structure of firm's organization. 3
   4. Contact is not likely to effect structure of firm's organization. 3
   5. Contact is likely to increase profit or surplus. 5
   6. Contact is not likely to increase profit or surplus. 1
   7. Contact does extend firm's network of external relationships. 6
   8. Contact does not extend firm's network of external relationships.
   9. Contact is likely to increase firm's efficiency. 4
   10. Contact is not likely to increase firm's efficiency. 2

Organization M10: Beecham Group Limited

1. Beecham's is a very large public company employing at the beginning of 1968 over 15,000 people at home and abroad. In the year ending March 1968 its total sales amounted to £115.5m., nearly equally divided between overseas and home sales. It has three main divisions—food and drinks with £32m. turnover in 1968, 'advertized toiletries and home remedies' with £50m., and pharmaceutical products with nearly £31m. turnover. It made a net profit of about £11m. with capital employed of £67m. It has had a long record of growth and its turnover has grown from £40m. in 1959, although there have been a number of acquisitions over the years. The company is noted for its modern marketing methods and it has grown out of the original Macleans toothpaste business, initially under the guidance of merchant bankers and more recently under the dynamic leadership of Mr Henry Lazell, noted for his marketing expertise.

2. In 1967, as a result of consultancy advice from Booz, Allen & Co. Ltd., the group was divided into four divisions. Beecham Products U.K. Division is the largest, mainly concerned with food, drinks, and toiletries, both at home and overseas. Beecham Pharmaceutical Division is concerned with research laboratories and the manufacture of pharmaceuticals. It has its own companies in Europe and Pakistan. Beecham European Division consists of manufacturing and sales organizations in the Common Market countries and in Austria, Denmark and Sweden. Beecham Western Hemisphere Division (Beecham Inc.) consists of major companies in Canada, USA, Latin America and Australia. The overseas business of the group is conducted through subsidiaries or manufacturing and distributing agents and by direct export from the United Kingdom.

3. Among its products are Lucozade, Ribena, Corona drinks, Coca

167

Cola (sold under franchise), Morton canned vegetables, Brylcreem, Macleans toothpaste, Silvikrin shampoo, a range of cosmetics with some brands only available overseas, a number of penicillins and other pharmaceutical products sold on prescription, 'home remedies' such as Beechams Powders, Beechams Pills, Eno Fruit Salts, and Venos Cough Mixture, and a group of veterinary preparations.

4. It was extremely hard to build up a comprehensive picture of such a large and diversified organization. We have had co-operation from nine informants over a number of visits, largely concentrated in the food and drinks division.

5. Because of the strong marketing orientation of the company, the marketing and brand managers have considerable power. Production depends on a marketing assessment, and the brand managers then strive to achieve the estimated sales within an approved budget. Each division has its own Board of Directors with specialized functional responsibilities. A management services manager was appointed in 1967, to the Beecham Products U.K. Division, concerned with exploiting the group's computers and supplying other modern management techniques to all members of the group.

6. The work of the brand managers, particularly in the Foods Division, compels them to make extensive use of advertising agencies, marketing research agencies, and specialist organizations that carry out psychological research to determine attitudes to the quality of products and the effectiveness of advertising. These agencies could be considered as suppliers of aid, or simply as suppliers of services who would thus be irrelevant to the present study. The categorization depends on whether the agencies offer advice and whether that advice is followed. It is usually impossible to identify the source of advice for any particular decision. Many joint meetings are held between marketing managers and agency managers, and it must be presumed that both sides contribute to the elucidation of policy. Probably on balance Beechams are less dependent on advice from their agencies than many less sophisticated firms and therefore all the marketing agencies should be considered as suppliers of services rather than sources of aid. One marketing brand manager said that he spent all his time with a variety of advertising and marketing agencies. That appears to be an exaggeration but these outside bodies are clearly important. Several advertising agencies are used by the group; each deals with one product or a group

of related products. But some market research information supplied by one agency would be relevant to a number of products.

7. The Beecham Group is a member of many associations and institutes. The decision to join or leave these organizations is tending to be taken by senior group executives, in view of the high subscription costs. In one case, the group decided to cease membership of a research association, and the divisions involved doubted the wisdom of abandoning that source of outside aid. The Food Division made use of the Institute of Marketing and Sales Management, the Incorporated Society of British Advertisers, and the British Institute of Management. The director concerned said that each organization was valuable and that he distributed information from them among his staff whenever he felt it was likely to be relevant.

8. The most important external aid used during this project was Booz, Allen & Co. Ltd., who investigated the general structure of Beecham's and from whose proposals the present organization emerged in 1967.

9. Little resentment was found among the staff about the activities of these management consultants, but one member of the organization, closely associated with the consultants, was highly critical of the decision to introduce them and of the abilities of one of their staff. There was probably a clash of personalities involved but the executive's attitude reflected a certain degree of anxiety about his future prospects; he considered himself to be a competent specialist in the relevant field and thus he felt that outside consultants were not needed. We were unable to discover the circumstances that led to the decision to use consultants, but we understand Mr Lazell decided that their services might be useful.

10. There can be little doubt about the high level of performance of this organization, judged by all the usual criteria. It would be difficult to determine the contribution of external aids to that achievement. As the organization becomes larger it seems unimportant whether external aids should be used and suppliers employed, or whether specialist staff should be engaged on a permanent basis. The quantity of specialist services used would partly determine the use of outsiders, but the need for fresh ideas and independent judgments would make outsiders more attractive than insiders in some cases. The firm's activities and success are not dependent on external aid or external suppliers within the marketing field, although the company is dependent on suppliers for

manufacturing purposes. Thus the role of external aid is almost certainly marginal in the case of Beecham's—but the marginal difference may be the crucial condition of its continuing expansion and prosperity.

No external contacts were reported or observed for the relevant period.

Organization M11: Petters Limited

1. Petters was established in about 1872. It began manufacturing internal combustion engines in 1895. It now manufactures diesel engines and a range of other engines. It became a subsidiary of the Brush Electrical Engineering Co. Ltd. in 1949. In 1957 Petters and the Brush Group became part of the Hawker Siddeley Group Ltd. who are now the only shareholders. The 1966 accounts show that it has assets of about £8m. and liabilities of about £6m., including £4,280,000 on loan from Hawker Siddeley Group Limited.

2. Petters manufacture a wide range of diesel engines up to 45 bhp, some of which are air-cooled engines and others water-cooled. The main factory is at Staines and a subsidiary factory at Hamble manufactures marine diesel engines, generating sets, air compressors and transport refrigeration units, as well as being a centre for spares for the main factory. The company employs about 2,000 people of whom about 800 work at Hamble.

3. The company exports directly 50 per cent of its output, and about another 25 per cent indirectly by supplying manufacturers with engines that are incorporated in final products. This extensive export business is carried out by an export manager and a world-wide network of agents.

4. So far as we could judge from our visits and the sixteen informants that we have met, Petters appear to be an efficient organization that is well managed, with a competent and contented labour force. It has invested heavily in research and is fully alert to the opportunities for expanding its sales in the light of many technological developments affecting a wide range of industries. It is always difficult to determine the respective roles of management in a subsidiary and in a group headquarters, and there seems no satisfactory method of allocating achievements and error between the two. Hawker Siddeley appear to allow considerable independence to Petters, who operate within a framework of expected performance; if Petters were unable to achieve a satisfac-

tory rate of profit, control from Head Office might be much more extensive.

5. So far as external aids are concerned, Petters belong to a large number of organizations, including the following trade associations:

Engineering Employers' London Association,
British Internal Combustion Engine Manufacturers Association,
Bradstreets Register,
British Refrigeration Association,
Transfrigeroute,
British Compressed Air Society,
Society of Motor Manufacturers and Traders,
British Internal Combustion Engine Research Association,
Agricultural Engineers' Association,
Marine Engine Manufacturers' Association,
Ship and Boatbuilders' National Federation,
The Confederation of British Industry.

The managing director instituted a review of memberships in 1967 but we did not have an opportunity of discovering how the appraisal was carried out.

6. Other organizations that the firm belongs to or makes use of include:

The London Chamber of Commerce,
The Export Services Branch of the Board of Trade,
Certain overseas trade commissioners,
The Industrial Society,
The Institute of Personnel Management,
The Ministry of Labour,
The National Engineering Laboratory,
The British Standards Institution.

7. In addition, a very wide range of publications from organizations and elsewhere are regularly received and made use of.

8. In the past consultants have been used but only on a specialist task for organizing the accounts department.

9. It must be remembered that Petters derive a number of benefits through Hawker Siddeley, and their group services are at the disposal

of Petters in many spheres of activity. In addition, the technical benefits obtainable from suppliers could well be important in this engineering company.

10. On the whole, however, Petters in no way seems dependent on any outside source of aid or any general contact, apart from its parent company. Most of the external relationships not directly related to manufacturing are not obviously essential. Over a long period of time, serious weaknesses might arise through inbreeding and narrowness of viewpoint.

11. We endeavoured to investigate in detail two particular activities in order to identify the role of external aid. The first concerned management development, and the second the Export Credits Guarantee Department.

12. One executive was sent on the four-week Oxford University Business Course. He was a much-respected production engineer with many years' service with the company, aged about thirty-five, and highly thought of by senior management as a person likely to go far in the company. It was appreciated that his experience was somewhat limited and that the course ought to be beneficial and broaden his outlook. At the time he was a production controller, which was more of an administrative than a technical post. The man himself found the course valuable and stimulating, and prized the opportunity of attending a university if only for a few weeks. The Oxford Business Course is largely concerned with economics, which was a new field for him. He also derived benefit from meeting the other people attending the course and has maintained contact with them since the summer of 1967.

13. Attendance did not have much effect on the man's work for nearly a year but in May 1968 he was promoted Production Manager. In the main his job did not change and it is still largely concerned with the administration of technical matters. But he does have wider responsibilities for short-term production activities. His superior believed that the main advantages of the course would become apparent in the future and that the man was in a better position to know where he was likely to go in the future. However, this particular external aid in the very important field of management development may not have been fully understood and exploited by the firm, and unless some more positive career planning is undertaken the main result of the course may be to create discontent.

14. The Export Credits Guarantee Department seems to work smoothly and satisfactorily and there were no problems for Petters. It is difficult for them to assess the value of E.C.G.D.: they rely on it and it works. Presumably they would hesitate much more over certain export opportunities if the credit insurance facilities did not exist.

ANALYSIS OF EXTERNAL CONTACTS
July 1, 1967 – June 30, 1968

NAME OF ORGANIZATION   PETTERS
CONTACTS OBSERVED   9
CONTACTS REPORTED   1

TOTAL CONTACTS ANALYZED   10

A. *Type of contact:*   1. Normal 'business' 6   2. Unusual 'business'
                  3. Aid—deliberate 4   4. Aid—indirect

B. *With whom*

1. Supplier 3	2. Management Consultant	3. Technical Consultant 3
4. Research Association	5. Trade Association	6. Public Body 2
7. Competitor	8. Training Board	9. Customer 1
10. National Economic Committee	11. Building Contractor	12. Local government authority
13. Professional practice	14. Government department	15. Foreign organization
16. Employment agency	17. Professional institute	18. Head Office
19. College 1	20. Research organization	21. Bank
22. Trade Union	23. International official body	24. Wholesaler
25. Retailer	26. Smaller Subsidiary Factory 1	27.
28.	29.	30.

C. *Purpose*

1. Give information—general	7. Give advice—general
2. Give information—technical	8. Give advice—technical
3. Give information—commercial	9. Give advice—commercial
4. Seek information—general 4	10. Seek advice—general 4
5. Seek information—technical—6	11. Seek advice—technical 5
6. Seek information—commercial 3	12. Seek advice—commercial 3
13. Buying operations	14. Selling operations 3
15. Research and development operations 2	16. General management operations 4
17. Financial operations 1	18. Personnel operations 1
19. Production operations 5	20. Other

173

D. *Duration of Contact*

1. Up to one hour continuously
2. Up to one day continuously
3. Up to one week continuously 2
4. Up to one month continuously

5. Up to three months continuously

6. Up to six months continuously
7. Up to nine months continuously
8. Up to twelve months continuously
9. Over twelve months continuously 7
10. From time to time irregularly 1

E. *Cost to Organization*

1. Free 1

2. Unassessed
3. By annual subscription (give amount if possible)
4. £.................
5. By professional scale— estimated at £.................

6. As % of main contract— estimated at £................. 1
7. Under £25 1
8. £26 – £50 1
9. £51 – £100
10. £101 – £1,000 1

F. *Nature of evidence*

1. Observation by researcher 9
2. Verbal report 10
3. Correspondence seen 2
4. Minutes of meetings
5. Technical reports 3

6. Financial statement
7. Organization's statistics 1
8. Special report for researcher
9. Information from outsider
10. Other (specify)

G. *Implications for Firm* (or other type of organization)

1. Contact is likely to effect firm's current performance. 10
2. Contact is not likely to effect firm's current performance.
3. Contact is likely to effect structure of firm's organization. 8
4. Contact is not likely to effect structure of firm's organization. 2
5. Contact is likely to increase profit or surplus. 10
6. Contact is not likely to increase profit or surplus.
7. Contact does extend firm's network of external relationships. 10
8. Contact does not extend firm's network of external relationships.
9. Contact is likely to increase firm's efficiency. 10
10. Contact is not likely to increase firm's efficiency.

Organization M12: Lion Case Company Limited

1. This firm was established in 1957 to manufacture cases and packaging material, mainly from wood and polystyrene. Its customers are in several industries and numerous orders come from government departments, particularly the Ministry of Defence. The firm occupies a small factory in Merton and employs about twenty people.

2. The managing director is Mr J. S. Neal, and his wife and son also work in the business. Mrs Neal is in charge of the office. Mr S. H. Butler is the works manager and has under him a foreman and between ten and fifteen operatives, according to the state of business. There are two drivers.

3. We have not been given any financial information but it is believed that total sales amount to about £45,000 a year.

4. The manufacturing process is relatively simple. When the works manager receives an order—and he often takes orders from customers over the telephone—he estimates the likely cost and frequently is able to quote a price as soon as he is asked for it. Once the order is given, the job is assigned to one of the operatives, given appropriate technical information. Much of the firm's competence is due to the works manager's ability; he is skilled in woodwork fabrication and he has been able in recent years to develop the moulding and cutting of polystyrene. The firm does a considerable amount of development work to improve packaging.

5. The managing director is actively involved in all the firm's activities. He has a down-to-earth, practical approach to management. He believes that there is only a limited need for consultants and that using them is evidence of the inadequacies of management. He is a member of the Institute of Packaging and he regards that as a professional qualification testifying to his ability. He has occasionally sought information from the Packaging and Allied Trades Research Association.

6. No deliberate use of external aid has been noted or reported during our visits. However, the firm is very dependent on its customers for supplying detailed specifications and for guidance on improved techniques. The firm's work brings it in touch with the electrical inspection directorate of the Board of Trade, formerly the Ministry of Aviation. The managing director takes advice from, and has had meetings with, such customers as the Royal Aircraft Establishment, the Admiralty, and the General Post Office. He also makes use of specialist subcontractors when necessary. About 5 per cent of turnover is sold directly to government departments and another 60 per cent indirectly through supplying other government contractors.

7. The company advertises on a small scale, mainly in the technical buying guide called *Compass* and in the Classified Telephone Directory.

8. We were surprised at its rather apathetic attitude to the shortage of skilled labour. The managing director complained of a permanent shortage but no action has been taken during the course of the project to study the problem thoroughly, if only to try to avoid the loss of existing staff.

9. The firm has grown considerably in ten years and seemed generally efficient.

10. The chief executive's extensive readership of trade papers is a notable source of guidance. The introduction of a new material—polystyrene—instead of dependence on the traditional use of wood for packaging, is a sign of willingness to change and to make use of new facilities. The use of this plastic has caused the firm to introduce new machinery at regular intervals.

ANALYSIS OF EXTERNAL CONTACTS
July 1, 1967 – June 30, 1968

NAME OF ORGANIZATION	LION CASE
CONTACTS OBSERVED	2
CONTACTS REPORTED	0
TOTAL CONTACTS ANALYZED	2

A. *Type of contact:*   1. Normal 'business' 1   2. Unusual 'business'
                    3. Aid—deliberate   4. Aid—indirect 1

B. *With whom*

1. Supplier	2. Management Consultant	3. Technical Consultant
4. Research Association	5. Trade Association	6. Public Body
7. Competitor	8. Training Board	9. Customer
10. National Economic Committee	11. Building Contractor	12. Local government authority
13. Professional practice	14. Government department	15. Foreign organization
16. Employment agency	17. Professional institute	18. Head Office
19. College	20. Research organization	21. Bank
22. Trade Union	23. International official body	24. Wholesaler
25. Retailer	26. Post Office 1	27. Labour Exchange 1
28.	29.	30.

C. *Purpose*

1. Give information—general	7. Give advice—general
2. Give information—technical	8. Give advice—technical
3. Give information—commercial	9. Give advice—commercial
4. Seek information—general	10. Seek advice—general
5. Seek information—technical	11. Seek advice—technical
6. Seek information—commercial	12. Seek advice—commercial
13. Buying operations	14. Selling operations
15. Research and development operations	16. General management operations
17. Financial operations	18. Personnel operations 1
19. Production operations	20. Other 1

D. *Duration of Contact*
1. Up to one hour continuously 2
2. Up to one day continuously
3. Up to one week continuously
4. Up to one month continuously
5. Up to three months continuously
6. Up to six months continuously
7. Up to nine months continuously
8. Up to twelve months continuously
9. Over twelve months continuously
10. From time to time irregularly

E. *Cost to Organization*
1. Free 2
2. Unassessed
3. By annual subscription (give amount if possible)
4. £.................
5. By professional scale— estimated at £.................
6. As % of main contract— estimated at £.................
7. Under £25
8. £26 – £50
9. £51 – £100
10. £101 – £1,000

F. *Nature of evidence*
1. Observation by researcher 2
2. Verbal report 2
3. Correspondence seen
4. Minutes of meetings
5. Technical reports
6. Financial statement
7. Organization's statistics
8. Special report for researcher
9. Information from outsider
10. Other (specify)

G. *Implications for Firm* (or other type of organization)
1. Contact is likely to effect firm's current performance. 2
2. Contact is not likely to effect firm's current performance.
3. Contact is likely to effect structure of firm's organization. 1
4. Contact is not likely to effect structure of firm's organization. 1
5. Contact is likely to increase profit or surplus. 2
6. Contact is not likely to increase profit or surplus.
7. Contact does extend firm's network of external relationships. 2
8. Contact does not extend firm's network of external relationships.
9. Contact is likely to increase firm's efficiency. 1
10. Contact is not likely to increase firm's efficiency. 1

Organization M13: A. Brown & Company Limited

1. This is a small private company with two owner-working directors, Mr Handley and Mr Griffiths, and twelve employees. It makes and repairs packing cases, particularly wooden crates and palettes. The firm's premises are in the goods yard of Merton Abbey Station, S.W.19, for which it pays annual rent and rates of £1,400. When it started in 1950 the rent was £102. Its annual turnover is estimated to be about £25,000 but we have not received any accounts. Most production is directly related to orders, and standard products for stock are not usually produced. It has in the past employed a total of thirty people.
2. The two owners divide up the management work between them, and the son of one has a junior management role. There are three skilled machinists who supervise the production of cases, and there is

177

a paint spray sub-department concerned with repairs. There do not appear to be any major production problems. Once the cases have been manufactured or repaired they can usually be stacked in the yard to await despatch. There is a friendly and co-operative atmosphere among all employees, and the partners work alongside the men for a considerable part of their time.

3. The firm is in a declining industry and there is no desire by the owners to diversify in order to grow. They are content to maintain a constant flow of work, so far as that is possible. There are about thirty main customers and that number is sufficient to maintain operations for the time being. The firm has benefited from the closing down of several larger competitors and has acquired additional business without any marketing effort.

4. The firm recruits and dismisses labour according to the state of business. The technology is very simple and does not appear to be changing. Such modification of products and processes as do take place are due to requests from customers. For example, one firm has asked for special boxes and steel-tipped cases for internal transportation during manufacturing.

5. A number of their customers operate seasonally, with consequent irregular demand for the services of Brown and Company.

6. The company does not belong to any trade or other association and does not use aid organizations. One director believes that the profits of the firm are too small to permit them to use or belong to such organizations. He mentioned that he would have liked to take up new methods of manufacturing ten to fifteen years ago, probably involving the use of plastics or other materials, but he did not feel that there was an appropriate source of aid which he could consult to guide him. For day-to-day work, the firm has all the necessary know-how for its simple technological needs.

7. The company has a display advertisement in the London Classified Telephone Directory costing about £10 a year and believes that some enquiries result from this insertion. It also advertises in a trade directory.

8. It is dependent on suppliers, such as timber merchants and road hauliers, particularly in relation to a major customer in the North of England.

9. The two owners were skilled craftsmen who decided at the end of

the 1939-45 war that they wanted to go into business on their own and to be independent. They have earned a satisfactory living from the business over the past twenty-three years and they may well continue to do so for the rest of their working lives, given sufficient minimal adaptability to the moderate changes in their customers' requirements. However, by all normal business efficiency criteria, particularly the assumption that firms ought to grow, be concerned with improved productivity, and plan management succession, the company would receive a poor assessment.

ANALYSIS OF EXTERNAL CONTACTS
July 1, 1967 – June 30, 1968

NAME OF ORGANIZATION	A. BROWN
CONTACTS OBSERVED	1
CONTACTS REPORTED	0
TOTAL CONTACTS ANALYZED	1

A. *Type of contact:* 1. Normal 'business' 1   2. Unusual 'business'
3. Aid—deliberate   4. Aid—indirect

B. *With whom*

1. Supplier	2. Management Consultant	3. Technical Consultant
4. Research Association	5. Trade Association	6. Public Body
7. Competitor	8. Training Board	9. Customer
10. National Economic Committee	11. Building Contractor	12. Local government authority
13. Professional practice	14. Government department	15. Foreign organization
16. Employment agency	17. Professional institute	18. Head Office
19. College	20. Research organization	21. Bank
22. Trade Union	23. International official body	24. Wholesaler
25. Retailer	26. Transport 1	27.
28.	29.	30.

C. *Purpose*

1. Give information—general	7. Give advice—general
2. Give information—technical	8. Give advice—technical
3. Give information—commercial	9. Give advice—commercial
4. Seek information—general	10. Seek advice—general
5. Seek information—technical	11. Seek advice—technical
6. Seek information—commercial	12. Seek advice—commercial

179

13. Buying operations
14. Selling operations 1
15. Research and development operations
16. General management operations
17. Financial operations
18. Personnel operations
19. Production operations
20. Other

D. *Duration of Contact*

1. Up to one hour continuously
2. Up to one day continuously 1
3. Up to one week continuously
4. Up to one month continuously
5. Up to three months continuously
6. Up to six months continuously
7. Up to nine months continuously
8. Up to twelve months continuously
9. Over twelve months continuously
10. From time to time irregularly

E. *Cost to Organization*

1. Free
2. Unassessed
3. By annual subscription (give amount if possible)
4. £..................
5. By professional scale— estimated at £..................
6. As % of main contract— estimated at £..................
7. Under £25 1
8. £26 – £50
9. £51 – £100
10. £101 – £1,000

F. *Nature of evidence*

1. Observation by researcher 1
2. Verbal report 1
3. Correspondence seen
4. Minutes of meetings
5. Technical reports
6. Financial statement
7. Organization's statistics
8. Special report for researcher
9. Information from outsider
10. Other (specify)

G. *Implications for Firm* (or other type of organization)

1. Contact is likely to effect firm's current performance. 1
2. Contact is not likely to effect firm's current performance.
3. Contact is likely to effect structure of firm's organization.
4. Contact is not likely to effect structure of firm's organization. 1
5. Contact is likely to increase profit or surplus. 1
6. Contact is not likely to increase profit or surplus.
7. Contact does extend firm's network of external relationships. 1
8. Contact does not extend firm's network of external relationships.
9. Contact is likely to increase firm's efficiency. 1
10. Contact is not likely to increase firm's efficiency.

H. Landseer Bailey Limited

1. This firm was our only failure. After four visits the following letter was received:

With regard to Mr Pulfrey's recent visits to our company we must now withdraw our sanction for further visits, since our staff find it quite inconvenient.

180

We hope that what information Mr Pulfrey received has been of some use.

Yours faithfully,
for H. Landseer Bailey Limited
F. W. Bailey (*Director*)

2. In reply, I wrote regretting that they had been inconvenienced and asked whether it would be possible at least to have a meeting in about three months, for not more than half an hour, and without in any way committing the firm to any further co-operation. No reply was received, and I wrote again on the same basis some three months later. No reply was received to that request either and I wrote finally four months later, again making a request for a short discussion. No reply was received and I then felt that I had done everything possible to try to maintain a source of information. A copy of this note was sent to them stating that it would be assumed that they had no objection to publication unless they said so within a fortnight. No reply was received.

3. We do not know why only this organization, out of the original twenty co-operating organizations, found it necessary to stop our enquiries after four visits. The first visit was made on March 8, 1966 and we had an amicable discussion with Mr Bailey about the possibilities of collaboration. He agreed to allow us to visit the firm regularly, and it was arranged that Mr Pulfrey would spend two days with the organization in the next week. Later, that was changed and Mr Pulfrey spent March 14th, in company with Mr Bailey, obtaining general information about the company and its activities. I had explained that it was our hope that Mr Pulfrey would be allowed to spend a day or two each quarter with managers, learning by observation from their activities. Mr Bailey did not seem to have a great deal of work to do on that day.

4. A third visit was made on August 1, 1966, and the day was spent with Mr Collard, the factory manager, reviewing the work of the firm. The last visit was made on September 20, 1966 and again the day was spent with Mr Collard.

5. In these circumstances, it is obviously extremely difficult to report on the firm and its use of external aids. Apart from the emotional factor, we did not spend sufficient time there to make any very thorough examination of it, although each of the three main visits lasted a whole

day. The following account should be treated with even more caution than that of the other organizations in the sample.

6. The firm was first set up by Mr H. Landseer Bailey in 1927 as metal merchants, primarily concerned with the buying and selling of scrap metal of all kinds. It was converted into a private company in 1957 as manufacturers of metal ingots for a range of metals, including copper. The firm now occupies modern premises in Mitcham and has fifteen furnaces in its works. Total space occupied is about one acre.

7. There are three executives of the company and about forty other employees, half of whom are employed on manufacturing. The firm appears to be very successful and prosperous, profits having doubled in the two years between 1964 and 1966. We were told that two-thirds of its output is exported and a great deal of it goes to West Germany.

8. There appear to be no formal contacts with external aids and there seems to be little need for them in view of the varied professional expertise possessed by the three senior managers. Some use is made of the specifications of the British Standards Institution but little else of external assistance appears to be necessary.

9. The smallness and specialization of the firm, coupled with many years of successful growth and profitability, has tended to make the employees of the firm feel that they belong to an organization that values them as individuals. There is considerable informality in the office, and in the dining room, at which free meals are provided for all staff. The managers cultivate outside leisure interests during the working week. It may be that the decision to allow visits from a research worker not directly connected with the company's technology or market was a misjudgment and that he was seen as something of an intruder into a close and intimate social group.

10. It should be noted that no complaint was made about the research worker and there is no evidence of any serious incompatibility.

11. From the point of view of the aims of this project, it would appear that this firm through its small specialized and long established activities had no need to break out of its organizational isolationism and that this detachment may well have been confirmed by the inability to maintain a relationship with the investigators. However, in view of our very limited knowledge of the firm, it will not be considered in analysing our findings.

Chapter 9

The Distributors

The enormous size and complexities of distribution in the British economy can be summarized with a few statistics. According to the first results of the 1966 Census of Distribution published in the Board of Trade Journal on February 23, 1968 there were 498,477 establishments in the retail trade plus 3,012 electricity and gas showrooms, 547 mail order houses, and fifty-six automatic vending machine operators, giving a total of 502,092 establishments. Their total turnover was approximately £11,665 million in 1966. This showed a reduction of 13.7 per cent in establishments between 1961 and 1966 and 14.7 per cent between 1950 and 1966. Turnover had increased by 22.8 per cent over 1961 and by 40.4 per cent over 1957. That figure takes no account of the increase in prices and it is estimated that the change in the volume of sales was about 7.1 per cent since 1961. There are some statistical problems in comparing the two years but broadly these simple figures illustrate major trends. Over two and a half million people work in distribution but some of them are part-timers. There is an apparent rise of ¼ per cent since 1961 but that may be due to an increase in part-time working—the final census results will provide the answer. On the whole, turnover per person engaged rose by 22 per cent, or 6.3 per cent at constant prices in the five-year period.

The average size of shop, as measured by turnover, has gone up substantially and at nearly £22,000 was 18 per cent higher in 1966 (at 1961 prices) than five years earlier.

The co-operative societies had 9.2 per cent of total retail turnover in 1966 as compared with 11.9 per cent in 1957. The multiples had 35.2 per cent of turnover in 1966 as compared with 24.8 per cent in 1957. The independents had 55.5 per cent of total turnover in 1966 as compared with 63.2 per cent in 1957.

Detailed figures about the share of turnover between firms of different sizes is not yet available for 1966. In 1961 there were 417,000 firms in retail and 34,000 in wholesaling. About 400,000 of the retailing firms accounted for two-fifths of the total sales, while the 700 largest retailing firms together accounted for nearly another two-fifths.

One of the first Economic Development Committees to be set up by the National Economic Development Council in 1964 was for the distributive trades. The aim of E.D.C.s, it will be remembered, is among other things to help bring about greater efficiency in their sectors of industry. The distributive trades cover the widest sector of any. In view of the comparative paucity of information about the distributive trades, the Committee has spent a considerable part of its energies in particular enquiries aimed at increasing knowledge. A whole range of new problems have occurred during the life of the Committee, not least of all the imposition of the Selective Employment Tax and changes in investment allowances that adversely affected distribution.

In a progress report on its activities dated May 6, 1966 the Committee stated that one of the best ways of increasing efficient distribution may be by the greater use of consultancy services both for the study of general problems and for giving advice to individual firms. 'It is considering whether it would be desirable to recommend government backing to get services started or extended. Information is being collected from trade associations about the consultancy services which they already operate.' In its fourth newsletter published in April 1967 a similar point is made but no evidence is provided that any progress has been made in this matter and the comment concludes with the following words: 'The E.D.C. is considering ways in which the development of associations' advisory services can be encouraged and stimulated.'

The role of trade associations in the distributive trades is confusing. It would appear that there are about 120 of these associations and there is general feeling of undesirable overlapping between some of them. At a conference organized by the Economic Development Committee in 1966, the study group concerned with associations included the following paragraph in their report: 'There was unanimous agreement that common issues and common services should be dealt with and provided through a common channel. But there was also a unanimous qualification that in the development of any machinery to that end, it was essential that the specialist trade association should be preserved and should remain in being to cater for the particular interests of specialized sectors of the trade . . . It was felt that if there is within the trade the will to improve the representation pattern, practical and administrative problems could be overcome.'

As a result of the conference, it was recommended that the Committee should enquire into the services offered by retail and wholesale associations and the results of that enquiry was published in a report entitled *Trade Associations in the Distributive Trades* that was considered by a conference of representatives of trade associations in May 1967. The report revealed a complex structure of a large number of trade associations of varying sizes which overlapped to some extent. The report concluded that although the complex pattern was justifiable to a certain extent in that it catered for a large and diverse field, there was duplication of membership and of services in several trades, and it was arguable whether many associations could provide the quality of services needed. The E.D.C. considers that there is great scope for co-operation and the provision of joint services by trade associations. Recently four of the leading retail trade associations have formed a consortium to deal with matters of common interest. The E.D.C. was encouraged by the number of associations who replied that they were considering extending the range of their services, particularly in consultancy and inter-firm comparisons.

In the survey on the use of productivity advisory services carried out by the National Economic Development Office and published in April 1967 it would appear that a lower percentage of firms in the services group (including distribution) have used productivity services as compared with manufacturing, according to the sample co-operating in the study. Part of the explanation for this difference is the larger number of small firms within the services group who have made less use of productivity services.

Organization D14: Jones & Homersham Limited
1. Jones & Homersham Limited is a private firm of builders' and plumbers' merchants in Kingston-upon-Thames. It was founded about 1850 and incorporated in 1949. Half of the shares are held by Mrs D. M. Leach, one-third by Mrs D. W. Amey and one-sixth by Mr P. G. Amey, the present managing director. For the major period of the

project the firm occupied two large warehouses, a showroom, a shop, offices and a store-room on one site in Kingston, but in the middle of 1968 it bought another firm of builders' merchants at Sheen, Surrey.

2. The business handles a wide range of goods that are used in houses and building generally, including copper tubing, copper ware, bathware, and sanitary fittings.

3. The builders' merchant is concerned with stocking and supplying the thousands of items of materials, components, fittings, and equipment that the builder needs. It has been estimated that 500 items are needed from eighty manufacturers to build a small modern house. All these products have to be obtained from the factories, taken into store, and delivered to building sites as required; a task which can involve daily journeys in view of the very limited space for storage at most sites.

4. In addition to the requirements of new construction, the builders' merchant will stock a wide range of goods that are needed in repair and modernization work, both by the professional and the amateur builder. There is, however, a difference between the builders' merchant and the ironmonger.

5. The firm employs one sales representative who deals with about 100 of their 400 customers and also makes visits to deal with such matters as kitchen planning. Two vans are owned and used in distribution, the larger of which has an hydraulic tail lift. The premises were remodelled in 1965 at a cost of £10,000 and appear to be well organized, so far as is possible in a business handling a wide range of goods, many of them bulky and occupying considerable space.

6. We have not been provided with any accounts or statistics but it is estimated that sales in 1966 were about £125,000, rose to £150,000 in 1967, and should reach £165,000 in 1968, excluding the turnover of the second shop, which is perhaps £50,000.

7. The business is organized round the managing director. He spends most of his time on the premises and deals with all aspects of the business when necessary. He will talk to customers and take orders on the telephone—a considerable quantity of business is obtained by telephone through a special telephone order office with four lines. Mr Amey sees many sales representatives and obtains considerable advantages from the information they give him about new products. Mr Amey was appointed a Justice of the Peace in 1968 and he is a director of the Kingston Building Society.

8. The staff at Kingston consists of four to five men in the shop dealing with both retail and trade customers, three warehousing staff, two drivers, four staff concerned with accounts and administration, and a representative—about fifteen in total.

9. The management and control of stocks are clearly a very important aspect of a business of this type. Where unavoidable, the routine checking of bins and trays is undertaken by one of the warehousing staff. Three other more accurate stock control systems are used as it is believed that no system is suitable for all kinds of goods. Checking the stock of an object one inch long raises different problems from checking the number of 5 feet 6 inch baths. Re-order levels are set as a guide for new demands from suppliers. The choice of stock, particularly of new products, raises several problems. Each member of the counter staff may feel differently about items not normally stocked by the firm. An order for a large piece of equipment which can be readily obtained in single units, will be accepted; items of stock for which there is little demand but which have to be ordered in some quantity beyond the immediate requirement of one customer, will be more critically considered. The final decision on orders is made by the managing director.

10. Equally important is the process of stocktaking, and until 1967 an outside specialist firm charging a fee of about £150 was used for this purpose. For the past two years the stocktaking has been carried out by the regular staff, and Mr Amey is pleased at the saving of money. However, it is difficult to calculate the precise saving. It would be necessary to know whether the internal stocktaking is as accurate as the external one, and also what the direct and indirect costs were of taking staff from their normal work for this additional task. But the results of the stocktaking are now available much more quickly.

11. The most important external aid is the trade association. The firm is a member of the National Federation of Builders' and Plumbers' Merchants. It appears to be a useful, progressive, and efficient body. It issues informative reports to its members, particularly about the internal layout of warehousing. Jones & Homersham have not made use of its consultancy services on warehousing but intend to do so in the near future. The Federation provides Mr Amey with valued opportunities to meet executives of other small builders' merchants. He is Past President of the West London Builders' Merchants Association within the Federation. Several members of staff have attended its courses, includ-

ing Mr Amey, and some have taken examinations organized by the Federation. The Federation has recently sponsored an Institute of Builders' Merchants and it is hoped that it will in time provide a recognized professional qualification.

12. The firm obtains considerable amounts of aid indirectly from manufacturers and from such bodies as employment agencies, the company's auditor, and banks. One less usual indirect aid was the local authority inspector who examined the premises after the alterations had been made to the shop and warehouse. He made a number of recommendations, all of which were acceptable and useful, and all but one of which were carried out. These suggestions dealt with the need for better lighting in the warehouse, the introduction of a safety rail on the staircase, and similar matters.

13. Without detailed financial figures, it is impossible to make any authoritative assessment of the firm or of its need for external aid. It seems sound and secure. The company has built up a good reputation for service in the Kingston area, and since Mr Amey became managing director in 1960 he has carried out a policy of increased investment and improvement in the business, primarily out of profits. The firm deals with well-established products and is relatively protected against major changes in technical processes and the upheavals of new building materials.

14. Progress in turnover has averaged about 8 per cent annually in real terms over the past ten years. The changes in the layout of the premises over the past few years have contributed to better performance, and the changes in many of the semi-skilled staff do not appear to have had an adverse effect on the business.

15. Mr Amey has chosen this policy of slow growth and appears to be well in control of the situation. He was half-way through a five-year development programme when the project started in 1966 and it culminated with the purchase of another firm of merchants. He has seen no need for professional external advice but does welcome opinions from friends and associates in similar firms.

No external contacts were reported or observed during the relevant period.

Organization D15: Tidmans Limited

1. This firm was selected as a distributor in accordance with the pro-

cedure described in Appendix 2. We discovered that in fact it was a manufacturer of sugar confectionery and that it had no unusual distribution functions. The explanation appears to be that it was selected from the directory under the name of the former occupants of the premises, who presumably carried out some distribution functions, probably as a wholesaler. However, in order to respect statistical impartiality, I decided to retain this firm in the sample and to endeavour to examine in some detail its distribution activities. But there is in fact nothing unusual about them.

2. From a wider perspective, this firm does highlight the economic role of small firms who are so tiny as to be primarily agents for distributing the products of others, although subjecting them to a minor processing operation.

3. Tidmans Limited is a private company owned by Mr and Mrs Tidman and they usually employ only two people. Mrs Tidman works part-time; she delivers goods to customers and keeps the accounts. Mr Tidman began his career as a sales representative, and in 1956 he became an independent merchant of imported almonds for the confectionery industry. His initial capital was £400, and with that he bought sugar almonds, wrapped them in cellophane, and sold them. By 1959 he was able to buy a declining business called W. Hancock & Son Limited, and he borrowed £2,500 from Barclays Bank Limited to acquire its factory, lorries and other assets.

4. The business produces special types of sweets by sugar boiling and panning. The sweets are a mixture of traditional old-fashioned brands such as 'gobstoppers', and small packets of cheap sweets in cellophane or miniature bottles. Some eight different types of sweets are turned out from time to time, and the production schedule is dictated by orders—no stocks are built up. The equipment is basically simple but would cost about £8,000 to replace. A sugar hopper was bought secondhand for £150 in 1968.

5. The company deals with about twenty-five customers and they are mainly manufacturers of confectionery requiring some of their goods to be further processed by Tidmans. Another type of customer is a toy manufacturer who uses sweets as part of his product. Mr Tidman thus sells most of his goods under other people's labels. He does not advertise and does not usually look for new business, but believes that there are a large number of potential customers available if needed.

6. We have no detailed financial information but the company's gross turnover is probably about £25,000 a year. Net profit before tax is probably about £6,500 (excluding the income of Mr and Mrs Tidman) and has probably doubled over the past four years. As a closed company, higher corporation tax on undistributed profits would be payable.

7. So far as external aids are concerned, the company is not a member of any association and makes no use of consultants of any kind. There is no evidence of information being obtained from other sources, except from trade papers. Mr Tidman's external contacts are restricted to customers, potential customers, suppliers, and local government authorities. His numerous contacts within the confectionery trade provide him with a great deal of valuable knowledge about sales and such matters as secondhand equipment. His suppliers include two sugar brokers; he seldom takes up options and buys at current market prices. He feels that there is an advantage in using two brokers.

8. For distributing its products, the company has its own van and makes use of British Railways, British Road Services, and other road transport contractors where necessary.

9. The local health inspector was dissatisfied with the cleanliness of the premises on one occasion, and that has led to a much greater concern with hygiene in the small factory, occupying an area of about 2,000 square feet. That has had an indirect influence on production processes, requiring some change of procedure so that refuse would be in a form suitable for regular collection by the local authority.

10. It is difficult to assess the efficiency of a very small firm. Tidmans is almost literally a one-man business, and the considerable achievements of the past ten years are due to the personality, shrewdness and energy of Mr Tidman. Within short-term goals, the business has been very successful. However, Mr Tidman has ambitions to grow larger, and if judged against the potentialities that exist within the confectionery industry, there should be more active planning for future growth. Thus if efficiency were to imply growth—and it does in this case because the owner says that he wishes to grow — the level of efficiency is disappointing.

11. Mr Tidman has planned the business so that it can survive within its resources and circumstances. He intended to keep it small enough to operate without any employees if the severe local labour shortage made that essential. Hence his consistent policy of processing the pro-

ducts of other manufacturers, instead of setting up his own full manu-facturing unit. He believes that the firm must remain small, despite his desire to grow, because of the unavoidable shortage of capital.

ANALYSIS OF EXTERNAL CONTACTS

July 1, 1967 – June 30, 1968

NAME OF ORGANIZATION   TIDMANS
CONTACTS OBSERVED   10
CONTACTS REPORTED   3

TOTAL CONTACTS ANALYZED   13

A. *Type of contact:*   1. Normal 'business' 9   2. Unusual 'business' 2
      3. Aid—deliberate 2   4. Aid—indirect

B. *With whom*

1. Supplier 10	2. Management Consultant	3. Technical Consultant
4. Research Association	5. Trade Association	6. Public Body
7. Competitor	8. Training Board	9. Customer 1
10. National Economic Committee	11. Building Contractor	12. Local government authority
13. Professional practice	14. Government department 1	15. Foreign organization
16. Employment agency	17. Professional institute	18. Head Office
19. College	20. Research organization	21. Bank 1
22. Trade Union	23. International official body	24. Wholesaler
25. Retailer	26.	27.
28.	29.	30.

C. *Purpose*

1. Give information—general 1	7. Give advice—general 1
2. Give information—technical	8. Give advice—technical
3. Give information—commercial	9. Give advice—commercial
4. Seek information—general 1	10. Seek advice—general 1
5 Seek information—technical 3	11. Seek advice—technical 5
6. Seek information—commercial 3	12. Seek advice—commercial 3
13. Buying operations 3	14. Selling operations 4
15. Research and development operations 1	16. General management operations 3
17. Financial operations 1	18. Personnel operations
19. Production operations 5	20. Other

D. *Duration of Contact*
1. Up to one hour continuously 9
2. Up to one day continuously 1
3. Up to one week continuously
4. Up to one month continuously

5. Up to three months continuously

6. Up to six months continuously
7. Up to nine months continuously
8. Up to twelve months continuously
9. Over twelve months
   continuously 2
10. From time to time irregularly

E. *Cost to Organization*
1. Free 7
2. Unassessed
3. By annual subscription
   (give amount if possible)
4. £...................
5. By professional scale—
   estimated at £..................

6. As % of main contract—
   estimated at £..................
7. Under £25 1
8. £26 – £50 1
9. £51 – £100
10. £101 – £1,000

F. *Nature of evidence*
1. Observation by researcher 10
2. Verbal report 9
3. Correspondence seen
4. Minutes of meetings
5. Technical reports

6. Financial statement
7. Organization's statistics
8. Special report for researcher
9. Information from outsider
10. Other (specify)

G. *Implications for Firm* (or other type of organization)
1. Contact is likely to effect firm's current performance. 11
2. Contact is not likely to effect firm's current performance. 2
3. Contact is likely to effect structure of firm's organization. 1
4. Contact is not likely to effect structure of firm's organization. 12
5. Contact is likely to increase profit or surplus. 8
6. Contact is not likely to increase profit or surplus. 5
7. Contact does extend firm's network of external relationships. 10
8. Contact does not extend firm's network of external relationships. 2
9. Contact is likely to increase firm's efficiency. 9
10. Contact is not likely to increase firm's efficiency. 3

Organization D16: Gosdens Limited

1. Gosdens Limited of 125 Chiltern Drive, Surbiton, is a retail news-agent, tobacconist, and confectionery shop that is now owned by Allied Retail Trades (London) Limited, a public company with more than 270 shops. It is one of their smaller branches as far as trade is concerned. We have investigated both the shop and the Head Office of the firm in order to obtain an understanding of its activities and of the role of external aids.

2. The shop is in a busy parade near Berrylands Station and has two competitors within a few hundred yards. The shop measures about 30 feet by 24 feet, there is a rear office, and the manager's flat is above

the shop. It is estimated that takings are about £400 a week. An extensive newspaper delivery business is carried on.

3. In one early morning period of ninety minutes 203 customers came in to buy papers, cigarettes, or confectionery. A census of visitors to the shop has been carried out over three different periods of the day and the results are summarized in the following table.

Gosdens Limited — Flow of Customers

	MALE			FEMALE			
	Papers	*Tobacco*	*Conf.*	*Papers*	*Tobacco*	*Conf.*	*Grand Total*
7.45–9.15 a.m.	108	42	5	27	12	9	203
March 28, 1968							
2–3.30 p.m.	2	6	1	6	1	3	19
May 3, 1968							
3.30–5.15 p.m.	11	7	5	19	1	14	57
June 7, 1968							279

4. The items that the shop has for sale are almost entirely controlled by Head Office, with a small number of special lines selected by the manager in conjunction with Head Office. Head Office is also responsible for the premises, the layout of the counters and display units inside the shop, the appointment and training of managers, and the placing of orders with manufacturers. There is one area supervisor for approximately every twenty shops.

5. The formal duties of the manager are to control the shop in all its aspects, particularly ordering stock in appropriate quantities, supervising staff and training them, selling and sales promotion, and ensuring that newspapers are delivered—a task the manager has to carry out himself occasionally if his delivery staff are absent through illness or other reasons. The only other full-time employee in this shop is the manager's wife. Part-time assistance is given on Saturdays and a relief manager attends on the manager's day off.

6. The manager is able to use his discretion within limits in ordering from a confectionery wholesaler when he runs out of stock. There are three categories of confectionery and stationery — compulsory (very popular) lines, optional lines, and specialities—as defined by Head Office. The manager is encouraged to participate in the choice of lines, and there are weekly communications from Head Office to assist him in sales promotion.

G

7. In June 1967 the company introduced an IBM 1440 computer into its Head Office organization and that has partially mechanized ordering and stock control for all branches. For cigarettes and tobacco, the manager has to record on sensitized cards the levels of stock at regular intervals and these are translated by the computer into replacement orders.

8. During the two main years of the project four different managers have been employed at this branch. Prior to that period, the same manager was in charge of the shop for many years and he has now transferred to one of the Company's newer branches at Reading. The four managers were for the most part inexperienced in the trade when engaged and had been trained by Head Office. They had had some relief experience whilst under training. We attribute this turnover of managers, which the company states is unusual, as being due in part to the appointment of people with more ability and intelligence than is really required for the running of a shop with such a small turnover and the change in responsibilities associated with the build up of Head Office control and centralized services.

9. The shop is more like a department of a single organization than a detached subsidiary. Geographical separation seems only to be important because it increases the difficulty of supervision. That problem is being overcome by reducing the activities that need supervision, mainly by standardizing stocks and ordering with the aid of a computer. Additionally, the company is constantly striving to improve its training to make more efficient managers, thus reducing its need for supervision.

10. During numerous visits to the shop no example of the use of external aids was observed, though this is not true of the company generally. Many representatives of manufacturers called on the manager, sometimes as a courtesy, as they well knew that orders were placed through Head Office, but occasionally they brought display material to encourage the manager to promote the sales of their own products. Occasionally competitions are organized by the manufacturer in conjunction with Head Office. Apart from these routine relationships, the shop looked to Head Office for guidance and support on all matters.

11. The company employs a training manager, and all recruits are subjected to a thorough training programme. Their induction into the company begins with two or three days at Head Office. Then they spend

some time as a trainee in one or two branches, return to Head Office for further training, then move on to being relief managers (in charge of shops on the manager's day off or during holidays) and finally are given a shop of their own—with frequent visits from the area supervisor in their early days.

12. Each potential manager has a training record card. It aims to ensure that the trainee learns about every detail of the shop's activities and his responsibilities. The instructor and trainee have to initial each section as the relevant training is completed, and the trainee reads the instructor's comments. Instruction is given by the training officer, Head Office executives, and certain experienced managers. There are training schedules for fourteen working days in Stage 1 of the record card, and twenty-four days in Stage 2. Stage 3 is concerned with any necessary additional training at Head Office.

13. The training programme is reinforced by a very detailed Branch Manual which lays down the procedures to be followed in all aspects of shop management. It contains about 150 duplicated foolscap sheets, together with copies of the main accounting forms used in the shops.

14. Training courses may also be held for experienced staff. For example, all managers were required to attend a two-hour course at Head Office to deal with the new ordering procedure associated with the introduction of the computer.

15. *Head Office.* Allied Retail Trades (London) Limited now occupies modern and extensive premises in East London. The buildings comprise offices, warehouses, which also house the computer, and a model shop. A major function of Head Office is to obtain requisitions from its 270 shops and to arrange despatches at fortnightly intervals to the shops. In addition, there is an extensive range of central services; the estates department is particularly important as it is concerned with acquiring additional shops and equipping them. The company possesses its own shopfitting firm which can be used by other firms.

16. The managing director is the son of the founder of the business, and two of the managing director's sons are now in the business, one being a director. There is therefore some of the atmosphere of a family firm, but the intimacy and informality that is possible in a smaller group is now more difficult to achieve. The computer symbolizes perhaps most clearly the transition from conventional small shopkeeping to modern multiple retail trading.

17. The company has used the services of Urwick, Orr and Partners Limited for some years. These management consultants tend to undertake one assignment every two years, dealing either with a particular activity or with general organization. This continual contact with such an experienced firm of consultants is acknowledged to be a vitally important influence on the firm's expansion and prosperity. The firm also uses the services of Research and Marketing Limited, a subsidiary of W. H. Smith and Sons Limited, the multiple newsagents and booksellers, which specializes in training retail staff and has prepared a training programme for shop managers; Urwick, Orr also assist with training. The computer installation was based on advice from Urwick, Diebold Limited, the subsidiary of Urwick, Orr and Partners that specializes in computer consultancy. We asked for permission to read the reports that the consultants had submitted but that was not granted.

18. The firm is a member of wholesale and retail trade associations and obtains all the usual benefits from them. It maintains good relationships with all sections of the trade.

19. As Allied Retail Trades is a public company we have been able to obtain detailed information on its finances from its published annual accounts. From 1958 to 1967 its trading profit, as a return on total net assets, has grown from 19.3 per cent to 21.5 per cent, which was the highest apart from 22.8 per cent in 1964. However, the percentage return on assets was 22.5 in 1966 and 21.6 in 1965. The number of branches in those ten years has increased from eighty-six to 245 in 1967 and to 270 in 1968. Sales have grown from £2,364,000 in 1958 to £10,142,000 in 1967.

20. It will be obvious that a business of this size is inevitably involved in an elaborate network of external relationships, many of which have aid characteristics. The individual shop that we studied benefited considerably from the services provided by Head Office and shared the protection the company obtained from manufacturers, consultants, trade associations, solicitors, and auditors, and such benevolent disciplinarians as the local authority inspectors for health and for weights and measures.

ANALYSIS OF EXTERNAL CONTACTS

July 1, 1967 – June 30, 1968

NAME OF ORGANIZATION   GOSDENS LTD
CONTACTS OBSERVED   4
CONTACTS REPORTED   4

TOTAL CONTACTS ANALYZED   8

A. *Type of contact:*   1. Normal 'business' 6   2. Unusual 'business' 1
               3. Aid—deliberate 1   4. Aid—indirect

B. *With whom*

1. Supplier 3	2. Management Consultant	3. Technical Consultant
4. Research Association	5. Trade Association	6. Public Body
7. Competitor	8. Training Board	9. Customer
10. National Economic Committee	11. Building Contractor	12. Local government authority 1
13. Professional practice	14. Government department	15. Foreign organization
16. Employment agency	17. Professional institute	18. Head Office 4
19. College	20. Research organization	21. Bank
22. Trade Union	23. International official body	24. Wholesaler
25. Retailer	26.	27.
28.	29.	30.

C. *Purpose*

1. Give information—general	7. Give advice—general
2. Give information—technical	8. Give advice—technical
3. Give information—commercial	9. Give advice—commercial 1
4. Seek information—general 1	10. Seek advice—general 2
5. Seek information—technical	11. Seek advice—technical 1
6. Seek information—commercial 1	12. Seek advice—commercial 1
13. Buying operations 2	14. Selling operations 5
15. Research and development operations	16. General management operations 1
17. Financial operations 1	18. Personnel operations 4
19. Production operations	20. Other

D. *Duration of Contact*

1. Up to one hour continuously 4	6. Up to six months continuously
2. Up to one day continuously 3	7. Up to nine months continuously
3. Up to one week continuously	8. Up to twelve months continuously
4. Up to one month continuously	9. Over twelve months continuously
5. Up to three months continuously 1	10. From time to time irregularly

197

E. *Cost to Organization*

1. Free   5
2. Unassessed
3. By annual subscription
   (give amount if possible)
4. £..................
5. By professional scale—
   estimated at £..................

6. As % of main contract—
   estimated at £..................
7. Under £25
8. £26 – £50

9. £51 – £100
10. £101 – £1,000

F. *Nature of evidence*

1. Observation by researcher   4
2. Verbal report   8
3. Correspondence seen
4. Minutes of meetings
5. Technical reports

6. Financial statement
7. Organization's statistics
8. Special report for researcher
9. Information from outsider
10. Other (specify)

G. *Implications for Firm* (or other type of organization)

1. Contact is likely to effect firm's current performance.   7
2. Contact is not likely to effect firm's current performance.   1
3. Contact is likely to effect structure of firm's organization.   1
4. Contact is not likely to effect structure of firm's organization.   7
5. Contact is likely to increase profit or surplus.   5
6. Contact is not likely to increase profit or surplus.   3
7. Contact does extend firm's network of external relationships.   6
8. Contact does not extend firm's network of external relationships.   2
9. Contact is likely to increase firm's efficiency.   5
10. Contact is not likely to increase firm's efficiency.   2

Organization D17: G. A. Dunn & Company

1. Dunn's are a well-known firm of men's outfitters with approximately 180 shops in most parts of the country. On average four new shops are opened each year including some transfers to better premises. The firm stocks suits, sports jackets, trousers, overcoats, umbrellas, men's accessories and hats and caps. Since 1966 the company has owned a subsidiary clothing manufacturing firm, Coop & Co. of Wigan, employing 800 people.

2. The firm was set up in 1887 and has evolved from a small family business into a private limited company incorporated in 1917, operating for the benefit of retired and present employees. No information about its financial activities are on public record and no financial information has been provided for us by the organization. A controlling trust to ensure pensions was set up in 1923. It was converted into a private unlimited company in 1968.

3. There are five directors and there are eight area directors who each supervise a group of shops. Each shop has a manager, some a deputy

manager, and several assistants. We concentrated our enquiries on the Kingston branch, and in 1967 it was moved from a small shop to much larger premises in the centre of Kingston. The move was carried out smoothly.

4. We made four visits to the firm's Head Office in North London to obtain a general view of the firm. Head Office is extremely important as it controls the stock and the policies of every shop, and all goods are bought by Head Office. It has an estates department for buying and renting new premises, and maintaining all the firm's shops. The main assets of the business are the freehold properties that it owns, and its biggest problem is its leasehold properties, with rents liable to double or treble on renewal. Sometimes the company decides to leave a site when a lease expires.

5. The shop manager is left largely undisturbed within the strict limits of policy on stock, prices, and staffing and he will have a considerable influence in the selection of staff. His main duty is to boost sales, ensure good relations with customers, and maintain the reputation of the shop with its local community. He will be responsible for window dressing; Head Office's display department provides detailed instructions for some displays. He and his staff will receive training. primarily on the technical aspects of shop management and window display. The company runs its own training courses for all salesmen and managers and there has been an increasing concern with management training in recent years. In the past five years, the firm estimates that it has spent £50,000 in meeting all the costs of its training activities and a training manager was appointed in 1962. Table A summarizes formal training since 1961.

6. Dunn's have always had a high reputation for supplying the conventional middle-class man with his hats, and also with suits and trousers, for over thirty years. There has been much less emphasis on hats since 1958. They cater for people who want something slightly better than the products of many multiple tailors. Dunn's have manufactured caps for over forty years, and since acquiring Coop & Co. they manufacture suits, jackets, trousers, coats, and fancy waistcoats.

7. Dunn's used to have a somewhat old-world atmosphere, and its conventional shop fronts and advertising reflected those attitudes. It is difficult to assess whether this image was cultivated deliberately to appeal to a particular type of customer or whether they merely failed

to move with the times. However, considerable modernization has occurred in the past seven years, and it appears to be a successful business as judged by its growth and by its contented labour force.

8. The staff are paid both salary and commission, including the manager. The manager is also paid 5 per cent commission on any increase over a basic figure, usually taken on an average over three years. There is a managing director's prize of £150 for the manager of the branch achieving the largest increase over the preceding year, with other prizes for runners up. The staff of the successful shops also receive prizes. In 1967 £852 was paid out under this scheme. There is an extensive pension scheme, and managers usually retire on over one-third of their final earnings. In 1968 there were 215 pensioners, including ninety widows of former employees.

9. The company is a member of the Multiple Shops' Federation and we were told that it can be of use in organizing joint objections to compulsory purchase orders and town planning, and in dealing with large landlords. Membership was also maintained of the Felt Hat Manufacturers' Research Association until it closed down in January 1968. None of these bodies played any part in the activities of the business during the course of this investigation, so far as our visits, questions, and observations enable us to judge.

10. We noted a considerable number of external contacts during our regular visits to the Kingston branch, but few of them were external aids. The comprehensive service provided by Head Office makes branch use of aids unnecessary. Managers, directors, and Head Office executives seem to have friendly and informal contacts with one another.

11. The firm as a whole makes use of lawyers, auditors, and suppliers. Some considerable use is made of colleges providing relevant training, as seen in the table; the College for the Distributive Trades, Cassio College, and Watford College of Technology predominate. Cassio College designed a special course to meet the firm's needs.

12. Competitors appear to have considerable influence on the activities of the firm and encourage it to adjust to new market threats and opportunities. In the past five years the firm has spent over £720,000 in modernizing its offices and shops. It has invested £900,000 in new premises, possibly an increase of 15 per cent in its total assets.

13. It is also enterprising in its own right. It was the first firm of multiple retailers to introduce a five-day working week for its staff. The

200

managing director believed such a change would eventually become inevitable and that it was better to make the change in a planned way instead of reacting suddenly to the initiatives of others.

14. Similarly, the change of emphasis away from hats to clothes in general was partly dictated by changes in fashion and demand, partly decided by management. It was carefully fostered throughout the firm and many older employees found difficulty in adjusting to this change. Turnover has doubled in the past ten years.

15. One important external influence on its activities was its advertising agency. Its views were not always accepted and not necessarily superior to Dunn's own. New agents were appointed in 1968 because the managing director believed that a fresh approach was desirable.

16. Perhaps because of its unusual legal status, the company is especially secretive about its sales and profits. There is no obvious reason for such an isolationist attitude. It may be felt that outside judges would criticize the level of financial achievement. It is more concerned with the welfare of its staff than the customary search for high profits, and it could be that the hidden trading results would show up adversely by conventional criteria. More importantly, there seems no obvious driving force towards better performance than an autonomous management — not always a reliable mechanism for optimum effectiveness.

17. The organization appears to be very inward-looking. It is also successful. Probably the nature of its trade changes very slowly so there is little need to expect many major policy changes. Providing the attitudes of customers change at the same speed as the company's, the firm could prosper indefinitely. The firm has kept up with changes in the habits and fashions of its main class of customers.

18. This is an interesting example of the relative unimportance of external aids in achieving a satisfactory level of performance, so far as that can be judged by external indications.

TABLE A   *G. A. Dunn & Co. Ltd.   Training — Courses used 1961-1968*

Year	Course	Venue	Attendance
1961	Display	College for the Distributive Trades	All Managers
1962	Display	College for the Distributive Trades	All Managers
1962	Sales	Dunn's School of Display, Watford	All Managers
1963	Sales	Dunn's School of Display, Watford	All Managers

ASSOCIATIONS AND CONSULTANTS

1963/4	Display	Dunn's School of Display, Watford	80 Staff
1964/5	Display	Dunn's School of Display, Watford	100 Staff
1965/6	Display	Dunn's School of Display, Watford	100 Staff
1965/6	Introductory	Kilburn School	47 Juniors
1966/7	Introductory	Kilburn School	35 Juniors
1966/7	Display	Dunn's School of Display, Watford	100 Staff
1967	Management	Cassio College, Watford	30 Managers
1968	Management	Cassio College, Watford	72 Managers
1968	Relief Managers	Dunn's School of Display, Watford	48 Staff
1967/8	Introductory	Kilburn School	33 Juniors
1968	Display	Dunn's School of Display, Watford	100 Staff
1968	Management	Cassio College, Watford	60 Managers

ANALYSIS OF EXTERNAL CONTACTS

July 1, 1967 - June 30, 1968

NAME OF ORGANIZATION	DUNN & CO
CONTACTS OBSERVED	2
CONTACTS REPORTED	3
TOTAL CONTACTS ANALYZED	5

A. *Type of contact:* 1. Normal 'business' 3   2. Unusual 'business'
3. Aid—deliberate 2   4. Aid—indirect

B. *With whom*

1.	Supplier	2.	Management Consultant	3.	Technical Consultant
4.	Research Association	5.	Trade Association	6.	Public Body
7.	Competitor	8.	Training Board	9.	Customer
10.	National Economic Committee	11.	Building Contractor	12.	Local government authority
13.	Professional practice	14.	Government department	15.	Foreign organization
16.	Employment agency	17.	Professional institute	18.	Head Office 5
19.	College	20.	Research organization	21.	Bank
22.	Trade Union	23.	International official body	24.	Wholesaler
25.	Retailer	26.		27.	
28.		29.		30.	

C. *Purpose*

1.	Give information—general	7.	Give advice—general
2.	Give information—technical	8.	Give advice—technical
3.	Give information—commercial	9.	Give advice—commercial
4.	Seek information—general	10.	Seek advice—general
5.	Seek information—technical	11.	Seek advice—technical
6.	Seek information—commercial	12.	Seek advice—commercial

13. Buying operations 1
14. Selling operations
15. Research and development operations
16. General management operations 1
17. Financial operations
18. Personnel operations 1
19. Production operations 1
20. Other

D. *Duration of Contact*
1. Up to one hour continuously
2. Up to one day continuously 1
3. Up to one week continuously 1
4. Up to one month continuously
5. Up to three months continuously
6. Up to six months continuously
7. Up to nine months continuously
8. Up to twelve months continuously
9. Over twelve months continuously
10. From time to time irregularly

E. *Cost to Organization*
1. Free 3
2. Unassessed
3. By annual subscription (give amount if possible)
4. £...................
5. By professional scale— estimated at £...................
6. As % of main contract— estimated at £...................
7. Under £25
8. £26 – £50
9. £51 – £100
10. £101 – £1,000

F. *Nature of evidence*
1. Observation by researcher 2
2. Verbal report 3
3. Correspondence seen
4. Minutes of meetings
5. Technical reports
6. Financial statement
7. Organization's statistics
8. Special report for researcher
9. Information from outsider
10. Other (specify)

G. *Implications for Firm* (or other type of organization)
1. Contact is likely to effect firm's current performance. 3
2. Contact is not likely to effect firm's current performance.
3. Contact is likely to effect structure of firm's organization. 3
4. Contact is not likely to effect structure of firm's organization.
5. Contact is likely to increase profit or surplus. 2
6. Contact is not likely to increase profit or surplus. 1
7. Contact does extend firm's network of external relationships. 3
8. Contact does not extend firm's network of external relationships.
9. Contact is likely to increase firm's efficiency. 3
10. Contact is not likely to increase firm's efficiency.

Findings

Chapter 10

The Process of Using Aid

The initial proposal for this project[1] hoped for five main achievements:

(1) A systematic and comprehensive understanding of the process of using help from outside the organization;

(2) Identification of the proper roles of (a) the user and (b) the supplier of aid in that process;

(3) Preparation of proposals for increasing the productivity of outside help within the user organization;

(4) Definition of a method for assessing the efficiency of an organization that could serve as a means of diagnosing its need for outside help;

(5) Preparation of proposals for the optimum organization and integration of all types of outside help.

These very broad aims had to be converted into more tangible and measurable concepts, which have to be applied to our data and the resulting inter-relationships considered. It seems impossible to provide precise statistical evidence about the role or organization of external aid, and such precision is only conceivable within a scheme of carefully controlled experiments, which would be beyond the context of the present study.

This part of the book will therefore attempt to analyse the findings about each co-operating organization within the framework of the five expected achievements of the project. This chapter will be primarily concerned with the user of external aid, Chapter 11 with the supplier, and Chapter 12 with the overall organization of aid. As aid does not exist for its own sake, it seems necessary to build this analysis around the user, and to consider the role of the supplier of aid and the organization of aid in the light of those conclusions.

[1] See pages 283-5.

It may help to begin with a logical analysis of the process of using outside aid. This analysis is based on the knowledge obtained from the seventeen firms who were users or potential users of aid but it would be tedious to substantiate each point. As the statement is only being used as a structural tool, the truth of each component element is not a matter of major importance. There is always a danger that such analytical devices may legitimize unsupported hypotheses but it is to be hoped that awareness of the danger will control it.

(1) THE PROCESS OF USING OUTSIDE HELP

This is divisible into four stages and a number of sub-stages. The four main stages are:

(i)   Selection of problems requiring aid;
(ii) Finding appropriate aid;
(iii) Organizational changes needed to adjust to aid requirements;
(iv) Terminating aid.

(i) *The selection of problems requiring aid involves*: (a) the existence of a need for outside help; and (b) the recognition by members of the organization of the need for outside aid.

(ii) *Finding appropriate aid* involves:

(c) awareness of sources of outside help;
(d) obtaining information about sources of help;
(e) making contact with sources of help;
(f) assessing competence of relevant sources of outside help;
(g) arranging preliminary discussions with aid organizations;
(h) agreement of the firm's management to a programme of aid;
(i) estimating cost of using aid.

(iii) *Internal organization to cope with aid* involves:

(j) allocating appropriate resources of firm to meet aid programme;
(k) arranging a system of progress reports on aid project;
(l) arranging for consideration by firm's employees of information or advice offered;

(m) arranging for advice to be accepted or rejected;

(n) preparing to change firm's activities in accordance with aid proposals;

(o) arranging for aid advice to be implemented.

(iv) *Terminating aid* involves:

(p) formal decision and communication of decision to terminate aid to aid suppliers and firm's own staff;

(q) assessing the value of aid;

(r) reviewing original problem and the consequences for that problem of the aid received at regular intervals in the future;

(s) assessing need for aid elsewhere in the firm;

(t) using aid to prevent problems arising.

It is proposed to make three assessments for each of our seventeen firms:

(1) its use of aid;

(2) its efficiency, and

(3) its environment.

From these assessments and their possible inter-relationships, a final indication of 'aid appropriateness' will be compiled.

Then the firms will be re-analyzed on their usual characteristics of age, size and technology, to search for any possible evidence or explanation of the role of aid for types of firms.

The Use of Aid

It will first be necessary to decide which of our seventeen firms were users of external aid, and then to see what we have learned from them about each stage of the aid process.

For this analysis, an organization will be defined as a user of external aid if it was a member of a trade association or a research association, or if it has made use of the services of a management consultant or a public aid body, during the period of our visits between 1966 and 1968.

The following table summarizes the position:

TABLE A   *Seventeen Co-operating Firms—Crude Aid Use Indicators*

Organization	Trade Association	Research Association	Management Consultants	Public Aid Body	Score	Grading
F1	X	—	—	—	1	D
F2	X	—	—	—	1	D
F3	X	—	—	X	2	C
F4	X	—	—	X	2	C
B5	X	—	—	X	2	C
B6	X	—	—	X	2	C
B7	X	—	X	X	3	B
B8	X *	—	—	—	1	D
M9	X	X	—	—	2	C
M10	X	X	X	—	3	B
M11	X	X	—	X	3	B
M12	X	—	—	—	1	D
M13	—	—	—	—	0	E
D14	X	—	—	—	1	D
D15	—	—	—	—	0	E
D16	X	—	X	—	2	C
D17	X	X	—	—	2	C
Total	15	4	3	6	28	

A = 4, B = 3, C = 2, D = 1, E = 0.

* ie, National Housebuilders Registration Council—perhaps a hybrid trade association / public body.

Not surprisingly with such crude indicators, all but two of the seventeen firms qualify as aid users. It would be much more difficult to separate the very dependent user from the very independent user, and also to separate absolutely the formal supplier of aid from the many informal suppliers. However, we appear to have two total isolationists among this sample, and that elementary degree of segregation will suffice, at least for this stage of the analysis.

It should be noted perhaps that the two non-users are very small organizations. One employs two or three people and the other about twelve. Both are based on very simple technologies and operate on a small scale. One has ambitions to grow but does not believe it to be possible, the other does not wish to grow.[1]

The small firm raises numerous problems and it would be unwise to suggest solutions or at least changes in the situation without an elaborate investigation of the small firm. However, it is worth noting that both these firms have numerous relationships with customers and suppliers, and they are also involved with the Inland Revenue! The main opportunities for influencing their behaviour lies within those relationships.

Selecting Problems Requiring Aid and Finding Aid

It was suggested that the first stage of the process of using outside aid—selecting problems—involved two activities: (i) the need must exist and (ii) it must be known to exist by management or other members of the organization. The second stage involved the finding of appropriate aid, and that is divisible into seven activities: (i) awareness of sources of outside help; (ii) obtaining information about them; (iii) making contact with them; (iv) assessing their competence; (v) arranging preliminary discussions; (vi) agreeing a programme of aid; and (vii) estimating cost of aid.

The following table comprises my assessments of the performance of the fifteen user firms on each of these nine variables, using a five-point scale ranging from 0 for total failure to perform the activity to 4 for optimum performance of the activity. I have made two assessments for each firm. The first is based on their known past behaviour in relation to at least one significant problem apparently suitable for external aid. The second assessment concerns their behaviour in relation to a continuing problem and I have tried to assess their aid behaviour in

---

[1] The eight non-users in the pilot project were managed by distinctive chief executives. It seems probable that a different policy to aid in these two firms would be adopted with a change of ownership. See Appendix I.

TABLE B *Fifteen User Firms—Selecting Aid Problems and Finding Aid*

Organization	Need exists	Need known	Sources known	Sources studied	Sources contacted	Competence assessed	Preliminary discussion	Programme agreed	Cost estimated	Score	Grade
F1 (i)	†	3	4	1	4	1	1	0	0	14	E
(ii)	†	1	3	0	0	0	0	0	0	4	
F2 (i)	†	0	4	0	1	1	0	0	0	6	H
(ii)	†	0	4	0	1	1	0	0	0	6	
F3 (i)	†	4	2	1	0	0	0	0	0	7	F
(ii)	†	4	2	1	0	0	0	0	0	7	
F4 (i)	†	4	4	4	4	2	4	4	0	26	C
(ii)	‡	—	—	—	—	—	—	—	—	0	
B5 (i)	†	0	4	0	0	0	0	0	0	4	J
(ii)	†	0	4	0	0	0	0	0	0	4	
B6 (i)	†	0	4	0	0	0	0	0	0	4	J
(ii)	†	0	4	0	0	0	0	0	0	4	
B7 (i)	†	4	4	2	2	2	4	4	4	26	B
(ii)	†	0	4	0	0	0	0	0	0	4	
B8 (i)	†	4	4	N.K.	4	2	4	4	N.K.	22	D
(ii)	‡	—	—	—	—	—	—	—	—	0	
M9 (i)	†	4	3	2	3	N.K.	1	0	0	13	G
(ii)	‡	—	—	—	—	—	—	—	—	0	
M10(i)	‡	No aid problems									
M11(i)	‡	No aid problems									
M12(i)	†	2	2	0	1	0	0	0	0	5	I*
(ii)	†	2	2	0	1	0	0	0	0	5	
D14(i)	†	4	4	2	0	0	0	0	0	10	I
(ii)	‡									0	
D16(i)	†	4	4	4	4	N.K.	4	4	4	28	A
(ii)	†	4	4	4	4	0	0	0	0	16	
D17(i)	†	0	4	0	0	0	0	0	0	4	J*
(ii)	†	0	4	0	0	0	0	0	0	4	

* Same problem. N.K. = not known. † Does exist. ‡ Does not exist.

The optimum score for each assessment would be 32, given that a need exists. As two assessments have been made, the maximum is 64. Only Beechams and Petters appeared not to have needed any additional aid at anytime during the project. Thus the remaining thirteen have been scored and graded.

1968. In some cases I consider that there is a need but management apparently do not (and of course I may be wrong and they may be right). In a few cases I believe that there is no problem requiring external aid at all or that aid is currently being received.

Internal Organization for Aid

The third stage of the aid process is concerned with the internal arrangements made by the firm to deal with aid, and these were divided into six sub-stages:

(i)   allocating appropriate resources of firm to meet aid programme;

(ii) arranging a system of progress reports on aid project;

(iii) arranging for consideration by firm's employees of information or advice offered;

(iv) arranging for advice to be accepted or rejected;

(v)   preparing to change firm's activities in accordance with aid proposals;

(vi) arranging for aid advice to be implemented.

The thirteen firms having a need for aid and using it during this project were assessed on each of these six variables on a five-point scale, with optimum behaviour receiving four points. The score for each of the six variables were added with a maximum score of 24, and the firms graded, as recorded in the following table.

It will be appreciated that we did not obtain adequate knowledge in all cases on all the variables and thus some scores involve more speculation than others. Whilst it would be difficult to justify any single score with objective evidence, the overall score probably indicates correctly the general situation regarding the internal arrangements for dealing with the provision of aid. Perhaps more importantly, the grading of firms on this stage of the aid process should help to identify overall relationships between aid need, aid use, efficiency, and environment.

TABLE C *Thirteen Necessary Aid Users—Internal Arrangements*

Organization	Allocating resources	Progress reports	Advice considered	Decision on advice	Arranging organization changes	Arranging implementation	Score	Grade
F1	2	0	1	4	0	0	7	H
F2	3	0	2	1	0	0	6	I
F3	3	3	3	3	2	2	16	E
F4	4	4	4	4	4	2	22	B
B5	4	4	4	4	4	4	24	A
B6	0	0	1	1	0	0	2	J
B7	3	4	3	2	4	4	20	D
B8	4	4	4	4	1	4	21	C
M9	2	2	4	4	4	4	20	D
M12	1	1	1	1	1	1	6	I
D14	1	1	3	3	3	4	15	F
D16	4	4	4	3	3	3	21	C
D17	1	1	1	3	2	2	10	G

Ending Aid Use

The final stage in the logical process of using aid concerns the activities involved in ending the use of aid. This can be seen most clearly in the firm's relations with a consultant, but similar considerations are involved in decisions to leave associations and to cease using the services of a public aid body.

We have no adequate evidence of aid termination to make an assessment of behaviour of our thirteen user firms. Two of the farmers reported terminating aid but these events occurred before this project. However, it may help the overall scheme of summarizing findings to predict each firm's behaviour in relation to aid termination by (a) assessing the likelihood of their ending aid appropriately, and (b) assessing the likelihood of their making intelligent arrangements to complete the five logical stages of aid termination, listed on page 209.

TABLE D   *Prediction of Aid Termination Tendencies*

Organization	Ending unnecessary aid	Completing termination process	Score	Grading
F1	4	0	4	D
F2	4	2	6	C
F3	2	2	4	D
F4	4	3	7	B
B5	2	2	4	D
B6	0	0	0	G
B7	2	2	4	D
B8	4	4	8	A
M9	2	1	3	E
M12	1	1	2	F
D14	1	1	2	F
D16	4	2	6	C
D17	4	0	4	D

Environmental Influences

In view of this project's major concern with external influences, it is necessary to assess the nature of the environment of each of our firms, in case there is a relationship between the environment and the firm's aid policy.

The four 'ideal types' of environment proposed by Emery and Trist are described on pages 297-298. Their classifications are extremely crude and most organizations contain elements of most types within their framework. It may help to refine the classification by adding a five-point scale to each type, thus enabling a firm's degree of similarity to the 'ideal' to be indicated. A high score indicates a close approximation to the 'ideal'.

I have followed the implied grading of the original scheme and taken a 'placid, randomized' environment to be relatively comfortable for management, and the 'turbulent field' environment to be extremely demanding. The comfortable environment receives a low score, the dangerous one a high score. I further assume that the 'dangerous' environment requires more aid. Thus the organization with a high score and grade would be expected to be a more frequent user of aid than the comfortable organization.

The following table records the assessments that I have made.

TABLE E   *Seventeen Firms and their Environment Type*

Organization	I *Placid, randomized ('Perfect competition') (1 - 5)*	II *Placid, clustered ('Imperfect competition') (6 - 10)*	III *Disturbed- reactive ('Oligopoly') (11 - 15)*	IV *Turbulent Field ('Positive environment pressures') (16 - 20)*	*Grade*
F1	4				I
F2	4				I
F3	4				I
F4	4				I
B5		8			F
B6		6			G
B7				18	A
B8		9			E
M9			13		C
M10			15		B
M11		9			E
M12	5				H
M13	5				H
D14			11		D
D15	5				H
D16			15		B
D17			15		B

Organizational Efficiency

The following table summarizes the two assessments of efficiency made by the research assistant in accordance with the criteria described in Appendix 2, pages 294-6:

TABLE F *Efficiency Assessment As Aid Need Indicator*

Org.	1967		Planning for the future 1968 Assessment				Social Awareness 1968 Assessment				Final rating	1968	
	Score	Grade	Market-ing	Produc-tion	Personnel	Capital	Market-ing	Produc-tion	Personnel	Capital		Score	Grade
F1	8	H	80	75	75	75	80	75	75	75	76%	8	H
F2	14	N	65	60	60	50	60	65	60	50	59%	14	N
F3	7	G	80	80	75	75	75	85	75	75	77%	5	E
F4	3	C	90	80	90	90	85	85	90	90	87%	3	C
B5	6	F	75	75	80	80	75	75	75	80	77%	5	E
B6	16	P	25	50	50	50	50	50	50	50	47%	16	P
B7	12	L	75	65	75	50	70	80	70	60	68%	12	L
B8	5	E	90	85	85	95	90	80	80	95	86%	4	D
M9	15	O	90	90	80	75	75	75	40	75	75%	10	J
M10	1	A	95	90	90	95	90	90	90	95	92%	1	A
M11	2	B	90	90	90	90	90	90	80	90	89%	2	B
M12	11	K	75	60	30	60	60	75	40	50	56%	15	O
M13	17	Q	30	45	55	50	80	40	65	25	46%	17	Q
D14	13	M	80	75	85	75	80	75	75	60	76%	8	H
D15	10	J	75	75	85	75	75	80	80	75	77%	5	E
D16	4	D	80	85	60	70	85	80	50	65	72%	11	K
D17	9	I	60	50	75	50	75	55	85	60	64%	13	M

¹ Average of eight percentages.

217

I disagree with the final grading to some extent but there is only a major difference in respect of Gaze's and Tidman. I should have placed Gaze's (B7) third in rank order and Tidman's (D15) thirteenth for reasons that should be clear from their descriptions in Chapters 7 and 9 and from the final impressions recorded in the next section of this chapter. The grading incorporated in the consolidated table (Table H) is this revised one.

Aid Appropriateness

This final assessment attempts to sum up my knowledge of the organization and its aid policy in order to decide whether that policy is sensible, given the internal and external circumstances of the firm. I have tried to be as objective as possible about external aid and to avoid any assumption that the greater the use of aid, the higher the status of the firm. If aid is unnecessary, its use, even if free of charge, reflects adversely on management. I have scored organizations on a ten-point scale, with 0 indicating a total absence of appropriateness and 9 indicating a fully appropriate aid policy. This wide range of scoring seems necessary to distinguish differences more clearly.

F1. *Highway Model Farm.* There would appear to be an obvious need for a wide variety of aid when an enterprising man lacking any systematic training in agriculture becomes involved in farming, handicapped by problems of death duties, stimulated by considerable ambitions. My impression is that more technical and specialized aid was necessary; given the comparatively secure environment in which he operates he ought then to achieve better current performance. Score: 6.

F2. *Horringdon Farm.* Appropriate aid has been used on technical matters, although his considerable reliance on informal guidance may be excessive and unwise. But on financial and farm management matters, including long-term prospects of security of tenure, there would appear to be a serious failure at least to find out about available aid.
Score: 5.

F3. *Anonymous.* A well-equipped and well-run farm that uses most aids sensibly. N.A.A.S. has not proved satisfactory but the farm manager's expectations may have been unreasonable. He prefers aid offered by cattle feed suppliers and seems unconcerned about the problem of their possible bias. Perhaps would benefit from aid on cream sales. Score: 6.

F4. *Anonymous.* A very efficient farm using a wide range of appropriate aids. Some doubt about plans for dealing with the problems likely to arise from the death of the senior partner in relation to the lease of the farm, capital gains tax and death duties, and some appropriate use of advice seems necessary. Score: 8.

B5. *Anonymous.* This building firm seems to be very competent and to make appropriate use of external aids in day-to-day activities. There is possibly an inadequate concern with optimum performance and long-term planning. Score: 7.

B6. *Anonymous.* Unsatisfactory performance in most spheres but it survives despite a failure to use needed aids. It is difficult to balance opportunities for improvement against modest management goals. Perhaps this firm constitutes more of a challenge to the aid suppliers than a failure of appropriate aid use. Score: 4.

B7. *Gaze's.* A very satisfactory development over the past nine years, making appropriate use of external aids to utilize the benefits of a well-established family firm. Yet some uneasiness from untapped opportunities. Odd that it agreed to collaborate on this project but refused to give us financial information—no risk of publication leading to take-over bid. Perhaps merely sensible caution? Score: 7.

B8. *Sibson.* An important example of how a tiny organization can tackle large tasks without acquiring extensive assets. It makes considerable use of external contacts and aids. Possibly, its nucleus would be too fragile to survive adverse conditions and its resources would appear to prohibit any significant growth. Score: 8.

M9. *Osway.* After a somewhat unimaginative approach to aid, this firm has found some aids very useful when faced with a major change and it now appears to be employing them sensibly. It might not have

219

done so without the compulsory furniture industry levy and the training levy.   Score: 6.

M10. *Beechams.* The only significant aid problem here is the lack of an effective appraisal procedure to ensure that all money spent on aid is necessary and used effectively. Perhaps as a result there was no attempt to determine whether the management consultants called in were needed. Apparently the chief executive saw them as preventing inefficiency.   Score: 8.

M11. *Petters.* Assessment is complicated by the imprecise role of the parent company which appears to supply a few but important aids, and the role of aid in relation to research has not been investigated. Broadly speaking, aids were neither greatly needed nor extensively used. Perhaps aid could play a greater part in obtaining marginal improvements in performance.   Score: 8.

M12. *Lion Case.* Little use of aid which was needed primarily for overcoming problems due to lack of skilled labour. That may be an aspect of fundamental importance. Otherwise, technical aid was usually supplied by customers. Two-thirds of turnover is dependent on government contracts and the firm may not be as 'free enterprise' as the managing director believes. If its aim were to achieve genuine competitive independence, many tasks would have to be undertaken that would almost certainly involve extensive use of external aid.   Score: 5.

M13. *A. Brown & Co.* No use of aid. No existing need. No ambitions to survive nor to grow, Hence,   Score: 9.

D14. *Jones and Homersham.* The only grounds for doubting aid appropriateness concerns its current level of performance. Higher goals could be set, given the resources available, and with aid management might achieve even more success. But there is no positive evidence to support this feeling.   Score: 7.

D15. *Tidman.* No aid is used or required for existing policies, yet the managing director expressed desire for growth but believes it

220

impossible to do so. As there is no objective evidence of this impossibility, aid might clarify the situation.   Score: 4.

D16. *Gosdens Ltd.*   Aid use by the parent company seems to be about right.   Score: 9.

D17. *Dunn's.*   Aid is needed to ensure that management satisfaction with current performance is justified. I suspect that financial policy could be strengthened. Its considerable efforts to modernize in recent years might have been easier and possibly more economical if they had used consultants to help them.   Score: 6.

TABLE G   *Aid Appropriateness*

Organization	Score	Grade
F1	6	D
F2	5	E
F3	6	D
F4	8	B
B5	7	C
B6	4	F
B7	7	C
B8	8	B
M9	6	D
M10	8	B
M11	8	B
M12	5	E
M13	9	A
D14	7	C
D15	4	F
D16	9	A
D17	6	D

TABLE H   *Summary of Assessments—Aid Users*

Organization	I Aid use	II Finding aid	III Internal arrange-ments	IV Ending aid	V Efficiency	VI Environ-ment	VII Aid appro-priate-ness
F1	D	E	H	D	G	I	D
F2	D	H	I	C	K	I	E
F3	C	F	E	D	F	I	D
F4	C	C	B	B	C	I	B
B5	C	J	A	D	F	F	C
B6	C	J	J	G	M	G	F
B7	B	B	D	D	C	A	C
B8	D	D	C	A	E	E	B
M9	C	G	D	E	H	C	D
M10	B	N/A	N/A	N/A	A	B	B
M11	B	N/A	N/A	N/A	B	E	B
M12	D	I	I	F	L	H	E
M13	E	N/A	N/A	N/A	N	H	A
D14	D	I	F	F	G	D	C
D15	E	N/A	N/A	N/A	K	H	F
D16	C	A	C	C	I	B	A
D17	C	J	G	D	J	B	D

Each of the assessments summarized in Table H were made in isolation and there was no conscious effort to make them consistent. But it will now be helpful to see whether the final overall impression of each organization's aid policy is justified by the earlier scores and grades.

If an organization uses aid sensibly, or decides that aid is unnecessary, it ought to achieve a high grade all along the line. But if its environment is difficult, its level of efficiency may be lowered. If its efficiency is low, particularly over policies for the future, it presumably ought to seek aid.

If it does not use aid, and its plans for efficiency in the future seem inadequate, its aid policy seems inappropriate, and its grade in column VII would be low.

Thus organizations F1, F3, F4, B7, M10 and M11 appear to have reasonably consistent grades. For example, F1 in a relatively comfortable environment has a relatively low level of 'future efficiency', and a similar grading for the appropriateness of its aid policy.

B6, on the other hand, is a high nominal user of aid (e.g. it belongs to and participates in a trade association), but it does not manage aid properly and its efficiency level is low. Its environment is comfortable in the sense that there is a considerable amount of work available in normal conditions and there are no 'monopolists'. But it is subject to the consequences of national economic policies, particularly in its construction work. It probably has at least two environments—one for its maintenance work, one for building. It could more easily influence the first than the second. Its failure to seek help in this complex situation suggests that its overall aid policy is inappropriate.

B8's aid policy seems appropriate for day-to-day activities but more doubtful in relation to 'efficiency for the future'.

Adequacy of the Aid System
It is worth reviewing the firms with the same aid appropriateness grade to see what guidance can be obtained about the adequacy of the supply of aid as a whole. Table I, summarizing the characteristics of firms, will help.

The most 'inappropriate' firms, graded F, are B6 and D15. B6 is a firm of builders and decorators. D15 is Tidman's, the tiny confectionery firm. The efficiency of both is comparatively low. Their environments are different with B6's slightly more dangerous. Their technology is similar. B6 has many more employees than Tidman but is comparatively small. Tidman also appears to be much more profitable. Their prospects for growth and better performance are equally poor but for different reasons possibly. Ultimately, however, their condition seems to be more within the potential control of management than would be true of firms exposed to major technological or economic challenges. The aid they need for future development exists and is known by management to exist, at least to some degree. For some reason, the available aid fails to impress management and they do not make use of it.

One firm graded E is M12 (Lion Case Co. Ltd.). It again is small but technologically a little more advanced and probably in a stronger financial position than B6 and D15. Its efficiency is reduced by a shortage of skilled labour that it believes is inevitable. It probably has inadequate capital for growth. It is heavily dependent on government departments and other government suppliers, and may be unwisely exposed to the risk of sudden economies in public expenditure. Perhaps a competent firm of management consultants could deal with all these problems, but such a firm is unlikely to use consultants particularly as the managing director believes such use is a sign of weakness. He derives considerable technical aid from his customers and that avoids short-term difficulties. But this source is unreliable for the future and not concerned with more fundamental weaknesses.

The other firm graded E is F2 (Horringdon Farm) and there seems no need to add to the comments on page 218.

The firms graded D are F1 (Highway Model Farm), F3, M9 (Osway) and D17 (Dunns). Their problems are much less serious, more a question of improving performance slightly and searching a little more vigorously for new opportunities. The inappropriateness of their aid policy is more a function of an inadequate supply of relevant aid, or perhaps simply that aid suppliers do not present their services in these less serious problem areas with sufficient emphasis.

Grade C firms are B5, B7 (Gaze's), and D14 (Jones and Homersham). Here again the problems are comparatively minor. They are distinguished from the grade B firms because they are all progressing well but could perhaps move forward more quickly and more comfortably if some suitable form of aid existed or emphasized its services for this purpose. The aid supplier would have to deal especially with the attitudes of management that may feel its achievements have been considerable and its plans satisfactory.

Grade B firms are F4, B8 (Sibson), M10 (Beecham) and M11 (Petters). The first two are very satisfactory in nearly all respects, especially aid policy, but they may run into difficulties in the future. Their use of aid for future planning would require the services of a very sophisticated supplier who would primarily have to help them make the best of legal and financial opportunities, so as to ensure that the high management potential was not hindered by arbitrary and unintentional difficulties such as death duties.

The A firms are A. Brown and Co. (M13) and Gosdens Ltd. (D16). The first has an aid policy appropriate to immobility and possibly stagnation. The second has done all that seems necessary, mainly through regular contacts with management consultants. Their only problem is to make sure that the consultants continue to be competent, and that is not the responsibility of the client.

EFFICIENCY ASSESSMENT METHOD

It was expected before we started work that this project would be able to 'define a method for assessing the efficiency of an organization that could serve as a means of diagnosing its need for outside help'. We have failed to produce such a method, at least in a form that could be used immediately and universally. The complexities of such a task have been noted on page 294, but we have made subjective efficiency assessments on two occasions for each firm, and they have been related to other assessments in this chapter.

We failed to devise a method because we could not obtain sufficient information about performance from most of our firms. Even if we had, conventional indicators such as return on capital, labour turnover, share of market, and input-output ratios, would not have demonstrated the need for outside help. They would perhaps have shown the need for change, although even that should be based on comparative information within the industry that does not exist in most cases. The changes needed would frequently require special staff rather than outside help.

A thorough investigation of this problem would have taken more time and resources than we had available. The need for aid is ultimately a psychological problem: if top management wants the help of consultants they will be brought in even if there is no evidence of necessity. Other employees will use aid if they want it and if they can obtain it— and that may be easy if no charge is made.

The objective assessment of the need for aid is a problem for the suppliers of aid. If they were able to demonstrate to a chief executive that his firm was not performing at the optimum level, and then showed him what help was available, the most sceptical manager would find difficulty in ignoring such evidence.

Such an objective assessment of the firm and its need for aid should spotlight the areas of uncertainty facing the firm. Current performance is difficult to appraise with certainty, even if information is provided, especially for indications of the need for aid. But everyone is confused about the future, and aid in dealing with the unknown is much more likely to be acceptable and productive, if only because firms can help

H

to shape the future by studying indications of its nature and acting on the more reliable indicators. I believe that planning for the future can be undertaken, and that management's ability in that function can be assessed. We need experimental validation of that opinion with users and suppliers of aid, and with experimental organizations.

TABLE I   *Characteristics of Seventeen Co-operating Firms*

	Year established	Numbers employed approx.	Income	Capital	Technology
F1	1962	5	£10,817	£38,000	Mixed farm
F2	—	4	£10,904	£16,443	Cows, barley
F3	1960	4	£13,500	£10,000 approx.	83 Jersey cows
F4	1939	12	£45,474	£42,000	Cattle, sheep and grain
B5	1930	40	£250,000 approx.	£30,000	Simple building
B6	1929	60	£161,976	£13,225	Simple building
B7	1879	1,200	£4.5m estimated	£1m approx. estimated	Advanced building
B8	1962	4	£43,613	£33,203	Building site development
M9	Incorporated 1954	30	£100,000 estimated	£20,000 estimated	Simple engineering (furniture)
M10	1928	15,000	£115.5m	£67m	Very advanced
M11	1895	2,000	£20m	£8m Assets	Very advanced
M12	1957	20	£45,000 estimated	£20,000 estimated	Simple
M13	1946	12-15	£25,000 estimated	£5,000 estimated	Simple
D14		12-18	£125,000 estimated	£50,000 estimated	Simple warehousing
D15	1956 started manufacturing	3	£25,000 estimated	£10,000 estimated	Simple confectionery
D16	1947	1,000	£7.422m	£1.085m	Simple retailing
D17	1887	1,000	Figures not available		Advanced retailing

Chapter 11

The Process of Supplying Aid

The supply of aid can be analysed into the following logical divisions:

(1) becoming and remaining qualified to act as an aid supplier;
(2) discovering the user's problem;
(3) carrying out the aid project;
(4) terminating the project.

(1) *Becoming qualified to act* involves:

 (a) appropriate general and professional education;
 (b) consultancy/advisory experience;
 (c) objective evidence of maintaining and improving relevant knowledge;
 (d) awareness of the client's psychological state regarding the use of aid;
 (e) possessing resources necessary for optimum professional behaviour.

(2) *Discovering the user's problem* involves:

 (a) Making contact with user and carrying out initial systematic general survey;
 (b) obtaining collaboration from all in user organization;
 (c) arranging working methods acceptable to client;
 (d) providing an estimate of direct and indirect cost.

(3) *Carrying out the aid project* involves:

 (a) Arranging work plan and programme;
 (b) obtaining and analyzing relevant information;
 (c) submitting agreed progress reports to clients;
 (d) reviewing project with colleagues.

(4) *Terminating the project* involves:
   (a) submitting final recommendations to client;
   (b) proposing implementation procedures;
   (c) assisting with implementation if so requested by client;
   (d) assessing need for additional aid and informing client;
   (e) arranging follow-up study.

Although this structure is imperfect, it can be used as a framework for reviewing the work and problems of the four aid organizations, and the examples of the use of aid by the seventeen firms involved in this study. The logical sequence is particularly relevant to the work of the management consultant, but it may not be so obviously relevant to the work of the Agricultural Advisory Service or a trade association. However, one analytical framework for all the main types of aid suppliers will clarify interpretation.

The management consultant, operating to the highest professional standards, represents an ideal that is suitable for all suppliers of aid to follow. He has the most difficult task in the aid spectrum: he has to make himself acceptable to clients who are paying large fees; he commits himself to achieving defined goals within a stated period of time; and those goals are translated by him into a precise financial estimate of costs and benefits. This does not mean that other suppliers of aid are inferior. All good aid suppliers resemble the best management consultant and most consultants do not achieve such ideal standards of work.

In any assessment of performance, trade associations and public aid bodies will achieve poor scores, given the above basis of judgment. Thus their scores and grades do not imply criticism of them, but merely indicate my estimate of the gap between their aid-giving functions and those of the ideal management consultant.

The phrases used to describe the process of supplying aid require some elaboration if they are to be properly understood. 1(a), dealing with education, implies that the supplier of aid must achieve the level of the best educated users. He should be a graduate or possess a professional qualification. 'Flair' is not enough because it is incommunicable, and the consultant has to help the client realize that knowledge exists and can be applied to solve many of his problems. 1(b), 'consultancy/advisory experience', emphasizes that an expert is not necessarily a competent adviser. He needs knowledge and experience of the aid situation in addition, and insight into its stresses for both the aider and the aided.

1(c), 'objective evidence of maintaining and improving relevant knowledge', recognizes that considerable knowledge is needed in most aid situations and that any supplier should ensure that his stock of knowledge is kept up-to-date and continually extended into associated fields. In particular, suppliers of aid should demonstrate some serious concern about acquiring knowledge of the process of giving aid itself.

Thus 1(d), 'awareness of the client's psychological state towards the use of aid', is of fundamental importance and appears to be frequently overlooked by aid suppliers. Many users or potential users resist the use of aid. Occasionally they recognize that they suffer from a sense of inferiority in relation to aid. Some believe that they know all that could be known about the firm's functions and they are unaware of the relevant knowledge that could be channelled to them through an aid supplier.

Many managers hesitate to bring aid into their organization because morale may suffer. There is widespread suspicion of the independence and integrity of consultants. The consultant will not behave objectionably if he takes the trouble to learn how to understand the client's attitude and to act in ways that do not reinforce the anxiety of employees.

At the other extreme, the user must be helped to act without aid in due course. If he becomes over-dependent on help, the supplier of aid will have been a failure. That does not exclude using the supplier for other problems in the future.

1(e), 'possessing resources necessary for optimum professional behaviour', emphasizes the need for the aid supplier to have sufficient financial reserves to act with professional concern for the user at all times. He must have a reasonable expectation of future income from new users. The aid supplier cannot easily act professionally when he is insecurely established and over-anxious to obtain work, without too close a regard for his ability to handle it. One or two established suppliers have adopted pressurizing techniques to sell their services They can produce statements of satisfaction by clients, and high pressure salesmanship need not be dishonest. But a conflict is likely between the long-term needs of the client and the short-term profit-seeking of the supplier. That is not necessarily an argument in favour of public aid bodies, since they could suffer from complacency, lethargy, and academicism.

The second and third sections, concerned with discovering the user's problems and carrying out the project, cover activities that have been discussed elsewhere. They are difficult to carry out successfully, but providing the user is encouraged to collaborate in the search for improvement, none of these tasks is impossible.

The fourth section, 'terminating the project', emphasizes the responsibility of the aid supplier to help the user maintain control of the situation, to continue to manage his organization, and to be capable of working again on his own after aid has been received.

My assessments of the performance of the suppliers in the four stages of the aid supply process are:

ANALYSIS OF AID SUPPLY PROCESS

TABLE A *Assessment of Qualifications*

	1a Education	1b Experience	1c Maintaining knowledge	1d Client awareness	1e Resources	S	G[1]
B.L.R.A.	4	4	4	3	3	18	A
N.A.A.S.	4	4	4	2	3	17	B
I.A.	3	4	3	4	4	18	A
B.C.P.M.A.	4	4	4	1	1	14	C

TABLE B *Assessment of Aid Supply Process*

	2a Initial survey	2b Obtaining collaboration	2c Working methods	2d Cost estimates	S	G
B.L.R.A.	1	3	3	1	8	C
N.A.A.S.	1	2	3	4	10	B
I.A.	4	4	4	4	16	A
B.C.P.M.A.	0	1	2	0	3	D

[1] S = score, G = grade.

TABLE C *Assessment of Project Management*

	3a Work plan	3b Information	3c Progress reports	3d Review with colleagues	S	G
B.L.R.A.	4	4	2	3	13	B
N.A.A.S.	4	3	1	4	12	C
I.A.	4	4	4	4	16	A
B.C.P.M.A.	1	3	2	2	8	D

TABLE D *Assessment of Termination Process*

	4a Final recommen- dation	4b Implemen- tation	4c Assist implemen- tation	4d More aid need	4e Follow- up	S	G
B.L.R.A.	4	1	2	2	0	9	C
N.A.A.S.	4	2	2	1	1	10	B
I.A.	4	4	4	4	4	20	A
B.C.P.M.A.	3	1	2	0	0	6	D

TABLE E *Aid Suppliers—Consolidated Assessment*

	i Qualification S G		ii User problems S G		iii Project S G		iv Termina- tion S G		Total score Max: 72	Final grading
B.L.R.A.	18	A	8	C	13	B	9	C	48	C
N.A.A.S.	17	B	10	B	12	C	10	B	49	B
I.A.	18	A	16	A	16	A	20	A	70	A
B.C.P.M.A.	14	C	3	D	8	D	6	D	31	D

INTERPRETATION OF ASSESSMENT

In view of the bias towards the image of the ideal management consultant, Industrial Administration could be expected to achieve the highest final score. But the subsidiary tables may help to identify some of the influences producing that result.

All four suppliers achieve a high score on qualifications to act as a supplier. The educational level of Industrial Administration is probably lower than that of B.L.R.A. and N.A.A.S. who emphasize their use of scientific specialists. The grading scale is not subtle enough to clarify the relevance of this difference. Industrial Administration is more concerned with the client's problems and state of mind than the other organizations appear to be. The manufacturers' association inevitably scores lower on client awareness and on resources because it is not designed to deal mainly with individual attitudes among its members, and members are not primarily concerned with ensuring that the association has ideal resources for all possible tasks. Both I.A. and N.A.A.S. provide some training in being an adviser and consultant.

Table B, concerned with the discovery of the user's problems, again places Industrial Administration in the lead because the firm is organized precisely for this purpose. A more subtle assessment procedure would reflect more faults in carrying out that basic function. The trade association scores badly because it does not carry out any initial survey of its members and is only too delighted to welcome any qualified firm into the fold. It has no opportunity for ensuring that all members of the firm that joins are concerned with the trade association, and most employees of member firms are totally unconcerned with the trade association. B.C.P.M.A. has arranged for one senior executive in each member firm to act as the firm's main contact on all matters. The association aims to carry out specific tasks, such as export market surveys and the preparation of its bi-annual buyers' guide, in ways acceptable to its members. N.A.A.S. seems to be a little too ready to deal with any relevant problem without worrying too much about the overall farm situation until it is invited to do so. N.A.A.S. does not hesitate to cost its recommendations, possibly because official grants are available for many of its proposals. The research association is not organized to undertake surveys of new members but it arranges a free visit each year by a technical officer to any member wanting to see him.

The consolidated assessment provides a basis for considering the difficulties faced by the aid suppliers.

Management consultants have many problems. Industrial Administration's status is related to its comparative smallness, and to its policy of working to the highest professional standards for high fees. It usually deserves its fees, but the fees are a condition of its achievement. The fees are too high to make them acceptable to every potential user of aid for every purpose.

A research association and a trade association need to resemble the best management consultants if they are to do their own special work properly. They need a thorough knowledge of each member and they would have to devote the same time and resources that Industrial Administration devotes to its clients to achieve that knowledge. If associations provided such services and charged higher subscriptions or fees, there would certainly be fewer members, but those services would be more valuable when used.

It seems clear that aid organizations are needed and that the demand is increasing. Trade associations, research associations, and various forms of consultancy have grown considerably in the past decade. Most aid is organized by private individuals and companies, but there is a very wide range of public aid services. Many organizations with other primary functons supply aid directly or indirectly.

None of these aid organizations has an entirely reliable source of income. The National Agricultural Advisory Service is never likely to be closed down, but as it is dependent on public funds, it can never be certain that it will receive the income it needs to do its work satisfactorily. Those functions change with the increasing technological and scientific complexity of agriculture, and N.A.A.S.'s growing involvement in management problems will extend the demand for specialists. The private management consultant is entirely dependent on clients, and most consultancy firms actively seek new clients. Trade associations, once established, seem to have less difficulty in obtaining a minimum income but face increasing uncertainty with every attempt to integrate associations. Research associations have often to persuade firms to join and to pay subscriptions, but receive a more secure part of their income from the Ministry of Technology. It is now more doubtful whether such official support will continue indefinitely.

A secure income for aid suppliers is necessary for them to be fully effective. Because real stability depends on secure capital from which an adequate income will flow, some capitalization scheme needs to be designed and implemented, which will combine public and private resources.

The aid suppliers are faced with unusual staffing problems. Some of their staff are inevitably rather amateur in approach because most of them are not trained and experienced directly in their aid work. Much more training is needed in the problems of being a supplier of aid, and also of managing an aid organization. The scientific interest of most aid suppliers should have encouraged a careful analysis of the necessary characteristics of consultants and the creation of helpful training procedures. There are many other aspects of this staffing problem, such as the need for greater mobility to ensure appropriate experience. The solution may lie in joint efforts rather than in the independent action of any one aid supplier.

Suppliers of aid show a surprising lack of concern with their own efficiency. Few of them assess their own performance, and few are usually concerned with improving it. This curious detachment from the problem that they are helping others to solve is partly due to the rapid growth of demand for their services. The best use of their skills is important and the people they employ cannot be wasted without serious cost to the national economy. Consultants need considerable independence and few want 'efficiency' if it involves restrictions or excessive bureaucracy. It is surprising that all the profit-seeking aid organizations are not closely controlled to maximize profit. The desirable forms of control would be difficult to evolve and no doubt every supplier exercises some control, consciously or otherwise. They need to pool experience and to debate efficiency criteria and methods so that each can evolve a suitable system.

THE ROLES OF USER AND SUPPLIER

The logical analysis that provided a framework for reviewing the findings also constitutes a basis for a role description of the user and the suplier of aid. If the two parties conform to the pattern of behaviour indicated by the analysis, the user is more likely to obtain optimum benefit from aid, and the supplier is more likely to provide optimum assistance. The supplier should be able to organize his operations efficiently and plan his organization's development if he can conform to the apparent requirements of his role.

The findings indicate the importance of aid as an essential element in a company's activities; it is not simply an insurance or optional extra. Aid should not be brought in or discarded at the whim of a manager. The distinctive characteristic of aid is specialized knowledge, based on a generalization of experience obtained from many organizations. The supplier of aid accumulates knowledge from a number of organizations and offers a distillation of that knowledge to the individual organization needing help.

Every specialist has a degree of independence because of his unique

234

fund of knowledge and skill. Management has to respect the independence of specialists, whether or not they are employed by the firm, if it is to obtain the full benefits of their expertise. The external specialist may be in a stronger position to protect his useful independence.

Aid is only likely to be successful when the managers of the organization using it recognize and follow an appropriate role. Making use of aid is not a passive activity; it requires the active collaboration of members of the user organization. The user must not be dominated by the aid supplier if he is to become self-reliant. Thus the user has to manage the process of aid and not allow the supplier to manage him.

All members of the user organization must supply all information required by the aid supplier and collaborate freely with him. Suspicion diminishes the productivity of aid; the internal policies and relationships of the user organization must be sufficiently harmonious to permit such unworried co-operation.

All proposals from the aid supplier must be very carefully examined and only accepted when management is satisfied that they will provide, at least on balance, benefit to the user organization. When unacceptable proposals are submitted, a thorough explanation of their faults ought to be given so that the supplier can consider other solutions. Aid proposals should only be rejected if they are genuinely unsatisfactory, not merely embarrassing or demanding.

The outcome of using aid should be to prevent the need for such aid recurring in the future. Some change in organization structure or policy is usually necessary and should be attempted.

The use of formal external aid should be reduced to a minimum. But aid opportunities existing within all the external relationships of the organization should be fully exploited before particular formal aids are introduced.

THE ROLE OF SUPPLIER OF AID

The supplier must ensure that he has relevant technical, managerial and psychological competence to deal with clients' problems. He is often unable to determine his competence until he has carried out a detailed analysis of the situation, as the potential user's own analysis is often unreliable.

The supplier must attempt to understand the problems the user faces in introducing aid and in working with an aid supplier.

235

The supplier must endeavour to provide the fullest possible information about the direct and indirect cost of aid before the potential user is charged for any service. If the aid is ostensibly a free service, the internal cost of proposed activities must be calculated and guidance given to the user.

The primary responsibility of the supplier is to enable the user to deal with his own problems without aid at the earliest appropriate moment.

INCREASING THE PRODUCTIVITY OF OUTSIDE HELP

Aid is most likely to be productive when it is linked to a major activity of the user organization. External aid as a form of insurance is almost certainly non-productive; it consumes the user organization's resources without necessarily providing benefits. Such a passive attitude is not truly analagous to insurance, for insurance is related to a known risk, whereas the organization that nominally belongs to a trade association, or merely allows certain publications to enter its offices, does not know what it is trying to achieve with those aids. Aid must be an additional tool for management, and management ought to know why it needs certain tools and how to use them. If it does not know then it ought to be helped to learn. The productivity of aid could be increased with more opportunities for the potential user to learn about the aid process. There is on occasions a considerable gap between the assumption of the aid user and the aid supplier. The supplier ought to take more initiative to reduce misunderstandings.

The most effective use of aid appears to occur when it is linked to a specific project being undertaken by the user organization or when the organization faces a new threat. Consultants are likely to be more productive, because they are more welcome, when management is faced with a difficulty that it has at least partially recognized. Trade associations flourish when members believe that they are faced by a major threat from proposed legislation. Research associations are most actively supported when genuine anxieties exist about manufacturers' ignorance in dealing with a particular process or material.

The introduction of help and its dissemination must be tackled by management as an overall organizational operation and not one restricted to a particular department or activity. It is the organization that receives aid from external sources, not only the individuals who are directly involved. There are of course degrees of involvement for different individuals and departments, but the introduction and implementation of outside help must be dealt with by management as a process affecting the entire organization.

Perhaps the greatest possibility of improving productivity lies within a concerted attempt to estimate costs and benefits, even when the aid is supplied without direct payment. The indirect costs of any organizational activity must be taken into account, even if it is no more than the cost of the work that an executive might have carried out if he had not spent time reading a particular report from an aid organization. Once costs are considered, management will examine aid more carefully and may try to put it to better use.

Chapter 12

Improving the Aid System

The final goal of this project was to prepare proposals 'for the optimum organization and integration of all types of outside help'. There are no grounds for expecting the existing range of aid suppliers to constitute a satisfactory structure, and the concept of 'the aid system' is somewhat optimistic as there are very few indications that a system exists. However, a system concept should help to link together the problems of the aid user and the aid supplier, and make it possible to consider solutions that may involve changes in the total aid situation.

There were four main stages in the aid user process and four main stages in the aid supply process. Although each logical analysis was made independently of the other, the four stages do run parallel to each other. The first stage for the user was concerned with the selection of problems requiring aid. One stage for the supplier was concerned with discovering the user's problems. Thus these two form a common dimension which one can label 'identifying need'.

The second stage of the user cycle was 'finding aid' whilst the second stage in the supplier's sequence was 'becoming qualified as a supplier of aid'. These two again link up, and perhaps the correct label for this dimension would be 'the need of the aid project'.

The third stage was concerned for the user with 'the internal organization for dealing with aid' and for the supplier with 'carrying out the aid project'. The dimension common to both can perhaps be labelled 'the conditions of aid success'.

The fourth stage for both the user and the supplier was concerned with 'terminating the aid relationship', and there is no need for any other label.

The existing aid system can be faulted when judged against these four primary aid requirements. There is no satisfactory method of identifying the need for external aid of an organization. Such an appraisal can only be initiated once it has called in the services of a supplier of aid, and it is then extremely difficult to be entirely objective in a situation that is inevitably biased towards the need for aid. There are many consultants and advisers who resist the temptation to propose aid in the same way that good doctors resist recommending medicine or surgery unless it is essential. However, it does seem desirable for some detached procedure to be followed that will indicate the probability that aid is needed. Ideally, managers ought to be able to apply such a technique independently of any other organization but it is then easy for them to ignore an indicator that is unacceptable. Therefore, some method of assessing efficiency and effectiveness is needed.

The 'needs of the project', the second common dimension, and 'the conditions of aid success', the third dimension, can only be properly investigated when the experience and knowledge of all aid suppliers can be systematically reviewed and interpreted. The existing aid system is defective because there is no common research organization that ensures the assimilation and exchange of information about supplying aid.

The fourth stage of termination and follow-up does appear to receive considerable attention from existing aid organizations in many cases, perhaps because of the prospect of further work being found necessary. But the final assessment of a project providing aid and the identification of the need for further aid are made by suppliers whose range of knowledge is inevitably limited. A production engineer may be fully satisfied with the overall performance of a manufacturing system and report that management has nothing more to worry about. It will be difficult to prevent management from believing that such approbation applies to marketing and finance as well as to production. Thus there are dangers of exaggeration of need for future aid and of failure to recognize the need for aid in unexpected areas of the organization. The aid system as a whole is not geared to making such comprehensive assessments although many management consultants will attempt it in their preliminary surveys.

The main opportunities for improvement clearly lie in three directions. The first concerns the improvement in the individual abilities of consultants and advisers of all kinds. The second opportunity will involve some positive collaboration between organizations supplying aid. The third source of improvement involves an appreciation of the proper role of government in the supply system.

INDIVIDUAL COMPETENCE

There are two main types of suppliers of aid. The first is the amateur, who operates on an informal basis and spends perhaps a very small part of his working life in giving help to others. He may not be aware of many occasions on which he gives aid because advice will be so closely linked with friendly conversation and casual professional chat. The other type of consultant and adviser is the professional who devotes himself exclusively to the identification of problems, and designs solutions to them. There is probably considerable movement from the amateur to the professional status, and the professional receives some form of training in his work. However, because there is such a widespread use of informal aid and because of the probable transition from amateur to professional, some general elementary training in the giving of aid would be desirable.

Such training should certainly be included in management courses of all kinds, and it could well form a topic for discussion at meetings of trade, research, and professional associations. The training would normally be very brief but it could usefully embrace a discussion of (a) the aid process, (b) the role of the aid supplier, (c) the need for continual advice by management, and (d) the wider effects of aid on the user organization. As to the professionals, such as full-time consultants, officials of associations, the staff of public aid bodies, and regular part-timers such as college lecturers, much more concern with the understanding of the aid process in training courses is necessary. Where no training is provided or undertaken, some training should certainly be promoted and awareness of the need to become competent in all aspects of the aid situation is most desirable.

Training in a formal sense can reduce the risks of bad work and help towards ensuring that the highest levels of achievement are reached. Continued improvement needs continual stimulus, which would be provided by a planned career that extends understanding through a widening range of experiences. Thus the consultant or official needs a combination of basic practical experience in the industry or profession that he is concerned with, followed by a period administering an aid organization, branching out into a period of work in government departments or research departments of colleges where appropriate, and then extending across a number of different aid organizations over the main span of his working life. This process involves some supervision of his work at all times, if only in the form of an occasional tutorial-discussion with a superior, but can extend into many other forms of training. It would also be helpful for each supplier to know more about other organizations supplying aid.

One purpose of this training is to improve the management of the supplier organizations, who are all faced with serious burdens and who lack any satisfactory opportunity to learn from one another's achievements and failures. There are a number of opportunities within particular types of supplier organization, such as the Management Consultants' Association and the Secretaries' Club (mainly for secretaries of trade and professional associations), and the activities of many professional institutes are relevant to the problems faced by suppliers of aid. But there is no central forum for the analysis of experience across different types of supplier organization and it is that wider interchange of knowledge that seems important.

LINKS BETWEEN ORGANIZATIONS

Training in its widest sense is merely one area in which there are opportunities for linking aid organizations. The confusion that exists in some industries and professions between the functions of associations and of public aid bodies indicates the need for a reappraisal of aid suppliers so that a more rational and integrated structure can be built up. The need for reform must not be exaggerated because proliferation may indicate that some confusion is a condition of effective aid. But some change is likely to be beneficial, provided the change is acceptable to all concerned. Many organizations supplying aid are in competition with one another, whatever their legal status, and there is no point in considering an imposed integration.

If voluntary methods only are desirable and sensible, there must be some incentive for suppliers to work together. That incentive will be found among the operating problems that they share, which may include obtaining clients, recruiting staff, obtaining information about appropriate methods and techniques, and seeking evidence for the efficacy of certain aid procedures.

There is another dimension to the integration problem. Should integration be attempted so as to bring together all suppliers of aid to one industry, such as agriculture, or should integration aim to bring together all management consultants or all advisory officers or all officials of associations or all civil servants working in public aid bodies? Fortunately, as the process of integration is to be voluntary, we do not have to recommend a single method. A simple framework for voluntary association and integration is needed and the exact form it takes will vary with the needs of those participating. On the whole, industrial boundaries seem to be preferred and desirable, so that we could hope for an integration of aid suppliers in iron or steel or in agriculture or in light engineering or in retail grocery more readily than in a wider meeting together of experts working in many dfferent industries. Perhaps industrial efforts will be more frequent and specialist links more occasional, probably emerging out of the intra-industrial integrations.

The suppliers of aid are unlikely to be more eager for adaptability than anyone else. Change can be encouraged by some positive action from the major users of aid. The survey of the use of productivity advisory services sponsored by the National Economic Development Office in 1966 showed that large firms used such services more than small ones and are more likely to do so in the future. Over 95 per cent of large firms in manufacturing and construction made use of these bodies. Government departments are themselves important users of aid, such as management consultants, as well as being suppliers through such bodies as the Export Services Branch of the Board of Trade. A few very large firms and a few government departments could readily state their views on the desirable qualifications, experience, and methods of working, of aid suppliers that they might engage in the future. There need be no compulsion on the firms and departments to abide by such a code of advisory practices, but private suppliers that hope for government and business contracts would clearly be unwise to ignore such opinions.

One particularly interesting possibility for promoting a more rational system of aid lies in the activities of numerous inspectors employed by public authorities to enforce certain legislation that lays down minimum standards in such matters as building, factory safety, and weights and measures, to say nothing of the more indefinable functions of education inspectors. These important officials are increasingly concerned with giving advice and less concerned with punitive measures that contain no promise of progress. Their work could be linked with other efforts to help management appreciate high standards and with sources of help that they might commend to those failing to achieve those standards.

THE ROLE OF GOVERNMENT

It would be easy to outline a comprehensive public system for supplying aid to all kinds of organizations. Such a scheme could be neat and economical and might achieve a great deal. But the evidence of this project suggests that such an official organization would be unacceptable to most users and, just as importantly, to many potential users. There is widespread suspicion of governmental activities, even when they are benevolent, and the vast range of government activities today is in itself a reason for opposing any further extension of government into the aid system. No political judgments are involved in such an appraisal; it is an attempt merely to note the existing atmosphere of relations between government and business. Even if the atmosphere were much more favourable, or even if a government believed that some rigid but efficient system should be introduced, the nature of the aid process suggests the advisability of privacy and multiplicity.

The private supplier of aid is not necessarily competent or efficient. The public aid body is not necessarily inefficient. The proper role of government is surely to encourage the better organization of aid and better performance by suppliers of aid, irrespective of their form of ownership. A great deal could be achieved by official support for a number of activities of potential value to all aid organizations. They would clearly include:

(1) Setting standards for the recruitment and training of all suppliers of aid, particularly those now under public ownership. Those existing public bodies that by this analysis ought to be 'denationalized', such as the National Agricultural Advisory Service, should be required as a condition of independence to conform to defined standards of management and organization and practice.

(2) Private suppliers of aid should be influenced by help and by money to want to improve their own performance. For example, a publicly sponsored body concerned with selection and training for public aid bodies could offer a similar service to private aid bodies. The

243

desirability of transfers between the private and the public sectors of aid is obvious, and such flexibility should ease the problem of career planning among small private aid organizations in particular. Government support for an information and research body into aid problems would also be useful and may well be acceptable to private firms. Some official system for identifying and registering competent consultants would be a valuable public service. Of course, it would not be easy to define an appropriate system but the experience of such organizations as the General Medical Council and the United Kingdom Architects Registration Council ought to be a valuable assistance to this project. The Institute of Management Consultants has already investigated the problem of assessing competence without using written examinations and there are numerous techniques now available for assessment that recognize the irrelevance of literary style to practical ability.

Another range of public support for improving aid would concern the management of aid supply organizations. Aid is not effective without an appropriate supporting organization, however good the individuals who try to deal with users' problems. An independent body that could appraise aid organizations and undertake some form of regular inspection would be to the public advantage. The initiative of the British Institute of Management in building up a register of management consultants, supported by information from clients, is a good beginning but is clearly not foolproof. The great opportunities for change in qualitative work mean that a once-and-for-all registration is unsatisfactory.

On a more positive approach, some public scheme that would enable competent and experienced aid organizations to increase their financial independence would make a major contribution to the future standards of aid. Perhaps a levy on the income of aid suppliers that could be invested in unit trusts or group life assurance policies could begin to provide a degree of capital growth that in turn would generate an income to enable aid suppliers to survive periods of bad business or to enjoy the luxury of turning down inappropriate assignments.

There does not appear to be any case for public subsidies to preferred organizations, and it is unfortunate that the NEDO report surveying users' attitudes led to an increase in government grant to such bodies as the British Institute of Management. If a supplier of aid is competent in every respect, particularly in planning its own existence and survival, management should want to use it. Perhaps government policy of subsidizing users of management consultants, in its pilot scheme for small firms in Bristol and Glasgow that started in 1968, is more sensible. But the £500,000 allocated for that scheme would have produced many more significant improvements in the supply of aid as a whole if it had been devoted to the public services outlined in the preceding paragraphs.

There are as always special problems about small firms. Perhaps all that need be said here is that some small firms do make use of all known forms of aid. It is not necessarily a problem of size if managers do not seek outside help for their internal problems that they cannot tackle successfully themselves. But the small firm does epitomize the general problem of using aid for the first time and it is essential for this aspect to be taken into account in any changes that may occur. The condition of successful aid is freedom of choice by management. Compulsory aid is meaningless. The complexity of the aid structure suggests that guidance is needed about the best form of aid and the most appropriate source of aid. There are now a number of opportunities for simplifying the search for aid, especially the Industrial Liaison Service of the Ministry of Technology. But it cannot reach every firm in the country and tends to concentrate on technical problems of manufacturing. Every firm does have some relationship with outside organizations, and most have contacts with one form of aid organization, whether it is a trade association or a professional institute or a technical college or a management consultant or a public aid body. Whatever the initial contact, each of the aid organizations should be encouraged to make sure that an enquiry is passed on to a central source of information that will arrange for the most appropriate aid organization to make contact with the potential user. Perhaps public money could properly be used to encourage and finance such a link organization, as an offshoot of the Industrial Liaison Service. If aid organizations were to collaborate more closely on the lines suggested earlier, such exchange of enquiries from potential users would emerge without the need for public funds. Even if public funds are provided, there is of course no need for public interference in the work of the collaborating suppliers.

THE PROBLEMS OF THE AID ORGANIZATION
The suppliers of aid do face considerable difficulties and the short-

comings of the present aid system is not due to incompetence or inertia only. In the course of this project, I obtained an opportunity to learn of their problems on a wider basis.

In November 1967 I was invited to talk to a group of members of the Chartered Institute of Secretaries who worked in trade associations, research associations, and professional institutes, about some of my views in the light of this research project. I later published my impressions of that meeting in an article in the March 1968 issue of *The Chartered Secretary*.

I suggested that the very great number of associations and institutes reflected a growing need of managers and members of professions to work together for a number of reasons. I thought that these organizations were potentially of great importance as sources of improved performance in many fields. They were faced with a number of complex management problems that needed to be solved if the potential benefits were to be fully exploited.

One of these problems concerned their internal government: difficulties arose from having very few full-time officials and many members. The members involved in the work of associations and institutes were usually eminent and busy people, but the majority of members seemed apathetic. There were opportunities for conflict and misunderstanding between members and the officials, because many members expected high levels of service for very low subscriptions. All these difficulties were increased by the existence of many associations, some of whom competed with one another.

I suggested that the solution would emerge with agreement to give much more power to officials and much stricter definition of members' powers and duties. The members would act as the 'policy makers' and the officials would become more professional and competent through the exercise of greater power. Such changes could happen only with a radical increase in the incomes of associations, and associations should earn larger incomes by charging for services and by extending very greatly the range of services they could provide and could charge for.

This brief article aroused some interest and led to a proposal for a conference to examine the problem of the management of associations and institutes. A one-day conference was held in London on September 26, 1968 of which I was the chairman. It was attended by forty-eight officials of associations and institutes, and was concerned with four main problems: (1) the organization of associations and the division of work between members and officials; (2) finance; (3) the network of associations and the problems of duplication and competition; and (4) future opportunities for the continuing study of the problems, and for changing the existing situation. Each person present completed a brief questionnaire indicating his views on a number of proposals that had been made, such as the need for training of association officials, the extension of services provided by associations for payment, and the possibilities of establishing a consultancy service for associations linked to a research programme into their management problems.

The conference was intended to be a forum to explore those problems and few precise conclusions emerged. My impression was that many difficulties existed but the incidence of difficulty varied with the size and type of organization.

Among the points stressed in discussion were:

(1) *The career of the association official.* There was no recognized qualification or training that ensured the initial competence of a new official. An increasing number had either a degree or a qualification in law, secretarial practice, or accountancy. An employment centre was desirable, concerned with the recruitment, selection, training, and promotion between associations of officials.

(2) *Members and officials.* The motives that encouraged members to join the committees or councils of their association provided no guarantee of competence or seriousness. Some members believed that their organization existed mainly to provide an opportunity to meet people with similar interests, and they cultivated friendships that were not necessarily linked to serious occupational problems. Others liked the glory of office, and changes in structure were sometimes delayed or frustrated simply because a few members did not wish to lose office nor give up free visits to London for meetings. One interesting proposal suggested that councils should be organized on a cabinet basis, with each member being responsible for a particular function, working closely with a full-time official. Such a structure existed in some institutes in the USA and it was suggested that this principle was followed already informally.

(3) *Finance.* This universal problem took many forms. One or two organizations, particularly the very old established and the very new

in such popular fields as computers, seemed to have some embarrassment of riches. The vast majority of associations and institutes could not meet the needs of members without increasing subscriptions, and increases discouraged recruitment of new members. It was suggested that incomes might be increased by activities for which members paid separately from subscriptions, such as courses, conferences, and exhibitions, and it was agreed that many other such opportunities existed that would be most profitable if several associations collaborated. Another suggestion was for an investment policy that ensured better returns on existing capital and led to capital growth, perhaps through unit trusts or group life assurance policies.

Two further conferences were held in December 1968 and January 1969, and I was asked to continue such meetings and to endeavour to provide some of the joint services. The officials could not undertake such tasks as their normal work was too demanding.

THE INCREASING VARIETY OF NEEDS

The administrators and technologists of aid are of fundamental importance in making aid more effective. But there is no certainty that the most enlightened bureaucracy will be able to meet the many changing needs that require help. The activities of most aid suppliers imply a common level of achievement among firms, a universal average for which their services are ideally suited. Beyond that level, difficulties arise. Even the most ambitious management consultant declines to help a firm that seems too near to bankruptcy. The research association is seldom concerned with the non-research firm. The trade association does not recognize the incompetent or the unambitious firm that is not a member. The public aid body is scarcely interested in finding out what use is made of its advice—its job is to churn out the information, not to overcome the difficulties faced by firms in applying it.

The user of one form of aid often does not know of other forms, particularly if they are unusual. The problem of estate duty in farming is not properly a N.A.A.S. problem. The man who so glorifies independence that he sets up his own business may believe that seeking external aid conflicts with his principles. He needs aid but the aid 'system' cannot communicate with him. Many other firms need aid and a major symptom of their need is their ignorance of available aid. How can aid be brought into contact with the needy?

The answer can only be through one of the firm's existing external contacts. For those are a condition of its existence, and they may influence the firm's behaviour. Customers and suppliers of goods are the unavoidable outsiders. The suppliers usually will be fewer and more identifiable than customers, and will have a vested interest in the prosperity of their customers. The Inland Revenue's interest in all organizations and individuals should also be used to effect a link with those possibly in need of aid. Tax allowances may be too much to ask for, but perhaps a scheme of grants for the proper maintenance of a firm's accounts may bring a little order into its affairs, and also provide the inspector of taxes with the annual return he seeks—something on the lines of the N.A.A.S. management grant schemes. If necessary, the suppliers of goods might contribute to the costs of such a scheme, as many pay to obtain an opinion of a customer's credit status.

There is no possibility of a simple procedure that will ensure that all firms assess their need for aid and then use it. But it should be possible to apply a range of techniques to ensure that every firm has an opportunity of tapping the vast resources of aid that now exist, through any of its external contacts. The NEDO guide to aid suppliers is too crude and biased to provide all the information required to select the most relevant source of help, but that should be possible with a more elegant information and appraisal system. The small firm, and the insecure firm of any size, needs a regular adviser who can listen and comfort and, occasionally, provide an immediate link with professional aid. Such independent and confidential advisers could be a boon to small firms, and such work could employ the increasing numbers in business education and in active retirement. A small annual fee for advisers should be agreed, and they should be offered training by colleges and the Industrial Liaison Service.

There is an undoubted conflict between the needs of an efficient economy and the freedom of the individual firm to 'go to the dogs' if the owner so wishes. But the conflict cannot be easily resolved. A ruthless policy of economic exposure may dispose of the incompetent eventually but that extreme solution involves considerable personal and social cost. Protectionism is equally costly and undesirable. There is no acceptable alternative to a general stimulation of managements to seek higher standards, whatever their size or ambitions. Official encouragement may help, but example is much more effective: deter-

249

mination to make government more efficient, and to ensure public aid bodies appraise their own performance, would be further contributions to action. But the decimation of the Inland Revenue would be the greatest possible liberation, although the major tax changes required to do that involve wider issues.[1]

ASSOCIATIONS AND CONSULTANTS

The myriad of aid services available to management could be placed on a continuum. At one end would be the association, consisting of numerous firms seeking to find the highest common factor on which they can all agree as a basis for joint activities. At the other end is the management consultant, devoting his energies exclusively to the problems of an individual firm. The two extremes are linked through the consultant's inevitable dependence on other firms to provide him with the knowledge and experience that enable him to serve his current client.

It would be unfortunate if these extremes disappeared in any improvement of the aid system. There are some needs that are common to all similar firms, but there are others that are peculiar to the individual, at least to the extent that effective therapy requires individual attention. Perhaps the aim should be to move the firm out of the care of the consultant into the sustained support of his peers in a continuing association that should concentrate more and more on attempting to reduce the dangerous uncertainties of the future.

The largest firms have special responsibilities and opportunities for improving the aid situation. They have vast influence on the associations they join and on the consultants they use, especially if they act together. The giant firms could make a rapid beginning to studies for greater collaboration between all types of aid available to an industry or an economic sector, and they could initiate a concern for appraising the performance of aid bodies. Their power imposes public duties on them, and their unique status would enable them to achieve more in this field than any other influential body. But they ought also to act out of self-interest: they cannot operate successfully without the support of efficient suppliers and customers, and the aid system provides the greatest opportunities for raising overall economic performance.

[1] See page 260.

This study has been concerned with aid in an advanced economy, but there are many obvious lessons to be learned by developing countries from this experience. In a way, foreign aid is an attempt to introduce a general aid system quickly where it has not yet emerged. All developing countries would benefit immensely from the extension of foreign aid into domestic aid, and the foreign aid should aim to leave behind at least a framework of essential associations and consultants. I have discussed elsewhere[1] the immensely important role in economic development of large foreign companies, and they could do a great deal to promote links between trade and aid by working through the aid system at home and overseas.

As an introduction to this book, I listed some questions that the reader might usefully ask himself whilst reading the evidence and analysis of this enquiry. I have provided my answers in my conclusions; it may help to summarize the knowledge and views provided by describing an ideal external aid system in universal terms.

THE IDEAL AID SYSTEM

(1) *It would provide aid to all types of organizations in society.*

Manufacturing industry employs less than half of the working population today, and its achievements depend on optimum performances in all other sectors of the economy;

(2) *It would provide all types of aid*—occasional or continual, dealing with technical, financial, managerial, and human problems of the organization;

(3) *It would ensure that the best source of qualified aid is available for every need;*

(4) *It would provide the potential user with an objective method for assessing his need for aid;*

(5) *It would assist users to derive maximum benefit from aid* through encouraging appropriate arrangements within the user organization;

(6) *It would provide an evaluation and follow-up service to users* to ensure that the aid provided was adequate and effective;

(7) *It would ensure that the process of supplying and using aid was constantly studied and improved* through research and development programmes;

[1] See my *Management and World Development*, 1967. Also *Consultancy in Overseas Development*, by C. Young, 1968.

251

(8) *It would provide links with aid supply and use throughout the world;*

(9) *It would ensure that aid was based on the latest available knowledge* from the physical and social sciences and from their application;

(10) *It could seek its own disappearance* through raising the level of management and organizational effectiveness so high that external aid becomes unnecessary.

Chapter 13

Implications and Opportunities

A number of wider issues have emerged during this long project, which require some consideration, even though they are not strictly part of the projects's goals, because they indicate the direction for future research. No project is complete without considering the need for further studies.

THE NATURE OF ORGANIZATION

The conventional concept of organization suggests an independent, integrated structure of people and activities, floating like a balloon in a vague area of space. As a result, the study of organization has been largely devoted to internal operations, with only cursory acknowledgement that boundaries and environments exist.

This project has demonstrated that the organization is in fact closely related to an active environment. If the organization is looked at primarily from the outside a different conception emerges which may be significant.

Organizations possess relatively permanent and relatively temporary resources. Machinery and buildings may last for many years. Raw materials used in the machines, and the products manufactured with them, may only stay in the firm for a few hours before they are transferred to customers. Employees stay longer than raw materials but not always as long as machinery. The 'permanent' resource is more lasting and more essential to the survival of the whole organization. The 'temporary' is intrinsically transitional and departmental.

The acquisition, processing, and distribution of resources constitutes an important social function. The organizations concerned provide some structural stability to a society that is not integrated by design. But none of the organizations is necessarily stable, and any may disappear, for many reasons. The function of organizations is to provide nodal points in society that are the meeting places for varied resources. The task of managers is to see that the nodal points operate effectively, and that effectiveness has to be judged by the journey of resources through them and by the transformations brought about by the organization, leading to an addition of value.

In addition to a temporary-permanent continuum, the organization of the firm has an essential-superficial continuum. At one extreme is the essential nucleus. The nucleus consists of the special attributes that characterize each organization. Distinctiveness may be due to the personal skill of one or more managers or a peculiar technological advantage, or the special service provided by the organization, or it may be a function of geographical location. There may be many similar organizations in existence, but each is distinguishable by its peculiar attribute.

The other extreme of the continuum is represented by the host of appendages that are linked to the nucleus and sometimes penetrate into its structure. The nucleus is a collection of separable parts temporarily agglutinated. Each part is linked with at least one external organization or individual, and can be detached from its nucleus by this outside force. The two parts of an organization are interwoven very closely, firstly by performance (machines are useless without materials) and secondly by changes in relationship (the appendage may be introjected into a nucleus, and part of the nucleus may be transformed into an appendage, as when a component ceases to be made in the factory and is 'bought-out' from a supplier, and vice versa).

There are only a few essential internal constituents of a firm. Its needs and the availability of external resources change over time, and the 'foreign policy' of the firm must be regularly and systematically reviewed.

There is a third continuum of 'interorganizational relationships', extending from competition, via bargaining and co-optation, to coalition. These constitute procedures for gaining support from the organizational environment; the selection of one or more of these is a strategic problem. 'It is here that the element of rationality becomes extremely important, for in the order treated above, these relational processes represent increasingly "costly" methods of gaining support in terms of decision-making power.'[1]

[1] *Organizational Goals and Environment. Goal-Setting As An Interaction Process,* J. D. Thompson and J. McEwen, American Sociological Review, February 1958.

Many of these 'relational processes' are informal and unbureaucratic. 'Unitary bureaucratic structure is just one way of consciously concerting action to achieve a goal . . . We need a theory of confederative organization or organization alliance. These interorganizational patterns . . . are the results of efforts to co-ordinate autonomous agencies, to unite effort without the authority of formal hierarchy and employee status . . . Delegation is largely lateral rather than vertical and voluntary rather than mandatory. It is heavily adaptive to the technical authority of experts . . . To comprehend the shift to interorganizational administration and leadership would be to understand better the changing nature of administration inside the giant organization where large size and deepening expertise have fragmented command. Since many complex single organizations resemble the more structured interorganizations, there is no sharp line between the conceptions appropriate to such formal organization and those necessary to the interorganizational scene.'[1]

This approach suggests that internal delegation, the growth of expertise and professionalism, and the increasing size of organizations leads to an organizational condition of permissive federalism that forms part of continua extending outside the organization. The optimum location of technical services—within a department, within an organization, or within a social agency accessible to a number of organizations —is a matter of convenience that should be conditioned by the nature of the technology concerned and the degree of use made of it on one organizational site, and not by considerations of ownership, the desire for isolation, or confused conceptions of competitiveness. The result should be a reduction of expense to the individual organization (and to society) and, more importantly, there should be much greater opportunity for management to concentrate on exploiting the unique characteristics of the organization.[2]

MANAGEMENT

Organization provides the framework for management. If the framework is not what it appears to be by common-sense standards, the functions of management may also be different.

The most obvious and pressing function of management is to ensure

[1] *Interorganisation Patterns in Education*, B. J. Clark, Administrative Science Quarterly, September 1965.

[2] See my 'Organizations and Society' in *Management International Review*, 1968 2/3.

that the organization operates efficiently now and that it will continue to be effective into the distant future. Managers therefore need to study, plan, and control internal activities with great care. But the beginning and end of any economic activity extends back to suppliers of raw materials and forward to the final consumers. In between, other external influences, such as trade unions and competitors, will also affect performance.

If the manager is to achieve his organizational goals, he is compelled to devote considerable effort to these external influences, some of which of course are benevolent. As they do not obviously link up with the operations inside the factory or office, they receive less attention than manufacturing and manning. External relationships demand more skilled behaviour from managers, if only because they do not know the outsiders as well as the insiders. Nor do managers usually receive adequate training in 'foreign affairs' and their efficiency may be lower in that external area.

But the external relationships are vastly important because they provide the major opportunity for improving efficiency and effectiveness. The intrusion of the outsider challenges the organization's domestic stability and its potential complacency. The external contact may demonstrate the superior achievement of the organization—and that status is worth knowing—but it is more likely to reveal the need for improvement. There is no evidence that exhortation will cause improved performance. Incompetent managers usually are ignorant of better methods and of ways of introducing and exploiting them. Managers who have allowed the organization to become inefficient are unlikely to transform themselves either through shame or good intentions.

They will need external help, not internal revolution. Thus the organizations set up to ease management problems are of major practical importance. They are also theoretically significant because they change the dimensions of organization and of management.

Our studies of management behaviour indicate the curious importance of the firm's relations with competitors and with government agencies. The 'folklore of capitalism' describes business as a battlefield in which the brave entrepreneur succeeds only by fighting competitors and governments. In real life, the entrepreneur devotes considerable efforts to restricting the battle with fellow manufacturers, despite legal bans on price agreements. They exchange information, compare performance, undertake industry-wide advertising, sponsor joint training schemes, finance joint market research programmes, and collaborate in exporting. They may be secretive about research and new products, but once on the market, a product is immediately known to competitors. Perhaps already news of future intentions is being exchanged to avoid wasteful duplication, and competition is likely to be more widely reduced with increasing technological complexity and the larger average size of firms resulting from mergers.

Consumer competition will continue—the consumer will still decide which product or service to buy, and the firm that does most to discover and meet the consumer's interests is more likely to succeed. But the obstacles to competition as understood in classical economics are so vast as to make the concept of competition meaningless and dangerously misleading.

Belief in 'competition' has created a conflict between the businessman's thinking and his actions, and such irrationality will complicate even further his understanding of the firm's environment and of aid organizations in particular. The suppliers of aid will achieve more for themselves and for their users if they tackle environmental problems seriously and imaginatively.

Every external relationship involves a reduction in the autonomous power of the organization. Each organization is involved in a complex network of relationships, any of which may control the prosperity of the focal organization. This is not necessarily a threat to the organization. Usually, management will be wise to know and use all appropriate outside resources. But it is important to recognize the practical and theoretical consequences.

As most of the firm's assets, opportunities, and threats are not under the complete control of management, the source of ultimate power cannot logically reside within the firm. Thus the concept of the management hierarchy is false. The external perspective suggests that the hierarchical structure should be laid on its side. It then becomes merely a network of roles, each with varying power and duties. Each role is part of a larger network that extends outside the firm—very far outside in some cases. The 'correct' area of the firm will vary according to the particular criterion of relevance. The legal area will be different from the purchasing area, and the financial area will differ from the

I

research area. The constant element in the many areas will be the firm's nucleus.

Thus the obvious but neglected truth that power is not concentrated but shared out, in unequal degrees, among all members of an organization, has to be extended—power is also distributed among all who contribute to the provision of resources for the firm's use and to the distribution of its output. A major task of management is to understand this widely dispersed array of resources and to determine appropriate procedures for learning about them and controlling those of value to the organization.

BUSINESS - GOVERNMENT RELATIONS
The major external constraint on the organization's independence is government, and relations between business and government are an important condition of achievement in modern societies.[1]

There is a sharp difference between the normal daily working relationships of business and government and the occasional major conflict over such issues as new taxation and nationalization. With public expenditure at almost half of the gross national product, government in all its guises regulates the general level of demand and is itself the most important customer of many privately-owned firms and indirectly of their suppliers.

Apart from its buying activities, government supports or maintains a wide range of aid bodies. The need for business and government to work together led to official encouragement for the establishment of trade associations. Government initiative created research associations, and the latest development of government aid policy was the 1968 scheme to subsidize the use by small firms of management consultants.

Yet this is no record of planned evolution. It is a history of fits and starts, with movements extending aid paralleled by movements threatening it. The consultants subsidy scheme was followed a few months later by the announcement of a policy aimed at reducing the activities of research associations. This confusing situation is inevitable when so many ministries are involved. The study group on productivity services sponsored by NEDO accepted that the interdepartmental consultative machinery in this field was satisfactory. It would be interesting to see the evidence for that surprising view.

[1] One outstanding example of management's attitude to government was contained in Mr Lazell's statement in Beecham's 1968 annual report.

Governments have traditionally been negative and inhibiting towards business, with occasional bouts of positive neutrality in which they offer grants and allowances for favoured policies. The negative, inspectoral role began with the first Factory Act of 1801. It had become a little more positive by the end of the century, with the complicated formula for grants to research associations as its highest point. But since 1914, the revolutionary increase in governmental economic power has made these gentlemanly manoeuvres absurd. For example, in an age of positive government planning throughout the world, many more positive actions to expand investment in development areas apart from offering grants and information are possible and would be acceptable to business.

This is not a problem of a Labour government in relation to private firms. The conflicts between nationalized industries and government since 1964 have been prodigious, and conflicts between Tory governments and private firms have a long history.

Trade associations now devote much of their energies to fighting unpopular official policies, such as the Selective Employment Tax. At the same time, they participate in official committees with civil servants and ministries. For example, the British Chemical Plant Manufacturers' Association has been involved in several enquiries by the Ministry of Technology since 1964 into the import and export of chemical plant, and the desirable size of the industry needed to reduce imports. It seems that little has been accomplished, and even the facts of international trading are still in dispute. The government has been pressing for special expansion, and the Association has been satisfied that normal management policies for growth are adequate. Meanwhile, time is passing, investment is taking place, and probably the industry will be large enough to cope with the next boom without an excessive increase in imports. All the committees may have been unnecessary.

More consultation is needed before official policies are decided; policies now are often formulated by civil servants that then have to be modified in the light of trenchant criticism from industry and commerce. The protective energies of trade associations could be put to positive use, as in wartime, with more benefit to all, for government is still very ignorant of management's problems, and the countervailing power of business is so great that unacceptable government policies will in time be defeated.

The clearest example of fundamental ignorance and conflict arises from economic policies aimed at reducing inflation and achieving a surplus on the international balance of payments. Those aims have led to a series of actions by governments since 1945 that have created sudden and unexpected obstacles to growth and to achieving management goals. These minor economic crises can be predicted with some difficulty, but the exact form of the corrective actions cannot be foreseen.

All the four sectors of the economy involved in this study have suffered from changes in government policies. The farmers have an annual ordeal of price reviews, and the results will largely determine their net incomes and their animal and crop policies. The building industry is one of the most vulnerable to changes in the economic climate because public authorities are responsible for half of the annual investment in construction. Manufacturing industry is currently favoured, with the hope of stimulating exports, but the motor car industry, for example, suffers from changes in demand arising from changes in purchase tax that can now be introduced at any time. The distributive trades suffer from purchase tax changes, the Selective Employment Tax, and problems arising from town planning policies.

These policies, inevitably seen by management as punishments, exist side by side with numerous other official schemes to modernize the economy, increase exports, reduce inflation, and develop backward areas of the country. Business managers take part in the work of many official bodies, particularly the economic development committees for all major industries. But that does not prevent serious new burdens descending without warning from the Treasury and the National Board for Prices and Incomes.

A fresh approach is urgently needed that will neutralize the tax burden, integrate government and company planning, and mobilize all sources of aid to management for promoting better performance. That programme must begin with taxation, which has become so absurd that some revolutionary change is needed. The only sensible solution is to tax the main public companies and to abolish all other forms of taxation. The tax on companies should be a proportion of their Stock Exchange value. In 1966 2,535 companies had a total market value of £44,448 millions. A tax of 33 per cent would have provided the revenue needed in that year by all public authorities. And the companies would

260

be free of tax on all their income after the tax on capital value had been met. Of course there would be major price increases—but consumer incomes would increase proportionately, and exports could be exempted from the price increases.[1]

Each of the tax-paying companies would have one government inspector to negotiate its tax liability and to approve its price increases. Special dispensations could be built in to those discussions so that company and government plans could be dovetailed. When company performance was comparatively or absolutely unsatisfactory, appropriate aid could be offered through public and private aid bodies, with immediate tax benefits.

Trade associations and research associations could be encouraged to co-ordinate their work round the framework of these 2,500 companies, extending outwards to their major suppliers and sub-contractors.

Business and government are inevitably partners in modern economies. It is time that the partnership became positive and creative and ceased to be a wasteful conflict through behaviour based on dead statuses and functions.

MANAGEMENT RESEARCH

The limitation on achievement of this project is due in part to the shortcomings of the investigators but also to the inherent difficulties of research into management. I have tried to describe our methods in Appendix 2 in some detail in case they may help beginners.

There is a need for many more studies in the field of inter-organizational relationships. They are crucial to any policy concerned with accelerating economic progress. They may be important to the solution of management problems in any firm and may provide the opportunity for a major development in management theory. Thus some attempt to suggest future programmes and methods of research seems justified.

Research is only possible within certain appropriate conditions. For studies of relations between organizations, research extending over long periods of time seems necessary: the relationships can only be discerned in actions, and the extent and consequences of actions can only be known by tracing them through space and time. All organizations undertake regular 'operations', and some unusual 'projects'. These

---

[1] See my 'Tax Reform—or Revolution?' in *European Business*, July 1968.

operations and projects provide the framework of organizational studies and of management research; by studying them over time, an objective model of the organization can be constructed. The methods and problems in achieving those activities provide the raw material for the study of management.

The inter-relationships have to be studied in their own right because they have economic and social consequences as well as consequences for the organizations immediately involved. These relationships have created direct and indirect link organizations, such as trade associations and insurance companies. The pattern of such inter-relationships for a group of organizations, in particular geographical areas, would indicate sources of maximum and minimum conflict which could then be studied and controlled.

None of this should be abstract research but very closely related to the normal activities of organizations. The research worker will have a distinctive role but it will involve him in training managers to be their own investigators—because good managers have to resemble investigators whether or not they are involved in research.

The strategy of this area of research requires the research worker to begin outside the primary organizations, with studies of the region and district where the firms are located, then the link organizations, and finally the firms, from the perspective initially of their external relationships.

The financing of such a research programme should begin with grants from firms and link organizations to an independent research trust. But the programme should be useful and self-financing after a few years, and could gradually extend into a separate consultancy service.

The ultimate goal must be an experimental programme. Organizations would be persuaded to act in accordance with defined goals and plans, and their consequences predicted, observed and measured. Preferably these organizations should be operating normally but if necessary special experimental organizations should be set up. They would in both cases have to be matched with control groups. The formulation of precise hypotheses is a major task and cannot be attempted here, but clearly they will be concerned very much with the consequences of policies of isolation from society or policies of integration with society.

SOCIOLOGY

Society comprises individuals, organizations, and social institutions who are not integrated together in accordance with a plan. Society is inherently chaotic so that achievement is the product of the initiative of individuals, many of whom are managers. Few of these managers are genuine dictators, although their style of management may reveal dictatorial ambitions. In practice, they rely increasingly on voluntary collaboration based on an awareness of shared benefits. Modern society is an anarchy, in the creative sense of the word.

The relationships between individuals and organizations, and between all organizations, are thus crucial to social stability and progress. This vital social mechanism cannot be analysed without a more specific concept that describes the search and choice processes involved in contacts with other organizations. A useful beginning has been made with the concept of the 'organizations-set' by Evan.[1]

Borrowing the concept of 'role-set' formulated by Merton—the complex of roles and role relationships that the occupant of a given status has by virtue of occupying that status—Evan proposes a similar term to describe the pattern of interactions of an organization with other organizations in its environment.

The point of reference he calls 'the focal organization'. Relations between focal organizations are mediated by (a) the role-sets of its boundary personnel (e.g. top management and sales representatives), (b) the flow of information, (c) the flow of products or services, and (d) the flow of personnel. He postulates a number of useful explanations that flow from an analysis of the organization-set of a focal organization. He concentrates on the impact of organization-set on decision making, and takes as his main variable in a group of possible hypotheses the degree of autonomy in decision-making. He implies that this type of autonomy is an important organization characteristic.

Perhaps because of his legal interests, Evan restricts the application of his analysis to relatively few organizational operations, mainly concerned with problems of conflict: disputes over contracts, the joint efforts of dealers against manufacturers, and the conflict of roles when people belong to two different but related organizations, such as employees who are also members of the trade union negotiating with

[1] *Towards A Theory of Inter-Organizational Relations,* William M. Evan. *Management Science.* Vol 11, No 10, August 1965, 217-230.

the employer. He fails to appreciate that the relations between organizations affect all the activities of the focal organization, not only those on the periphery.

The 'organization-set' concept implies that we must begin with an organization and study the relationships that emerge from it. There is, however, a no-man's land of inter-organization, represented by a network of activities that link many organizations together. Organizations are linked through their functional activities and not through the organization, which has no relevant material entity. Each department links itself with many other organizations in its daily activities. Each executive creates his own external relationships, some of which are more or less permanent, some temporary, some almost invisible because of their brevity.

Every external relationship involves a reduction in the autonomous power of the organization. Each organization is involved in a complex network of relationships, any of which may be of decisive significance to the prosperity of the focal organization. This is not necessarily a threat to the organization. Usually, management will be wise to know and use all appropriate outside resources. But it is important to recognize the practical and theoretical consequences and these have already been discussed.[1]

There is an urgent need for sociology to provide much more positive guidance to society in dealing with its problems. That guidance can only be based on knowledge of how that society works. The sterility of sociology is due to many causes. One is an inadequate concern with the living realities of action. Action in advanced societies is through organizations, and the network of relationships between organizations constitutes the most solid evidence of social structure. Perhaps management studies have some contribution to make to sociology to reciprocate all that they have drawn from sociology.

Social scientists are increasingly concerned with the application of the knowledge they acquire. They have identified many reasons for the failure to use sociological knowledge even if they have not discovered many ways in promoting application.[2] A great deal of knowledge has

---

[1] A review of the literature on this approach is given in 'The Evolution of Organizational Environment', Shirley Terreberry, *Administrative Science Quarterly,* March 1968. Her attempts to extend the concepts of Emery and Trist described in Appendix 2 are unfortunately unhelpful.

[2] See for example the unpublished 'Bibliography on Social Science Policy', Loughborough University, Centre for Utilization of Social Science Research, June 1968.

been applied in education, the social services, and prisons. But even in those fields, little has been accomplished. The situation in industry and commerce is infinitely worse although there may be some outstanding exceptions within a few companies.

It is popular to talk of managers as 'change agents' and of course to some extent they are. But change working through millions of individuals is slow. Some intermediate agency is needed to transmit knowledge to managers more speedily. That agency exists in the organizations created to help managers, especially those organizations set up by managers themselves. They have the greatest chance of acceptability and achievement. The improvement of those organizations may provide the best means of social progress. Helping to improve them may provide some of those new laboratories that sociology so urgently needs.

The Pilot Project

It was agreed with D.S.I.R. that the pilot project should seek answers to the following questions:

(1) What external help is available to firms in the Kingston area?

(2) To what extent is it used? How many firms use it? How much is it used by those that do?

(3) Which firms have special administrative arrangements for exploring for information and help and for making it available to the management?

(4) Which firms use such help and with what results?

(5) What are the characteristics of the firms that have such arrangements and use such help? (a) Are they larger than the others? (b) Are their markets and products of a similar kind? (c) Have they similar technologies which differ from the others? (d) Do their managers differ in background, education and training? (e) Are they more efficient? (f) Are they more stable?

I obtained from the Ministry of Labour a list of (a) all firms in their Kingston area employing more than fifty people and (b) a random selection of firms employing fewer than fifty people. The total number of firms in the Kingston area was 1,647. We interviewed 216 firms, including twenty-seven organizations supplying aid, most of whom were not located within the Kingston area. Table A shows a comparison between the structure of local industry, according to the Standard Industrial Classification, and the make-up of our sample.

The number of interviews was based on the time available within the twelve months at our disposal. I estimated that we could hope to interview 280 firms altogether, representing different sizes and industries. It was also planned to include a more thorough investigation of a few organizations so as to increase the qualitative value of the information obtained from only one visit.

TABLE A *Comparison of Local Industry and Firms Interviewed*

MANUFACTURING	Area Total	%	Interviews	%
Food, Drink and Tobacco	18	1	5	2.3
Chemicals and Allied Industries	15	1	5	2.3
Metal Manufacture	3	—	1	.5
Engineering and Electrical Goods	190	12	44	20.2
Shipbuilding and Marine Engineering	7	—	3	1.2
Vehicles	22	1	5	2.3
Metal Goods not elsewhere specified	47	3	5	2.3
Textiles	2	—	1	.5
Leather, Leather Goods and Fur	1	—	—	—
Clothing and Footwear	9	—	1	.5
Bricks, Pottery, Glass, Cement, etc	13	1	—	1
Timber, Furniture, etc	32	2	4	1.9
Paper, Printing and Publishing	43	2	4	1.9
Other Manufacturing Industries	30	2	12	5.6
	432	25	91	42.0
NON-MANUFACTURING				
Agriculture, Forestry, Fishing	32	2	3	1.4
Quarrying and Mining	1	—	—	—
Construction	224	14	12	6.0
Gas, Electricity and Water	7	—	2	1.0
Transport and Communication	58	3.5	7	3.2
Distributive Trades	364	22.5	33	15.2
Insurance, Banking and Finance	58	3.5	7	3.2
Professional and Scientific Services	127	8	21	9.9
Miscellaneous Services	318	20	34	15.3
Public Administration and Defence	26	1.5	6	2.8
	1,215	75	125	58.0
TOTAL:				
NON-MANUFACTURING	1,215	75	125	58.0
MANUFACTURING	432	25	91	42.0
GRAND TOTAL:	1,647	100.0	216	100.0

The following sample was aimed at:

	Manufacturing	Non-Manufacturing	Total Interviews
1–49 employees	20	60	80
50–999 employees	20	60	80
1,000+ (all in area)	19	21	40
Depth interviews (multiple, 1 firm)	6	14	20
Building firms		20	20
Aid organizations			20
			280

Initially, we wrote to 364 employers. 332 were in the area served by the Kingston office of the Ministry of Labour. Thirty-two were large organizations employing more than 1,000 people in the immediately adjacent Ministry of Labour areas. Fourteen of the organizations were suppliers of aid located in the London area. Forty-three of the 364 firms approached employed more than 1,000 people, 186 employed between 50 and 999, and 135 employed between 0 and 49 people. We also visited thirteen aid organizations who were not in the original list of firms approached but were mentioned in other interviews.

Later we wrote to another eighty-six firms employing between 0 and 49 people. These firms were selected on a random basis, confined to particular industries and services chosen for more intensive investigation—retailing, electrical engineering, building, and professional practices.

The following table shows the number of firms approached and the number that we interviewed.

FIRMS APPROACHED AND INTERVIEWED

	No.	%
Manufacturing firms interviewed	91	25
Other 'user' organizations interviewed	98	27
Aid organizations interviewed	27	8
Firms approached but without response	65	18
Interviews refused by firms	43	11
Interviews offered but declined *	15	4
Firms interviewed by telephone only	25	7
	364	100

* Mainly because firms had moved away from Kingston.

The questions that shaped this project raised numerous problems of definition. We used a small jury of informants to guide us towards operational solutions. I invited a group of students on a part-time advanced management course to discuss with their colleagues and superiors at work the meaning of such terms as 'external aid' and 'efficiency'. There appeared to be little confusion about the meaning of 'external aid' or 'external help'. I decided to restrict the meaning to cover management consultants, technical consultants, research associations, trade associations, and certain services provided by government departments and public bodies. However, we later discovered that suppliers of goods and services often were of considerable help in an unselfish way, and we had to include them within the concept of external aid.

Identifying the use of external help presented more subtle problems. Most of our informants were managing directors and senior executives; they would not necessarily know the full range of external aids used by subordinates, particularly when they were available without charge. We sought additional interviews in a few large organizations so as not to be dependent on one source of information. But the study almost certainly did not cover the total supply of aid.

We were asked to identify the characteristics of firms that have 'special administrative arrangements' concerning external help and we had to consider whether we needed a definition of that. We simply asked whether they had such special arrangements and the question seemed to make sense. Such arrangements were generally assumed to include (a) technical libraries and (b) at least one person who searched for appropriate information and then circulated it to executives who ought to find it useful. Only three organizations appeared to have anything like 'special arrangements' and even that number included two doubtful cases.

We were required to assess the technologies of firms having 'special administrative arrangements' and to compare them with other firms. We therefore had to record the technology of each firm visited. We could not know in advance whether the firm had 'special administrative arrangements' until the whole subject of external help had been explored in the interview. As we were not omniscient, we could not make a technical appraisal of all firms and usually we were unable to inspect the workshops or laboratories. Moreover, only about one quarter of Kingston firms are manufacturers. We decided that we would assess 'technology' on the basis of information given by our informant and that we would ask about (a) the age of the organization, (b) whether its equipment of all relevant kinds was old, modern, or an average of both, and (c) whether its major operations were based on manual labour or were mechanized, and if mechanized, whether it could properly be described as mass production. Our informants did not try to mislead us but there were many opportunities for misunderstanding. We did not assess the firm's 'technology' directly but merely recorded the information given to us.

We decided that for our purpose 'size' was reflected in the number of employees. The Ministry of Labour classified organizations into three size groups: 0 - 49, 50 - 999, and 1,000 plus. These categories are unsatisfactory in many ways but we could not obtain others and no great harm was done by restricting ourselves to those classifications.

We were also asked to find out whether the firms with special administrative arrangements had markets and products that were similar to other firms. That raised many difficult and nebulous problems, and we restricted our marketing enquiries to questions about importing and exporting.

We were required to find out whether the managers of the firms having special administrative arrangements for aid differed in background, education, and training from managers in the other firms. We decided that we could only seek some elementary knowledge about our informants; we classified them into one of three age groups, according to the average age at which the managers completed full-time education, and the typical social class of the managers of the firm, based on the social class of the informant's father, as reflected in his occupation. There are many reasons for doubting the validity of the information obtained but at least we tried.

Were the special firms more efficient than other firms? As there is no agreed objective definition of 'efficiency', we decided to ask the first six firms that we visited how the informant would try to assess efficiency. There seemed to be general agreement on three factors:

(a) the success of the firm in reducing its costs over several years;
(b) the degree to which productivity was increasing, measured by (i) output, (ii) number of customers in relation to staff, and (iii) general improvement to services supplied; and
(c) the attitude of management to new ideas about products, methods and markets.

We asked each informant at subsequent interviews to assess their firm on these three criteria.

Were they more stable? We designed in a similar way three criteria of stability:

(a) the steadiness of their net profit in recent years;

270

(b) their attempts to control 'uncontrollables'—those influences in the economy and society that are frequently said to be outside the control of management, such as taxation, government economic policy, and cut-throat competition; and

(c) their market reputation, innovation record, and goodwill.

I need scarcely emphasize that these were subjective appraisals based on terms not precisely defined and on reported information.

For assessing the use of external aids, we asked informants about membership of associations, and whether their organization had used management consultants, technical consultants, or government and official bodies during the past two years, and if so whether they had used them on two or three occasions. We then invited them to give us an average assessment of their efficiency and competence, as judged by the influence they had had on (i) increasing profits, (ii) modernizing the firm or (iii) increasing the confidence of management. We also asked them how they had made contact with the consultant or the public body, and suggested that the alternatives were: (a) recommendations, (b) response to an advertisement, or (c) a direct invitation from the firm to the aid organization. We asked them to decide which role they had expected the consultants to play from the following three: advisers, executives, or researchers. We then asked them to take the largest project that they had been involved in and say whether it was primarily concerned with manufacturing, marketing or personnel. Finally, we asked them to tell us how long the longest project had lasted—up to four weeks or over four weeks.

FINDINGS

It is difficult to summarize the facts and opinions obtained in these elaborate interviews and to interpret them objectively. However, such summary and interpretation are essential and must be attempted.

Appendix A gives the facts of membership and use of aids for 189 firms, divided into (a) manufacturers, (b) distributors, and (c) personal service industries, sub-divided by (d) the number of employees, and (e) ownership—for this purpose classified as 'independent', 'subsidiary', 'family firm', or 'parent (head office)'.

Appendix B analyses the use made of aid organizations, and Appendix C summarizes the attitudes and opinions of users of aid.

271

Appendix D describes the aids used, the technology of firms, and the characteristics of the management of the firms.

Few firms had coherent policies about their membership of aid organizations and about using consultants. Most informants found difficulty in telling us why they belonged to associations. After a time, we suggested some possible reasons, and most of these terms were used by respondents at our prompting. Few of the firms undertook any regular review of their annual payments to associations, nor did they try to evaluate the benefits obtained from them. When financial difficulty indicated the need for economy, membership was often ended, possibly to the disadvantage of the firm. As the decision to join was not rational, it was more difficult for management to evaluate the services obtained.

Some large firms were also irrational in choosing their representatives for committees or meetings of associations. Sometimes they were the people most readily available and not necessarily the most suitable.

The very large firm, public or private, has many real difficulties in deciding which associations to join, as their activities may extend throughout the whole economy and there would be some case for belonging to every association.

The attitudes of managers are more important to the proper use of available aid than mere membership. Some managers regard the use of aid as an admission of their own incompetence and failure. The evidence for this attitude is the statements of some managers and their failure to use appropriate aid organizations, even when faced with difficult technical or commercial problems.

Of course, some organizations do not need any outside help, and they may be of any size and in any industry. If a firm is meeting the policy laid down by its management and owners with reasonable efficiency, they cannot be expected to seek specialized guidance. But managers can seldom be objective about their own achievements and some operational criteria of effectiveness are needed. Such guidelines may have to be created and assessed by the consultant, and the reputable consultant will not propose an assignment if his initial survey indicates a clean bill of health.

An equally unsound management attitude is the magical expectation of sudden solutions from aid. That hinders the sensible use of help. Similarly, some managers are unrealistic about the time needed to formulate initial proposals, to carry out investigations, and to bring about changes proposed by aid organizations. Some managers expect associations and consultants to appear at a moment's notice and to carry out a complex task in a few days. Management consultants were criticized for failing to make clear how long they would take and what their fees would be for an assignment. Whilst that is a perfectly reasonable criticism in most cases, it is extraordinary that businessmen should allow themselves to enter into contracts without knowing their financial obligations.

Most of the firms we visited were manufacturers, and a great number of external aids are slanted towards manufacturing industries. But the structure of aid suppliers concerned with distribution and personal service industries and with organizations outside business altogether may have to be changed because the nature of their work is so different.

We interviewed some members of professions in private practice—six architects, two solicitors, one accountant, and one surveyor. We were surprised at their numerous external relationships, many of them due to the increasing complexity of their tasks. We found a need to distinguish between (a) the external division of labour within professions, (b) the consequent increase in specialization among members of a profession, and (c) the use of outside help as normally understood. The clearest examples of outside help in the professions are the management consultancy service of the Law Society, and the activities of the Royal Institute of British Architects aimed at increasing the efficiency of architectural practices. The Institute has published a pioneering survey of the efficiency of architectural practices, and it has since set up a management advisory service for its members.[1]

The existence of large practices, particularly among solicitors and architects, is related to the increasing complexity of their work, requiring the services of more and more specialists. But large organizations are unpleasant to many professional people, who prefer to work in small groups, perhaps even in isolation. Nevertheless, some form of joint enterprise among different specialists within a professional group, occupying separate accommodation yet readily available as a team, appears to be growing. This reflects on the role of outside aid because this type of loose federation may mean that the aid that is usually external will be internalized, although it may not be fully utilized all

[1] *The Architect and His Office*, R.I.B.A. 1962.

K   273

the time by the official membership of the federation. Presumably there are many examples of this half-in and half-out use of aid; a continuum may exist whereby, for example, a technical consultant gradually increases the time spent in one firm and may in the end be indistinguishable from a full-time employee.

Exporters

Fifty-two of the firms interviewed were exporters. They made use of external aids, such as the Export Advisory Service of the Board of Trade and the Export Credits Guarantee Department. Opinions differed widely as to their adequacy, some being highly critical, others regarding them as excellent. It is extremely difficult to make any overall appraisal, partly because of a general distrust of government offices by many business firms. There was some indication that exporters misunderstood the functions of these public bodies, and some expected them to obtain orders from foreigners, not simply to provide information or insurance.

Non-users of Aid

Those organizations that do not use external aid need special study and raise many research problems. It was difficult to make sure that help was never used, particularly informally or accidentally. Reading a news item, or talking to someone at a party, may lead to a valuable idea and could be categorized as help.

However, of the 216 interviews carried out, eight of them were with firms who appeared to be non-users of outside help by all normal criteria. They were not members of associations, they had never used consultants, and they appeared to have no contact through suppliers with the changes in technology. Because of their importance, the following detailed notes are provided to complete the picture.

There are few similarities statistically: five have fewer than 49 employees, three have over 50 but less than 250 employees. There are five in manufacturing, two in distribution and one in service trades, three are over 20 years old, three are from 10-19 years old, and two are from 0-9 years old. Only two have modern equipment, three have old equipment, and three have average equipment. As to ownership types, four were independent, two subsidiaries, and one family and one parent firm.

In three of them, the average age of management was 50-60 years, and five had an average of 35-50 years. In six firms, management left school at 14-15 years of age, and in two firms management left at 18. As for social class, five firms' management derived from the working class, and three from the middle class.

As regards efficiency, two firms seemed to rate fairly well, and four firms had steady profits with a growth trend, whilst three were among acknowledged leaders in their trades.

All their managing directors had abnormal attitudes, in the view of the interviewer. For example, one 'was unique for his conceit and contempt for all bodies charged with attempting to provide help for management. I gained the impression he was a megalomaniac—and after a second interview, maintain this impression. Undoubtedly his firm has achieved notable success, and is very efficient, whilst the management generally may not share his conceit or greed for power. There is some evidence, however, for the view that as a whole, the management is unscrupulous, and are exploiters of people and situations without regard to normal requirements of human decency.'

Another 'is abnormal in that the managing director established and runs the firm merely to provide a poor livelihood and keeps himself busy. He has no family, and apparently few friends; is old, partly deaf, and quite disinterested in his or the firm's future. He takes a "garden allotment" attitude towards business—somewhere to go, to occupy the mind and body, which takes precedence over business success or failure.'

THE ANSWERS TO THE QUESTIONS

1. *What external help is available to firms in the Kingston area?* It is impossible to say because there is so much available. We were told that the following types of aid organizations had been used in the course of the interviews and the relevant names are in our records:

Management consultants	19
Technical consultants	13
International and foreign miscellaneous organizations	5
Professional institutes	35
Research associations	31
Trade associations	103
Government departments and public bodies	53
Miscellaneous organizations	23
Total	282

275

2. (a) *To what extent is it used? How many firms used it?* Eight organizations visited claimed that they made no use of external aids.

Thus 181 of the 189 firms visited claimed that they used external aids, defined by us to mean membership of trade and research associations and users of consultants, government aid services, and advice from suppliers.

(b) *How much is it used by those that do?* It is extremely difficult to obtain information needed for a comprehensive reply but the appendices give some indication of use.

We have excluded casual use of associations, such as brief telephone calls. It must be remembered that frequency of use is an estimate of the informant and not based on any records of actual use. Our statistics may not therefore indicate maximum use.

3. *Which firms have special administrative arrangements for exploring for information and help and for making it available to the management?* This question raises many difficult problems of interpretation and verification. We decided to exclude technical libraries that are available to individuals if they wish to use them, and to ignore the unsystematic distribution of technical and learned journals. As a result, only three firms appeared to have a special arrangement to deal with aid facilities. They were unusual primarily because of an active technical information service that took the initiative in distributing information as well as answering individual queries. They also kept in touch with universities, research associations, and consultants. On close investigation, however, it appeared that only one of these three firms came near to a satisfactory administrative structure to make full use of information and help.

4. *Which firms use such help and with what results?* Presumably this question was intended to reveal the differences between firms having special administrative arrangements and those firms that do not. In view of the small number of 'special arrangement' firms, and the lack of clear evidence about the nature of these special arrangements, there seemed little point in trying to make such a comparison. If, on the other hand, the question is taken to refer to users in general, we have presented the available information in appendices.

As to results of using help, we asked firms that had used consultants and public bodies to make an average assessment of the benefit derived on a crude scale—useless, valuable, and very valuable. Appendix C (a) gives the results for those firms that were willing to make this appraisal. We also asked members of research and trade associations to state their reasons for membership, under the four categories of: (i) convention, (ii) joint defence, (iii) knowledge, and (iv) obtaining information about competitors. The results are given in Appendix C (b).

For those who stated that suppliers provided them with aid, we asked them to assess such aid as useless, valuable, or very valuable, and to analyse the type of aid received into one of three categories—(i) completion of orders, (ii) product development, and (iii) research. Finally they were asked to judge the value of suppliers' aid on the criteria of (a) helping to retain a customer or (b) increasing profits. The results are given in Appendix C (d).

5. *What are the significant characteristics of the firms which have such arrangements and use external help? (a) Are they larger than the others? (b) Are their markets and products of a similar kind and do they differ in this way from the others? (c) Have they similar technologies which differ from those of the others? (d) Do their managers differ in background, education and training? (e) Are they more efficient? (f) Are they more stable?* There are too few firms with special arrangements for external aid to answer this question properly. In order to seek the answers, however, it was necessary to analyse certain characteristics of all organizations interviewed, and severe problems of terminology and definition arose. Appendix D summarizes the information obtained about size, technology, management characteristics, efficiency and stability for (a) the special arrangement firms, (b) firms using external aids, and (c) firms claiming not to use external aid. Two of the three 'special arrangement' firms had more than 1,000 employees, the largest category used in the classification of firms. Only 0.5 per cent of all firms in the Kingston area come into this category. The three special firms were all more than twenty years old, whereas 73 per cent of firms giving such information came into this category. The only similarity of the products and markets of the 'special arrangement' firms, so far as they can be discovered and are known, is that (a) they serve modern needs, (b) are strongly based on scientific knowledge or

277

processes, and (c) serve international markets. Many other firms would also qualify for these categories.

So far as management background is concerned, the average age at which management completed full-time education was stated to be fourteen or fifteen in one of the special firms, eighteen years of age in the second, and over twenty-one in the third. For 184 firms in the sample, the education age distribution was:

Age of completion	No. of Firms	Percentage of all firms
14–15	120	65
18	55	30
21 over	9	5

As to efficiency, all three claimed to have increased productivity, to be receptive to new ideas, and one claimed to have reduced costs over the last two years. Thus, they are similar to other manufacturing firms of equal size. There was no clear pattern among the three in relation to stability.

In order to obtain a more thorough view of the availability, use and appraisal of aid, we asked for additional information about the means of initial contact, the expected role, and the criteria of appraisal in relation to management consultants. The answers are summarized in Appendix B and Appendix C.

APPENDIX A   *Analysis of 189 Interviews by External Aids Used*

Employees Ownership	'MANUFACTURING'							'SERVICE'							'DISTRIBUTION'							GRAND TOTAL
	0/49		50/999		1,000+			0/49		50/999		1,000+			0/49		50/999		1,000+			
	Ind.	Sub.	Ind.	Sub.	Ind.	Sub.	Total	Ind.	Sub.	Ind.	Sub.	Ind.	Sub.	Total	Ind.	Sub.	Ind.	Sub.	Ind.	Sub.	Total	
FIRMS	17	4	29	20	7	14	91	*(2)23	5	*(6)16	8	*(6)7	1	60	18	2	*(2)8	4	*(1)6	0	38	189†
R.A.	5	3	12	8	6	9	43	2	0	6	3	4	0	15	0	0	2	1	6	0	9	67
T.A.	8	2	26	15	7	11	69	7	3	12	4	7	1	34	11	0	5	4	6	0	26	129
M.C.	0	1	5	6	3	6	21	2	0	1	1	4	1	9	0	0	4	2	4	0	10	40
T.C.	1	0	6	9	3	8	27	8	1	3	3	4	0	19	1	0	1	0	3	0	5	51
Govt.	10	1	17	11	6	11	56	12	2	10	3	5	0	32	4	0	4	0	4	0	12	100
Supp.	11	3	18	9	5	11	57	11	3	10	5	4	1	34	13	2	4	3	5	0	27	118
AID	8	3	13	0	3	0	*(7)27	—	—	—	—	—	—	—	—	—	—	—	—	—	—	27†

NOTES: Ind. = Independent firms owned and managed, together with government departments and public bodies.

Sub. = Subsidiary of a holding company.

R.A. = Research Associations   M.C. = Management Consultants   Govt. = Government Bodies and Research Stations

T.A. = Trade Associations   T.C. = Technical Consultants   Supp. = Suppliers

*figures in brackets indicate government owned

APPENDIX B   *Analysis of the Use of Aid Organizations*

(a) *Use of Consultants*

	M.C.	T.C.	Govt.	Totals
Firms using once in 2 years	25	5	6	36
Firms using twice in 2 years	2	3	3	8
Firms using thrice in 2 years	13	43	91	147
Longest project manufacturing	17	24	31	72
Longest project marketing	5	5	6	16
Project period 0–4 weeks	4	3	1	8
Project period 4+ weeks	4	6	4	14

(b) *Use of Associations and Suppliers*

	R.A.	T.A.	Supp.	Totals
Firms using 0–5 times in two years	21	42	11	74
Firms using 5+ times in 2 years	43	79	107	229
Participation, e.g. committee members	8	19	0	27
Members of one association	41	51	0	92
Members of two associations	13	37	0	50
Members of two + associations	13	41	0	54

N.B. Answers are not available on all points from all interviews.

(c) *Aid from Suppliers: Type of aid received*

Completing order	40
Product Development	68
Research	49
	157

(d) *Management Consultants: Means of Initial Contact*

Recommended by friend	20
Advertising by consultant	10
Invited by client	3

APPENDIX C   *Attitudes and Opinions of Users*

(a) *Assessment of Benefit Derived from Consultants and Public Bodies*

	M.C.	T.C.	Public Bodies
Useless	10	1	5
Valuable	20	10	43
Very Valuable	11	39	49

(b) *Reasons for Membership of Trade and Research Associations*

	R.A.	T.A.
Convention	17	30
Joint Defence	11	52
Knowledge	45	64
Information about competitors	3	9
	76	155

Sixty-seven firms were members of research associations, 129 were members of trade associations. Some informants give more than one reason. 113 did not make this assessment in relation to research associations, and 34 did not make it in relation to trade associations.

(c) *Aid from Suppliers: Assessment of Value*

Useless	0	
Valuable	40	
Very Valuable	78	
	118	= total using suppliers for aid

(d) *Aid from Suppliers: Criteria of Judging Value of Aid*

Customer retained	72
More profits	41
	113

(e) *Management Consultants—Role expected by Clients*

Adviser	26
Executive	17
Researcher	2

(f) *Management Consultants—Client's Criteria for Judging Performance*

	Total	Judged Useless	Valuable	Very Valuable
Increased profits	7	—	3	4
Firm modernized	14	—	10	4
Management confidence increased	23	—	17	6
General	10	9	1	—
	54	9	31	14

APPENDIX D *Analysis of Firms — Age, Technology, Management*

N.B. Information was not available for all firms on all items

INTERVIEWS		Special Firms Total	Users	Non-Users	TOTAL
Firms:	Manufacturing	2	87	5	92
	Service	1	58	1	59
	Distributive	0	36	2	38
			181	8	189 *

Technology:					
Age of	0–9	0	14	2	16
firm	10–19	0	29	3	32
where known	20+	3	131	3	134
			174	8	182
Equipment:	Old	0	10	3	13
	Mixed	0	54	3	57
	Modern	3	104	2	106
			168	8	176
Production:					
Process:	Manual	0	49	2	51
	Mechanized	2	89	6	95
	Mass	1	35	0	35
			173	8	181
Management:					
Age Group	25–35	0	24	0	24
Average	35–50	2	117	5	122
	50–60	1	40	3	43
			181	8	189
Age full-time	14–15	1	114	6	120
education	18	1	53	2	55
completed (average)	21+	1	9	0	9
			176	8	184
Social Class:	Working	2	134	5	139
(average)	Middle	1	45	3	48
	Upper	0	1	0	1
			180	8	188
Efficiency:	Costs reduced	1	103	2	105
	Productivity increased	3	119	2	121
	Open to new ideas	3	134	2	136
			356	6	362 †
Stability:	Profits steady	1	119	4	123
	'Uncontrollables'	1	93	2	95
	Industry Status	3	64	3	67
			276	9	285

* The other 27 firms were suppliers of aid.
† Each firm could claim three achievements under 'efficiency' and 'stability'.

Appendix 2

Research Methods

ORGANIZING THE PROJECT
The main project followed from the pilot study completed on May 31, 1965. After discussion with the Social Science Research Council the following aims for a new project were agreed:

'It is intended to investigate the use of outside help by four firms in agriculture, four in building, four in distribution and four in manufacturing. In addition, a study will be made of one research association, one trade association, one firm of management consultants, and one public advisory or aid body. A pilot project on External Aids to Management was carried out between June 1, 1964 and May 31, 1965, under a D.S.I.R. grant.

The organizations will be selected at random from those operating within twenty miles of Kingston (but outside the central London area). It may be necessary to approach several firms in each sector before finding those willing to co-operate in this investigation.

A series of visits will be made to the twenty organizations at three-monthly intervals. At each visit, interviews will be held with the chief executive, the main departmental managers, supervisors, and operatives or similar workers in non-manufacturing organizations. The purpose of the interviews will be to discover the nature and organization of the firm's main activities, and to observe the role of outside help in established activities and in new developments as they occur. The same people will be interviewed at each subsequent visit, or other representatives of their category of employment. The interviewees will be asked to describe their current work, or a particular project that they are involved in at that time. An attempt will be made to discover whether any outside help is being used on that project, whether the use is known to management, whether any cost arises from the use of help, and what effects the outside help is having on management and the organization.

At each subsequent visit, the particular project that formed the basis of the second interview will be raised by the interviewer and further development of the project, and the subsequent use of outside help, will be discussed. At each interview after the first, it is likely that a new activity will be mentioned by the interviewee. These will be checked on throughout the three-year cycle as long as they appear to be relevant to the activities of the organization. Wherever possible, the subject raised by one interviewee will be mentioned to other members of the organization, to discover whether they have any different version of the event described by the first informant. First-hand observation of the problems raised by the interviewee will be sought wherever possible.

In the organizations supplying help, it is proposed to begin with a survey of their organization and methods of working, including an analysis of clients or members, and of current activities. It is hoped that the investigator will be able to accompany, say, a consultant on an assignment, and to attend meetings of committees of association as an observer.

It is proposed to conduct this investigation over three years in view of the long period taken by many firms to plan, develop and complete projects, particularly those concerned with automation, computers, personnel selection and research.

The first three months of this investigation will be devoted to designing the programme in detail, to obtaining co-operation from firms, and to negotiating with the aid organizations. The final three months will be needed for writing up the findings. Of the remaining thirty months, there will be a maximum of twenty days available for interviewing in each month, and it is thought that approximately three days will be needed at each organization for each visit. Thus each organization should be visited ten times in the three-year period.

EXPECTED ACHIEVEMENTS
The following results are expected to emerge from this investigation:

(a) a systematic and comprehensive understanding of
    (i) the process of using help from outside the organization, and
    (ii) the proper roles of both the user and the suppliers in that process.
    From this analysis proposals for increasing the productivity of outside help within the user organization should be possible;

(b) a set of proposals for the optimum organization and integration of all available types of outside help, so as to maximize the benefits that can be obtained by a user from the wide range of existing facilities for help;

(c) the outlines of a method for assessing the efficiency of an organization that could serve as a means of diagnosing its need for outside help.'

The first step in the organization of the project was to appoint a senior research assistant. Mr R. B. Pulfrey is a Cambridge graduate and had attended a two-year course for the post-graduate Diploma in Industrial Sociology at Liverpool University. He had spent three years as an assistant personnel manager in industry. He was twenty-eight years of age at the time of the appointment.

Our next task was to find the twenty organizations willing to co-operate. Interviewing the management of these organizations took a considerable amount of time. More than 50 per cent of the firms approached declined to co-operate, but most of the refusals came from small building firms that had only one or two managers and hesitated to take on more commitments. By June 30th eighteen organizations had been recruited. The fourth building firm and the trade association were not selected randomly and both were recruited by September 23, 1966.

On November 2, 1966, one of the manufacturing firms, Landseer Bailey, wrote to say that they could no longer continue to co-operate on the project as our visits were taking up too much of the time of their executives. We then asked to be allowed to visit them three months later merely to discuss changes that had taken place during that period. No reply was received then, nor to a similar request three months later. Several other firms in a similar industrial category were approached and two of them agreed to co-operate. As they were very small organizations it was decided to study both of them. The first visit to A. Brown & Company Mitcham Limited, manufacturers and repairers of boxes and packing cases, was made on December 5, 1966, and the first visit to the Lion Case Company Limited, manufacturers of crates, cases and moulded packs, was on January 6, 1967.

SELECTION OF THE SAMPLE

Most of the sample of firms in this study was selected by random choice from a known population.

The firms were chosen with the use of random number tables.[1]
The different populations were drawn from the following sources:

(a) The London Classified Telephone Directory;
(b) Kelly's Directory of Kingston-upon-Thames, Surrey;
(c) Kelly's Directory of Surbiton, Surrey;
(d) Lists supplied by the National Union of Farmers' office at Guildford, Surrey.

The Standard Industrial Classification published by the Stationery Office was used in selecting the different sub-universes.

The Classified Telephone Directory was found adequate in finding manufacturers but I decided to ensure that two of the manufacturing firms employed more than 1,000 people. A list of forty organizations employing over one thousand people in the Kingston and neighbouring areas of the Ministry of Labour was used. Beechams Limited and Petters Limited were selected.

The research and trade associations approached were selected from a list of 134 given in an appendix of the pilot project report.

The management consultant was selected randomly from the six members of the Management Consultants' Association listed in their 1964 report.

The National Agricultural Advisory Service was chosen to represent public bodies without statistical selection. The pilot survey showed it to be unusually interesting to this project and would complement our knowledge derived from the four farmers.

Nineteen builders were approached over the first six months of the project, and three agreed to co-operate. Despite many attempts it seemed impossible to obtain a fourth one and eventually a large local firm, W. H. Gaze and Son Limited, was asked to co-operate and agreed to do so on July 25, 1966.

PROGRAMME OF WORK

To a surprising extent we kept to the original scheme of work, but the quantity and quality of each activity was far from perfect, in part because of the nature of the problems we were investigating. Some-

[1] *Tables of Random Sampling Numbers: Tracks for Computers 24*, M. G. Kendal and B. B. Smith, Cambridge University Press, 1939.

times we could not find enough informants in an organization, and sometimes the intervals between visits prevented us from observing the cycle of events of new activities that we had planned. Even if we had been able to do everything that we hoped to do, we should still have obtained an imperfect result because of the complexity of organizational analysis, particularly from our special perspective of external relationships.

The basic challenge we faced was the need to build up a procedure that would provide us with useful knowledge of each organization over a period of three years. At the same time, we wanted to identify and appreciate external aid. In order to do that we had to attempt to assess the efficiency of the organization as an indicator of the need for aid.

The original project scheme provided for three days each quarter to be allocated to each of the participant organizations. It rapidly became obvious that we could not in fact spend three full days at each organization, partly because we would be unwelcome for such a continuous period in many of the organizations, partly because there were many other activities that had to be undertaken within the limited time available. For example, reports on visits had to be written up and the implications of the visits discussed by me and the visiting research assistant. Then we needed time for planning the next visit and in some cases we were involved in planning a series of visits to each organization where particular topics would be discussed. I felt it essential to allow time for quarterly meetings to review each organization and the project as a whole. At the fourth of such quarterly meetings it was necessary to review the whole of one year's work and to prepare a report for the Social Science Research Council on what had been achieved. Out of that annual review came the need to plan broad targets for the subsequent year's work.

In addition to this work directly connected with the sample organizations, it rapidly became apparent that there were a large number of other sources of information that we ought to consider, each of which would make further demands on our time. Nearly all of our firms were members of associations and we could not exclude all of these bodies from our attention as they were at the heart of our project. Many firms were in industries that were under the care of a government department, or an economic development committee of the National Economic Development Council, or of an industrial training board, or closely connected with a college. In order to appreciate the problems and opportunities of our firms we had to try to keep up to date with trends within each of their industries and to keep careful watch on changes in government policies and in new, relevant legislation.

Gradually it became clear that we had to ensure that at least one visit was paid to each organization in each quarter; each visit was usually for one day, including time for travelling, plus several hours for report writing. In a few cases, particularly one or two of the farms, it was inconvenient for visits to last a whole day and therefore we restricted ourselves to a half-day visit. At the other extreme, it seemed essential to spend more than one day in a quarter investigating a firm or its associated organizations or sources of knowledge. The statistical tables summarize the distribution of our time among the available resources.

Mr Pulfrey devoted all his time to the project and I devoted about nine hours per week either to visits, meetings, report writing, or to study of relevant documents.

We had stressed from the start that we wished to be allowed to move around the organization and that we did not wish to be simply lectured to by informants. I believe that it is essential to obtain information from direct observation wherever possible and thus we asked for Mr Pulfrey to be allowed to accompany our informants in their normal working activities. In many cases that was impossible for many months. By a gradual process of education it was found that the research assistant did not conflict with the activities of the executive concerned and we were able to observe how the organization operated, and in particular to note anything that appeared to be an external contact, which later we were able to classify as an external aid where relevant. In some cases, again particularly with the farmers, our request that Mr Pulfrey should participate in normal activities of the farm were taken very literally and on one or two occasions he did some heavy manual farm work. Most of our information came from discussions with informants at work, and we were able to observe some external contacts and aids in actual operation in most organizations.

It would be tedious to record in detail all the changes that were made in our procedures but the importance of this should be stressed, particularly in a long project, because the interesting or even the uninteresting fact or experience has to be available for integration and assessment many months or years in the future. Thus the visit procedure had to be designed in detail, and elaborate methods for recording, filing, and retrieval of information are absolutely vital. It is impossible to discover the perfect system solely by cogitation at the beginning, and we had to make many difficult changes in our procedures.

Most of the first year of the project was devoted to gathering information about the activities, and obtaining an understanding, of the members of each organization, at many different levels. The second phase of the project emerged, at different dates for each organization, when we found it necessary to explain the main focus of our interest, and we gradually moved away from the simple explanation that we were studying management problems. The outcome of this evolution was the decision to begin a new phase of recording information for the twelve months from July 1, 1967 to June 30, 1968. At every visit during that year a separate report form was completed for each external contact observed or reported during visits. We aimed to obtain as much information as possible about different types of external contacts, some of which were external aids. The results of this elaborate procedure are summarized at the end of the report for each firm. I have resisted the temptation to compile elaborate statistical analyses of these reports. Their unavoidable imprecision would not justify too serious a treatment. They are reported here because of their methodological interest and because they provide some degree of evidence for my conclusions.

During that year from July 1, 1967 we realized that we had to devote time to consolidating the knowledge that was being obtained, in some cases from more than a dozen visits. A comprehensive review structure was therefore planned, and the information about contacts and aid was consolidated. Particularly interesting events were written up as case studies.

Owing to illness, Mr Pulfrey was unable to make any visits between July and November 1968. I made a few visits during that period but most of my available time in the last six months of the project was concerned with drafting reports on each organization, negotiating with informants for permission to publish their names in our findings, and compiling this report.

Whatever difficulties there might be in collecting information, the question of relevance was a constant predicament. What types of information are needed to know an organization? Is anything and every-

L   289

thing desirable? Even if that all-embracing process could be followed, what was to be done with the mass of facts and feelings that would emerge? Professor Burns's exhaustive review of the problem leads him to conclude that there are seven analytical categories that taken together 'serve to distinguish organizations from other institutions They are:

1. Relationships between the organization and its environment.
2. Definitions of tasks and division of labour.
3. Communication system.
4. Authority structure.
5. Systems of engagement and rewards.
6. Involvement (responsibility).
7. Definition of individual social identities in organizational settings.'[1]

I believe that the descriptions of the co-operating organizations provide some information on all these categories. But it must be stressed that the project was not designed to constitute a comprehensive account of all aspects of a group of organizations. We were primarily interested in Burns's first category and we studied the others to the extent necessary to know the first. That constitutes a difference in kind and not merely of degree, but it is extremely difficult to define it. One or two examples may help.

We were not interested in the details of the authority structure as we knew from the pilot project that some external relationships and some requests for aid were initiated by 'unauthorized' members of the organization. But we were concerned with the attitude of the senior and other executives towards outside aid as they could significantly influence aid policy and practice. Similarly, we were not interested in the system of engagement and rewards except to the extent that inward or outward looking behaviour was considered by members to be more conducive to their status within the organization.

It seemed best to begin with an open and unstructured approach and to be guided by our informants in learning of their work and the

---

[1] *Methods of Organizational Research,* ed. by V. H. Vroom, Chapter 3: The Comparative Study of Organizations' by Tom Burns, p. 130, University of Pittsburgh Press, 1967.

organization they worked in. We were deliberately vague when talking to them about the aims of the project so that we should not be presented with selective information. Our intention was to be more like a sponge than an X-ray machine although it was appreciated that these two approaches were not opposites nor in conflict with one another. Gradually familiarity made analysis unavoidable. But we were frequently surprised at the change of view that emerged from new information obtained at later visits. The furniture manufacturer, the management consultants, and the building merchant, for example, demonstrated innovative initiative beyond our expectations. More and more we had to concentrate on relevant 'external' facts (such as using consultants) and on identifiable self-contained activities (such as the decision to stop cultivating a particular crop) so as to order our impressions.

In all this, the personal variable of the research assistant is of major importance. The onerous psychological tasks of learning about an organization through a series of visits were hard enough, but they were multiplied by twenty-two different groups of people and processes, and then magnified by the heavy demands I made on his ability to report accurately and succinctly.

One methodological problem of some possible significance is that the bulk of the information obtained was derived from a number of relationships between the research worker and a major respondent in each organization. This problem of research worker-informant relationships has frequently been discussed. For example, Karl E. Weick states: 'Field researchers report that when they become friendly with their informant, they are tempted to see the world solely from his point of view. If this occurs, the field man finds less and less that requires explanation. A related problem exists in the supposedly minimal and "programmed" contact between an experimenter and a subject.' He goes on to report an experiment involving firstly groups of five to eight and then a single subject in a number of tests. It seemed that the subject of the experiment, when a single individual, behaved differently from the members of a group of people, and the following explanation is proposed: 'Despite the experimenter's deliberate attempt to behave identically in both experiments, inevitably a more personal relationship resulted in the two-person experiment. In this two-person study, the subjects felt free to ask questions and make comments and frequently did so, resulting in a relationship more informal than in the group setting, where almost no subject seemed to feel uninhibited enough to comment freely.'[1]

We were somewhat protected against the disadvantages of this person-to-person effect in the present study through having a number of informants from each organization, although only one informant normally provided information at one interview. The other protection is that in nearly all of the organizations at least one visit was made both by the research supervisor and the research assistant, and on some of those occasions corroborative evidence was obtained to justify the attitudes and interpretations of the research assistant. On occasions, conflicting evidence emerged. The other and more important protection against emotional involvement and thus distortion is that the visits were made at regular intervals over a period of nearly three years and thus considerable opportunity was presented for the stereotype that may have been formed in the first few visits to become modified as a result of wider experience. In a number of cases, the image of the organization certainly did change in the light of objective additional information.

DISCUSSION OF DRAFT REPORT

One research technique that was expected to be, and proved to be, of considerable value was the submission of a draft final report about each organization to our major informants. The draft was submitted in order to check on the accuracy of the facts and to seek relevant additional information that the informant believed was needed to complete the reader's understanding. We also wanted to know what he thought should be deleted, particularly when opinions were expressed about the organization.

Although at least two preliminary drafts were prepared before a report was despatched, I did not expect that a perfect version could emerge without the informant's contribution. In some cases, some mildly provocative but tentative conclusions were included and they produced helpful reactions. In several cases, new and valuable additional information was given.

I wanted to publish the reports under the name of the co-operating

[1] 'Organizations in the Laboratory' in *Methods of Organizational Research*, edited by V. H. Vroom, p. 39.

organization because I believe that it gives a desirable authenticity to the account provided. It may also enable other researchers to go back to the organizations to check up on and to supplement our information. It would also encourage the reduction of undesirable and unnecessary secrecy in management research. There may have been a price to be paid: perhaps more could have been said under the shroud of anonymity. Each organization had an absolute veto—if they disliked my account of what we had learned about it and its use of external aid, they simply said that their name should not be used. I then had to rewrite the report so as to disguise their identity.

I was pleasantly surprised at the very large number of organizations who agreed to their name appearing, and I am not aware of any substantial sacrifice of information being necessary to obtain their consent. Of course, the analysis and interpretation of the findings in general were not involved in the process of consultation, and the organizations are not responsible in any way for my conclusions.

In the few cases where anonymity was requested, there were personal and organizational factors that made their attitude understandable.

EXTERNAL RELATIONSHIPS

Our main interest was in the external relationships of the organizations studied.

It seemed simple at first to identify external relationships in general and then to isolate external aid relationships from the totality. But it was not long before we realized that, for example, there were many degrees of involvement in being a member of a trade association, and thus a simple note of formal membership was only useful as an indication of the need for further analysis.

It seeemed necessary in the end to supplement barren fact with an assessment of particular relationships. The only relationships we could begin to judge properly were those that were observed during the visits. Hence the special report to describe and assess each observed external relationship. Sometimes informants reported on what they considered to be important external relationships but which we did not observe, and these too were analysed and assessed although the second-hand nature of the information was appreciated. The analysis of these relationship reports appears in the report on each firm and some general conclusions are given in Chapter 10.

None of these techniques was completely satisfactory. We have not resolved in particular the role of the supplier of goods and general services, primarily because we did not have the opportunity of examining the problem from the supplier's perspective.

EFFICIENCY AND EFFECTIVENESS

One difficult task has been to attempt to assess the efficiency of each organization as an indicator of the need for the use of external aid. If an organization is functioning satisfactorily without using aid, there is no basis for proposing that it should or could be used. But if a non-user is operating unsatisfactorily, then the situation is more interesting and may indicate reasons for the absence of aid that will highlight the nature of the aid relationship.

The study of assessment of organizational efficiency (or effectiveness —the more popular and more meaningful term today) has formed a central part of other research projects that I have been concerned with and there is no need to deal with the concept exhaustively here.[1] I agree with Katz and Kahn that there is no obvious solution to the problem of satisfactory criteria of organization performance and that the difficulty is essentially theoretical and conceptual. But I do not share their conclusion: 'Organizational effectiveness has become one of those handy but treacherous pseudo concepts, connoting a sort of totality of organizational goodness—a sum of such elements as productivity, cost performance, turnover, quality of output and the like. This rudimentary model as Seashore (1962) states "is false to most of the data we have examined so far and more complex models need to be invoked".' Their solution is to say that organizations are systems and that the frame of reference or definition of system boundaries in space and time varies with the problem under analysis. For most situations, a simple engineering concept of efficiency—output related to input— seems appropriate. Moreover, that kind of efficiency tends to produce immediate increases in profit which in turn creates the opportunity for building up a store of resources and is thus conducive to long-run growth and survival. That involves a wider concept and, following Barnard, they use the concept of 'effectiveness' to mean 'the maximization of return to the organization, by economic and technical means (efficiency), and by political means'. 'Political' covers a range of external

---

[1] See my 'How To Be Efficient', *Management Today*, May 1968.

and internal actions aimed at persuading people to provide more benefits to the organization than they would spontaneously.[1]

Seashore's criticism of the 'total' approach to effectiveness that they quote has not been published but is based on one study. Any such criticism involves serious problems of definition and method. Whether or not it is methodologically desirable, managers feel a need to consider the overall performance and status of their organization and hence they use efficiency in a wide sense, perhaps meaning something like effectiveness. Such a concept is meant to be a combination of several performance indicators plus an indication of the organization's potentiality for long-term survival.[2] The fault is not really with the concept but with the indicators usually employed to identify it. It is not simply the levels of performance achieved that matter but management attitudes to performance and survival. A new firm may score badly on most criteria, a firm may record a high profit figure because it spends no money on research or training, and a firm may be manufacturing at minimum cost but be entirely incapable of selling its output. The main influence on effective performance is an awareness of and concern with external dangers and external opportunities, and organizations need to be assessed on objective criteria indicating their awareness of the very active and penetrating environment within which they operate.

Argyris has summarized the problem neatly: 'Concepts of organizational effectiveness typically focus on the degree to which the organization accomplishes its objectives. A business firm is effective if it makes a profit . . . ' But two dimensions must be added to make the concept of organizational effectiveness more valid. 'They are first the organization's capacity to maintain its internal system in working order so that it can solve problems effectively and, second, the relative cost of transforming the human energy inputs into useful organizational outputs.

'Organizational effectiveness, then, is the balanced or optimal emphasis upon achieving objectives, problem-solving competence, and human energy utilization.'[3]

[1] *The Social Psychology of Organizations*, D. Katz & R. L. Kahn, John Wiley, 1966, p. 150.

[2] See *Functional Analysis of Organizational Effectiveness*, Seashore & Yuchtman, Administrative Science Quarterly, December 1967.

[3] *Organizations: Effectiveness*, Chris Argyris, International Encyclopaedia of the Social Sciences, 1968, Vol. 11, p. 311.

Thus in our attempts to assess performance (called 'efficiency' for the sake of familiarity and simplicity), we not only looked at output and productivity but we tried to decide whether the firm was alert to new opportunities in marketing, manufacturing, and personnel policies. However, our appraisals were largely impressionistic through lack of time and information and we would claim no more for them than they were elementary indicators of the potential need for external aid or the presence of unnecessary or inessential aid. They were at least disciplined impressions, based on an attempt to assess definite criteria some of which have been described elsewhere.[1] Moreover, the assessment was repeated 'blind' after the interval of about a year and thus some defences against faulty judgment were provided. Clearly, this problem of assessing overall performance of organizations is extremely important and the most urgent subject for future research.

THE ENVIRONMENT

As this study is particularly concerned with the relations between an organization (assuming that it can be properly considered as having clear boundaries) and the environment within which it operates, it is necessary to define and understand the nature of environment. If organizations cannot properly be seen to have definite boundaries, it is difficult to differentiate between the internal and external forces operating to produce particular situations. A train strike will delay the arrival of employees at their place of work—at what stage in the total process of work on that day does the influence of the strike begin and end? From one perspective it is simply a question of assessing the amount of working time lost as measured by the difference between the time of starting work on the day of the strike and the normal starting time. But some people will spend time describing their journeys to one another, and others will spend time worrying about their journey home. Some people will leave early because of the strike and some will have stayed at home altogether. Some sales representatives and some managers will not have made certain journeys during the day that they would have carried out but for the strike. How can the inner and outer influences be separated and why should they be?

There can be little doubt that general socio-cultural influences from the external environment must be considered in any assessment of

---

[1] 'How to be Efficient', *Management Today*, May 1968.

296

organizational performance. That broad concept does not act as a very precise indicator of external influences and in any case all organizations within a society share the same socio-cultural context, at least in the most generalized sense. Some differentiating concept is needed to demonstrate the special situation of each organization, particularly as it may be related to differences in organizational structure or external relationships. One interesting proposal is the suggestion of Emery and Trist that there is a need for a concept to describe 'those processes in the environment itself which are among the determining conditions of the exchanges (between the organization and its environment)'. This they call 'the causal texture of the environment' and they distinguish four 'ideal types', approximations to which 'can be thought of as existing simultaneously in the "real world" of most organizations—though, of course, their weighting will vary enormously from case to case.'

The first type is 'the placid, randomized environment'—something like the classical free market of the economist. It is distinctive because organizations have no need to distinguish between tactics and strategy, with the best strategy being the simple tactic of trying to do one's best on a purely local basis.

The second type is 'the placid, clustered environment'—something like imperfect competition, in which a strategy is needed as survival is linked to what an organization knows of its environment.

The third type is 'the disturbed-reactive environment', akin to an oligopolistic situation. Each organization has to consider other organizations and must base its strategy on the realization that what it knows is also known by the others. As a result it may be important to absorb other organizations, to attempt to become their parasite, to come to terms with them, to know when not to fight to the death.

The fourth type are 'turbulent field' environments. Unlike the third type, dynamic processes arise from the field or environment itself, create significant variance for the component organizations, and increase the area of relevant uncertainty for organizations. This situation arises from the growing interdependence between the economic and other facets of society and the increasing reliance on research and development to meet competitive challenge. This type of environment requires some relationship between dissimilar organizations whose fates are positively correlated. 'This means relationships that will maximize co-operation and which recognize that no one organization can take

297

over the role of "the other" and become paramount. We are inclined to speak of this type of relationship as an "organizational matrix". . . . Professional associations provide one model of which there has been long experience.'[1]

It is clear that a great deal of individual judgment is needed in determining the classification appropriate to any organization in this typology and it is a pity that more effort was not made to develop objective criteria. However, the concepts may be helpful and our firms have been allocated to one of these four categories in order to see whether any pattern of relationships emerges, especially with their efficiency assessment. In many cases, organizations will move from one type of environment to another over time but our assessment is made about the situation in the middle of 1968 and we have noted any that has been subjected to radical change during the course of the project.

THE ROLE OF THE RESEARCH SUPERVISOR
My role in this project is clearly relevant to understanding its methods, the difficulties encountered, and the resulting shortcomings of the study. It is impossible to be objective about oneself but some impressions may be useful to others about to take up this role.

Perhaps the most important need is for the investigator to consider very carefully the burden that he will be putting on himself when designing a research project and when carrying it out. While a great number of problems can be anticipated and planned for in a project, there is an inevitable assumption that the person in charge will fill in all the gaps that may occur and make good the shortcomings of the planning. I believe that it is possible and desirable to make very detailed plans for a research project and to apply all relevant management techniques to ensuring that the process of research operates as smoothly as possible. I have discovered no conflict at all between the requirements of orderly management of the project and the maintenance of intellectual freedom. There seemed to be no grounds for assuming that intellectual freedom requires a slovenly approach to the organization of work. There are certainly phases of a research project that are entirely creative and perhaps cannot be systematized. But the vast proportion of

---

[1] 'The Causal Texture of Organizational Environments', F E. Emery & E. L. Trist, *Human Relations*, 1965, No. 18, p. 29.

research work, at least in the field of management, is eminently suitable for disciplined organization.

Nevertheless, it is extremely difficult to make a realistic estimate of the amount of time that the investigator will need to manage a project. I anticipated that I should need six hours per week and that was the amount of official time I received as relief from teaching duties to carry this project through. There is little doubt that that period was exceeded very considerably, particularly in the work that I did during official vacations: official work commitments refer only to thirty-nine working weeks in the college year. However, the major problem is not time but the psychological and particularly emotional strains resulting from trying to reconcile other work commitments with a research project, particularly one of this size and complexity. Physical resources were far from ideal—for example, I shared an office with a secretary and two research assistants throughout most of this four-year period.

Perhaps it is worth mentioning that there were a number of official pressures operating on me in connection with this project. It was the first time that a grant had been obtained from the Social Science Research Council or its predecessor by any member of the college staff and it was also the first major research project within the management department.

So far as my relationship with the collaborating organizations is concerned, I had to allow the research assistant to decide the number of my contacts because of his needs as a continuing visitor. After the initial arrangements had been concluded, I did not make contact with the organizations unless they approached me or unless the research assistant asked me to contact them. That was occasionally necessary when we wished to move into a different phase of the project or where there was some complaint or misunderstanding about the research assistant's activities. On the whole, however, the research assistant was in contact with the organizations and I was concerned with planning those contacts and analyzing the results. This seems to be a necessary and satisfactory situation although there were frequent temptations to intervene. That would have complicated the task of the research assistant, and I feel that this procedure has worked reasonably well.

The most demanding intellectual aspects of the project arose from the need to translate the initial proposal into exact working procedures. These procedures had to be practical in terms of time, people and cost;

they also had to be suitable for subsequent evaluation. I was always conscious of the need to write a final report and therefore the activities of each phase had to be considered as a contribution to our findings. There have been a number of failures of this kind but I do not see any ways of avoiding them, given the size of the sample and the available resources. I am not a statistician and I feel sure that there were a number of statistical opportunities that have been missed. However, I have consulted statisticians from time to time and I am not convinced that the lost advantages were substantial, given the somewhat complex and subtle nature of the problem under investigation.

THE FINDINGS

The analysis of the material we obtained raised numerous problems, some of which have been reflected in this discussion. The preparation of the final conclusions seemed in prospect an enormous, almost impossible task. After considering many possibilities, I found that I was being guided in my thinking by the initial statement of expected achievements. They did not require precise numerical support for every view, and therefore a systematic framework for thinking about our work was the first requirement. The rather elementary logical structure that emerged did provide an opportunity for stating certain sequences that have become obvious to me but were by no means obvious to the layman—nor even to many aid suppliers.

Hence the most important requirement of research into management is a very precise initial programme, including specific goals.

TABLE A *Statistics of Visits to Organizations*

Organization	*No. of visits during project*	*Visits*	*Report writing*	*Travel*	*Total*
		H O U R S			
F1	15	53	23	15	91
F2	14	69½	19½	14	103
F3	16	58¾	33¼	17½	109½
F4	11	41¼	21¾	16½	79½
B5	23	61¼	41	37	139½
B6	23	141¾	42	34½	218¼
B7	21	74	30½	32	136½
B8	10	46	21¼	50	117¼

M9	13	59¾	30½	22½	112¾
M10	19	70½	35½	28½	134½
M11	14	100½	28½	17½	146½
M12	6	28¼	8½	9	45¾
M13	6	7	8	7½	22½
Landseer Bailey	4	29½	5½	6	41
D14	13	45¼	23¾	9¾	78¾
D15	13	71½	20¼	21	112¾
D16	18	70½	27	18	115½
D17	21	60½	35¼	21¼	117
A18 (B.L.R.A.)	13	85	36½	60¾	182¼
A19 (N.A.A.S.)	24	103¾	45¼	69	218
A20 (I.A.)	12	87¼	24¾	36	148
A21 (B.C.P.M.A.)	14	43½	21½	35	100
Initial visits to potential collaborators	8	17	4½	15¼	36¾
Extra Farm visits re N.A.A.S.	10	17¼	16¼	19	52½
Builders—Associated visits	6	7¼	10	12¾	30
TOTALS	347	1,449¾	613¾	625¼	2,688¾

TABLE B *Consolidated Visit Statistics*

Type of Organization	*No. of visits during project*	*Duration of visits*	*Time report writing*	*No. of hours travelling*	*Total*
			H O	U R S	
FARMS	56	222	98	63	383
BUILDERS	77	323	135	153	611
MANUFACTURERS	62	296	116	91	503
DISTRIBUTORS	65	248	106	70	424
AID BODIES	63	320	128	201	649
PRELIMINARY VISITS	8	17	5	15	37
EXTRA FARM VISITS	10	17	16	19	52
EXTRA BUILDING VISITS	6	7	10	13	30
	347	1,450	614	625	2,689

Bibliography

AGRICULTURE, MINISTRY OF
(1) *A Career in the N.A.A.S.*, 1967.
(2) *The Structure of Agriculture*, HMSO, 1966.

ARGYRIS, C.
'Organizations: Effectiveness', *International Encyclopaedia of the Social Sciences*, Vol. II, p. 311, 1968.

ASSOCIATION OF CONSULTING MANAGEMENT ENGINEERS (USA)
Professional Practices in Management Consulting, The Association, 1966.

BOARD OF TRADE JOURNAL
First Results of the 1966 Census of Distribution, February 23, 1968.

BRITISH CHEMICAL PLANT MANUFACTURERS ASSOCIATION
Annual Report for year ending December 31, 1967.

BROWN, R.
Explanation in Social Science, Routledge, 1963.

CENTRAL OFFICE OF INFORMATION
Agriculture in Britain, HMSO, 1967.

CHERRINGTON, J.
'The Civil Service Land Army', *The Financial Times*, July 31, 1968.

CLARK, B. J.
'Interorganizational Patterns in Education', *Administrative Science Quarterly*, September 1965.

CONFEDERATION OF BRITISH INDUSTRY
A Review of Mechanical Engineering Trade Associations, 1966.

EDWARDS, R.
Co-operative Industrial Research, Pitman, 1950.

EMERY, F. E. and TRIST, E. L.
'The Causal Texture of Organizational Environments', *Human Relations*, No. 18, 1965.

EVAN, W. M.
'Towards a Theory of Inter-Organizational Relations', *Management Science*, Vol. II, No. 10, August 1965.

FEDERATION OF BRITISH INDUSTRY
Industrial Research in Manufacturing Industry: 1959-60, FBI, 1961.

FRASER, T. C.
'Economic Development Committees—A New Dimension in Government/Industry Relations', *Journal of Management Studies*, May 1967.

HAMMOND, A. B. and OTHERS
Industrial Research Associations in the United Kingdom, OECD, Paris, 1966.

HAMMOND, P. E. (ed.)
Sociologists at Work, Basic Books, 1964.

HIGGIN, G. and JESSOP, N.
Communications in the Building Industry, Tavistock Publications, 1965.

HYMAN, S.
'How to be Efficient', *Management Today*, May 1968.
Introduction to Management Consultancy, Heinemann, 1961.
'The Management of Associations', *The Chartered Secretary*, March 1968.
Management and World Development, Pitman, 1967.
'Organizations and Society', *Management International*, May 1968.
Society and Management, Business Publications, 1964.

JOHNSTON, J.
'The Productivity of Management Consultants', *Journal of the Royal Statistical Society*, Vol. 126, Pt. II, 1963.

KATZ, D. and KAHN, R. L.
The Social Psychology of Organizations, John Wiley, 1966.

LAZELL, H.
Annual Report, Beecham Group Ltd., 1968.

ASSOCIATIONS AND CONSULTANTS

LEARNED, E. P. and SPROAT, A. T.
Organization Theory and Policy, Richard D. Irwin, 1966.

LOUCH, A. R.
Explanation and Human Action, Basil Blackwell, 1966.

LOUGHBOROUGH UNIVERSITY
Bibliography on Social Science Policy, Centre for Utilization of Social Science Research, June 1968.

MIDLAND BANK REVIEW
The 'Neddy' Experiment — A New Approach to National Planning, February 1968, Midland Bank Ltd.

MILLARD, P.
Trade Associations and Professional Bodies of the United Kingdom, 4th edition, Pergamon Press, 1968.
The Management of Associations, (Editor): Kenneth Mason, 1969.

NATIONAL ECONOMIC DEVELOPMENT OFFICE
(1) *Trade Associations in the Distributive Trades*, 1967.
(2) *Business Efficiency*, 1968.
(3) *Productivity*, 1967.

ORGANIZATION FOR ECONOMIC CO-OPERATION AND DEVELOPMENT
Industrial Research Associations in France, Belgium and Germany, OECD, Paris, 1965.

P.E.P.
Industrial Trade Associations, Allen & Unwin, 1957.

PRICE, J. L.
Organizational Effectiveness, Irwin, 1968.

R.I.B.A.
The Architect and His Office, 1962.

SWETMAN, E. W.
'What's Next?', *ABLC Journal* (Association of British Launderers and Cleaners), pp. 126-30, March 1968.

TATHAM, L.
'The Efficiency Experts', *Business Publications*, 1964.

TERREBERRY, S.
'The Evolution of Organizational Environments', *Administrative Science Quarterly*, March 1968.

THOMPSON, J. D. and MCEWEN, J.
'Organizational Goals and Environment. Goal-Setting as an Interaction Process', *American Sociological Review*, February 1958.

URWICK TECHNOLOGY MANAGEMENT LTD.
The Organization of Co-operative Research in the Wool Textile Industry, Wool Textile Research Council, 1967.

VROOM, V. H. (ed.)
Methods of Organizational Research, University of Pittsburgh Press, 1967.

WARREN, R. L.
'The Interorganizational Field as a Focus for Investigation', *Administrative Science Quarterly*, December 1967.

WESTON, DR. J.
'Building Research', *The Financial Times*, November 13, 1967.

YOUNG, C.
Consultancy in Overseas Development, Overseas Development Institute, London, 1968.

Index

Printed and bound by CPI Group (UK) Ltd, Croydon, CR0 4YY

01/05/2025

01858372-0002